THE THEATRE OF THE HOLOCAUST

THE THEATRE OF THE HOLOCAUST

VOLUME TWO

SIX PLAYS

edited and with an introduction by

ROBERT SKLOOT

The University of Wisconsin Press

The University of Wisconsin Press
2537 Daniels Street
Madison, Wisconsin 53718

3 Henrietta Street
London WC2E 8LU, England

1 3 5 4 2

Printed in the United States of America

Library of Congress Cataloging-in-Publication Data
PN6120.J4T4 1982 809.2'93458 81-69829

ISBN 0-299-16270-2 cloth; 0-299-16274-5 paper

For my students

Contents

Acknowledgments

For their advice and assistance in the publication of this anthology, I am grateful to Rachel Brenner, Alvin Goldfarb, Rabbi Kenneth J. Katz, Louise Root Robbins, Claude Schumacher, the playwrights and their agents, and especially to Steve Salemson, Associate Director of the University of Wisconsin Press, and its talented editor Juliet Skuldt. A special thank you to my friend Waldek Dynerman, who provided his paintings for the cover images for both volumes one and two. Above all, thanks to JoAnn, who watched over me while I watched over this book.

THE THEATRE OF THE HOLOCAUST

Introduction

1. History, Theatre, and the Holocaust

Since the first appearance of volume one of *The Theatre of the Holocaust* in 1982, the old discipline of theatre and the new field of Holocaust studies have undergone astonishing transformations. Both the old and the new have changed and been changed by the academic and cultural turbulence that has forced the boundaries defining art and history to be altered, even eliminated. The six plays that are found in this second volume of *The Theatre of the Holocaust,* beyond their intrinsic merits as theatrical texts of extraordinary quality, provide proof of this turbulence and these changes, which are the subjects I want to explore in this introduction.

Foremost among the changes has been the incorporation into the field of Holocaust studies of new and different voices with new and different points of view concerning this catastrophic historical event. As the progress of time has moved all of us further away from the Holocaust, the voices of those who were reluctant to speak earlier, were too young to speak before, or were not yet born have begun to appear in great and varied profusion. In the last decades, for example, the public has needed to accommodate itself to the outpouring of memoirs of Holocaust survivors and their children which, by the 1990s, had filled many shelves in book stores in the United States and abroad. Still these memoirs represent only a small fraction of the stories that could be told about "ordinary" people in times of extraordinary duress. These survivors' tales have also been accompanied by the stories of their oppressors and tormentors, further enlarging the record of Holocaust testimony available to the general reader.

In addition these memoirs, and the many critical investigations to which they were subjected, have appeared and been disseminated not just in the traditional forms of autobiography, drama, and poetry but in different and newer forms: the comic book (as in Art Spiegelman's two-part *Maus*), performance art, and the austere videotapes made of interviews with Holocaust survivors. Implicit in the proliferation of Holocaust literature (in its broadest sense) is the final laying to rest of the dubious critical perspective that art cannot explore or attempt to explain the tragic events of 1933–1945.

In fact, the Holocaust chronology has itself been opened up to other times, influences, and voices. In studying the Holocaust, we now admit easily into our discussions portraits of the world that preceded the start of the Second World War, as when we investigate the societies destroyed during the Shoah (see Theo Richmond's *Konin* or Eva Hoffman's *Shtetl*) or the effect of the Shoah on second and third generations after Nazi Germany's defeat and the liberation of the concentration camps (see Aaron Hass's *In the Shadow of the Holocaust: The Second Generation* or Hank Greenspan's *Recounting the Holocaust: Survivors and Their Listeners*). And we concentrate also on Holocaust experiences too long neglected, as when we attend to the stories of women (see Carol Rittner and John Roth's *Different Voices: Women and the Holocaust*). From the vantage point of the 1990s, clearly we know more about the Holocaust than we did when volume one of this anthology was first published.

But enlarged chronology and perspective are only two reasons for the new abundance of Holocaust investigations since the early 1980s. A second reason for the proliferation of Holocaust literature is the phenomenon of critical reappraisal, a phenomenon with both positive and highly negative implications. On the positive side are found the contributions of academics who apply to Holocaust studies the theories of postmodern criticism that in recent years have received considerable attention in the culture of higher education. As a result, we not only know more about the Holocaust, but we know it differently as well.

Many recent critics have taken advantage of what has long been understood as the liberal historian's prerogative: they have engaged in the reassessment of historical incident demanded by newly perceived and differently understood relationships between society and the individual. Holders of historical or cultural theories impervious to reassessment find the power of their orthodoxy threatened by those who seek new insights into human and social behavior in the face of reconfigured historical and cultural understandings. Inevitably, professional and personal disputation can result from the clash of diverse interests and the ideologies that motivate them.

For some, reassessment fails because the "revisers" of history (itself a negative term frequently linked to Holocaust deniers), in books or on stage, betray survivors and destroy objectivity by tampering with Holocaust "truth." Deeply held beliefs occasion outrage from those, frequently survivors, who fear their experiences are being assaulted and rejected. This problem is discussed in Albert Lindemann's *Esau's Tears: Modern Anti-Semitism and the Rise of the Jews,*[1] which argues implicitly for the disciplinary intersection of the historical and artistic imaginations and a generous spirit in evaluating this overlap. In his epilogue, Lindemann summarizes a crucial point.

> It has been a key assertion of these pages that although no historian can be free of love or hatred, a determined effort to understand the opposing tugs of those two passions must be made, for one of them alone typically does not lead to "genuine history" but to skewed, tendentious versions of it, conducive to self-righteousness and new cycles of misunderstanding and hatred. . . .[2]

By acknowledging "the opposing tugs," Lindemann expresses the belief that even historians write from subjective and emotional perspectives—even as they must move beyond those perspectives in their attempt to achieve coherence and fairness in their judgments. Here we can see how the search for historical "truth" in general, and Holocaust "truth" in particular, is controlled by the

1. Cambridge: Cambridge University Press, 1997.
2. Ibid., p. 510.

contextualizing forces that have determined one's individual nature, status, or professional training.

At the close of the twentieth century, this view of historical and artistic overlap, and of personal and professional overlap, can probably withstand most attacks by doctrinaire and dogmatic critics whose anger, it must be said, finds justifiable expression when focused on flagrant examples of Holocaust revisionism, the kind that seeks to exploit the victims, relativize the evil of the victimizers, or, most repugnantly, to deny the Holocaust altogether. It is also likely that we can accept a term such as "Holocaust truths" so long as we are free to criticize writing that seeks ideological, psychological, nationalistic or commercial advantage, or that refuses to admit the historical events themselves.

Later in his conclusion, Lindemann argues forcefully on behalf of the historian who attempts to re-create the life of the past through both the accumulation of incident and the power of the ethical imagination.

> Imagining oneself into such situations and answering the question "what would I have done?"—either as concentration camp inmate or ordinary citizen—is more than most people are able to do confidently and honestly, although the question nonetheless needs to be confronted, the effort made.[3]

Nevertheless playwrights, novelists, film makers, or poets, the artistic "imaginers" who seek newer, often harsher insights, suffer critical reactions to their works that can be discomfiting and hostile. As the philosopher Tzvetan Todorov reminds us, "Truth, it seems, is incompatible with inner conflict, and most of us prefer comfort. . . . I do not think we can change this state of affairs, nor do I even wish we could. I do believe, however, that from time to time we need to disrupt it."[4] For what else can the sincere artist do than seek through verbal and visual image to understand an event that, because it contains both opacity and ambiguity in

3. Ibid., p. 529.

4. *Facing the Extreme: Moral Life in the Concentration Camps,* tr. Arthur Denner and Abigail Pollak (New York: Henry Holt, 1996), p. 257.

many of its aspects, because it raises the most urgent of human issues, and because it is forever receding in time, compels the desire for some kind of immediate emotional and intellectual engagement with it? Inevitably, in the service of an artistic impulse shaped by the cultural pressures of the age and the individual's mission, the artist may either reaffirm conventional understanding or, instead, search for a different kind of expressiveness that moves the reader or viewer to contemplate differently than before the event known as "the Holocaust." Working to deconstruct a text (and for postmodernists the idea of what a text is has expanded enormously) means not a diminution or denigration of the Holocaust, its victims, or perpetrators but rather a new attempt to come to grips with a historical catastrophe of astounding complexity. I believe that a reading of the six plays in this volume will confirm the value of this strategy, for the plays courageously, even defiantly, validate how the supple, ethical imagination, mediated by a profound emotional sympathy, can propose new ways to approach historical truth—some even by asserting the "death of history" in the process.[5]

Among the best books that deal with the anxiety of imagining Holocaust "truth" is Saul Friedlander's *Probing the Limits of Representation: Nazism and the "Final Solution."* In his introduction to the volume of essays, Friedlander writes of how the search for the monolithic interpretation or the totalizing narrative of the Holocaust must give way before the need for "a multiplicity of equally valid approaches" to the subject. He writes:

> Thus on the one hand, our traditional categories of conceptualization and representation may well be insufficient, our language itself problematic.

5. Pierre Vidal-Naquet, a most conservative historian who condemns the kind of revisionism that preaches Holocaust denial, asks: "Does this mean that one should capitulate in the face of such denial, sliding bit by bit toward a world in which all things are equivalent, the historian and the forger, fantasy and reality, massacres and car accidents?" He answers no and offers "In the Guise of a Conclusion" the lyrics of a tango "Cambalache" by an Argentine poet! See *Assassins of Memory: Essays on the Denial of the Holocaust,* tr. Jeffrey Mehlman (New York: Columbia University Press, 1992 [1987]), pp. 139–42.

On the other hand, in the face of these events we feel the need of some stable narration; a boundless field of possible discourses raises the issue of limits with particular stringency.[6]

There is no better place on this "boundless field" than in the work of playwrights to test the accuracy of Friedlander's divided assessment of the limits of representation. For while all serious Holocaust literature attempts to manage the tension between the compulsion to reenvision and the need for stability, the theatre's flexible, performative nature magnifies the tension considerably, even unbearably. Indeed, discussing theatre without discussing the range of interpretive opportunities inherent in any play or production of it, can lead only to the tendentious and self-righteous criticism that Lindemann rightly deplores. As we shall see, the work of Holocaust playwrights in recent years raises certain formal challenges to earlier dramatists who resist and reject the changes in structure and subject that have come to be seen as the most challenging and provocative in contemporary theatre.

In volume one of *The Theatre of the Holocaust,* I advanced five reasons for the work of playwrights who engage the Holocaust experience: 1) to pay homage to the victims; 2) to educate audiences; 3) to provoke emotional responses; 4) to raise moral questions; and 5) to draw conclusions about the possibilities of human behavior.[7] Missing from the list is explicit reference to the necessary ways in which playwrights can achieve these specific objectives through

6. Cambridge: Harvard University Press, 1992, p. 6. The American critic Irving Howe, writing a decade before Friedlander, addressed the same questions:

> For some decades now philosophers and literary critics have been agonizing about the question: Can imaginative literature "represent" in any profound or illuminating way the meanings of the Holocaust? Is the "debris of memory" (as one survivor has called it) a proper or manageable subject for stories or novels? Are there not perhaps extreme situations beyond the reach of art? Should not art have a sufficient sense of its own limitations to keep a certain distance from the unspeakable?

"Preface," *The Art of the Holocaust,* ed. Janet Blatter and Sybil Milton (New York: Rutledge, 1981), p. 10.

7. Madison: University of Wisconsin Press, 1981, p. 14.

new approaches to their subject at a time when cultural and political understandings have become less monolithic or universal than a generation ago. Indeed, to speak of "universality," just as to speak of a unified "truth," raises substantial critical problems that no simple or single dogma can resolve.

An instructive case in point concerns the recent controversy attached to the most famous work of Holocaust literature, *Anne Frank: The Diary of a Young Girl.* In a passionately misguided essay in the *New Yorker* magazine, the novelist and critic Cynthia Ozick asked the important question through her title "Who Owns Anne Frank?" In her survey of the literary and cultural legacy of the diary in the half-century since its original, textually altered publication, Ozick excoriates all those who have attempted to engage with it, judging them inept, rapacious, and indecent. "Almost every hand that has approached the diary with the well-meaning intention of publicizing it has contributed to *the subversion of history,*" she writes [emphasis added].[8] Ozick concludes her sweeping cultural and artistic reprimand ("the conversion of Anne into usable goods") with the reputedly satirical conclusion that the diary would have been better off burned than reduced to so cheap and shameful a fate as it has received from its adapters, all of whom are incompetent, opportunistic, or mendacious. I believe that whatever the tone or intention of Ozick's judgment, it is based on an understanding of history and culture that is as mistaken as it is difficult to sustain.

Ozick's "answer" keeps its distance from the inquiry that provoked her ruminations. A more appropriate response would have incorporated the knowledge that neither historical documents nor the interpretation of them are fixed or exempt from the pressures of culture or time, and that this awareness being absent, Lindemann's "new cycles of misunderstanding and hatred" will result. There is, of course, plenty of blame to spread around the "boundless field" that is to be found in Anne's cramped hiding place. Yet,

8. *New Yorker,* 6 October 1997, p. 78.

there is much useful striving for some truth as well, not the kind that exists only to subdue and destroy other truths but the kind that seeks restlessly to grapple with different "ways of knowing" than that possessed by keepers of the cauterizing, critical flame. Whether sad knowledge or not, it is inescapable that *everyone* owns Anne Frank, even those who don't deserve her.

Thus, in an essay assessing the legacy of the diary, Alvin H. Rosenfeld examines how Anne's personal memoir has been received differently by different groups (Americans, Germans, and Jews), each of which creates from Anne's short life and agonizing death meanings and images that can contradict those held by others. "Thus," he writes, "in both Germany and Israel one finds a common history marked by a common symbol but shaped by very different motives and yielding diverse interpretations of the past."[9] Rosenfeld then focuses on the condition that must result in multiple interpretations of the same text.

> The past, we know, is never permanently fixed but rather shifts in contour and meaning with the changing shapes of symbolization and interpretation. . . . There is nothing particularly surprising about this development, although the pace at which it seems to be proceeding and the degree of divergence that it may yield are matters that warrant serious pondering by anyone interested in observing how the past is variously reconstructed and transmitted to diverse publics.[10]

In the theatre, differing or contradictory interpretations of the same text are often the result of differing interpretations of the same historical event. Indeed, journalistic commentary about

9. "Popularization and Memory: The Case of Anne Frank," in *Lessons and Legacies: The Meaning of the Holocaust in a Changing World,* ed. Peter Hayes (Evanston, Ill.: Northwestern University Press, 1991), p. 277. A more recent example of the same phenomenon involved the international reception of Steven Spielberg's film *Schindler's List.* See *Spielberg's Holocaust: Critical Perspectives on Schindler's List,* ed. Yosefa Loshitzky (Bloomington: Indiana University Press, 1997), especially chapters 8–11.

10. Ibid., pp. 277, 288. Rosenfeld's essay appears in an anthology whose subtitle confirms the struggle of the public to reach comprehension through accommodation with the alterations of time and perspective: *The Meaning of the Holocaust in a Changing World.*

the recent Broadway production of the dramatization of Anne's diary in December 1997 finds contemporary cultural importance in the incorporation into the "revised" script words, themes, and images from the diary that had been altered or excluded purposely from the "original" 1955 version of *The Diary of Anne Frank* by its adapters Frances Goodrich and Albert Hackett. In the 1997 *revision of a revision,* the latest producers seek a history "made right" and a truth "made pure" (though not forever, of course, and probably not even for long).

In the context of performance, we need to acknowledge that altering the form or content of this re-revised text represents only one way to approach the issue of interpretative variations of a script. Another very significant way to "change" a dramatic text through performance is *to play against the text* (i.e., to perform the script differently than the playwright would appear to have intended). One example might be to deliver the 1955 version's most famous, optimistic, and, perhaps, most criticized line (spoken by Anne's "Voice"): "In spite of everything, I still believe that people are really good at heart," as bitingly satirical rather than earnestly hopeful. Or, the line could be placed elsewhere in the performance than at the final curtain. In a postmodern "reading," where subjectivity is splintered and other media incorporated, the line might be spoken by an embodied Anne, or several Annes, on stage or on videotape, who appear neither innocent nor clean, but rather scabrous and stained, expiring alone or together in agony, in rags, in view. Of such a production, not a few critics would inquire: Who owns that Anne?

What then can the arts do for a world where values are made cheap by cultures that participate in acts of horrifying cruelty? What humane function remains to artists who create stories and images that reassess the many actions and the complicated characters involved in the flourishing of atrocity? What ethical place can be occupied by audiences whose familiarity with history is *inevitably* biased or partial, and therefore in some absolute sense, *always* mistaken? These are the continuing aesthetic and moral questions that are raised by artists and, in their individual ways, answered by the plays in this anthology. The six plays, specifically and intentionally, contribute new perspectives to understanding the Holocaust while, at the same time, they force readers and audiences to deal with the issues of interpretation and representation that, in the public space of the theatre, earn the kind of immediate, volatile, and often contradictory responses that their historian colleagues usually are spared.

Peter Haidu, in his essay in Friedlander's anthology, is forthright and uneasy with the instability of linguistic strategies to deal with what he calls "the Event." He sees danger not in negligent or careless witnessing to the Holocaust but in the very attempt to confront and explain the experience itself. "It is rather the ineluctable structures and risks inherent in the representational process, *including history as well as fiction,* historical discourse as well as any other form of discourse. These structures and risks would appear to be the inherent cost of any and all representations . . . ." Haidu finds the solution to this problem in an approach that is both "ethical and religious" and advocates a proper way to address the Event: "with a requisite sense of responsibility toward the dead, their suffering, and the piety appropriate" to it.[11] Yet, heartfelt and humane as it is, even Haidu's modest prescription has an imaginative latitude that is made even greater in the arena of the theatrical event where the combination of history and fiction and the uniquely layered strategies of impersonation and "reality" produce diverse and divergent perspectives on the subject of the Holocaust.

All the playwrights in this volume abide by a well-earned moral compass. They convey responsibility for the dead, move us mightily, and provide images that provoke intense discussion. They also raise issues of historical and aesthetic importance without losing their ethical grip. For some, the primary focus is on those persons whose anguish finds no relief and whose understanding lacks any certainty. Many brood on the legacy of evil and

11. "The Dialectics of Unspeakability: Language, Silence, and the Narratives of Desubjectification," in Friedlander, pp. 280–81.

the surprising appearance of goodness, though some suggest that, where the Holocaust is concerned, the line between is difficult to discern. Their treatment of historical fact is mediated by performative interventions that endow the texts' theatrical efforts not with clarity or reconciliation but rather with mystery and desperate unease, the latter sometimes provoked or softened by laughter. What they all do, and I believe appropriately, is withhold easy hopefulness or sentiment, avoid advocacy for causes other than profound concern for life's moral basis, and reject the simple answers to profound questions concerning justice, faith, suffering, and truth that are aligned with ideological or doctrinaire explanations of the Holocaust. And though they may resist promulgation of a single meaning or truth for their work, even dispensing with formal closure to their version of the Holocaust story (a common postmodern strategy), they participate nonetheless in the theatrical discovery of some kind of essential though provisional and unstable truth. In sum, they do what good historians do, historians who have not lost "a sense of theatre" in their attempt to "redress" reality.

> In an age which has experienced horror beyond measure from the perversions of true believers, we are well educated to the interpretation of signs. . . . The brilliance of the theatre is that it represents experience and offers us the conventionalities by which the representation can be interpreted. . . . Experience represented in the theatre is dressed with the same particularities of everyday experience and has the larger-than-itself quality of everyday experience, but is transformed by being selected and shaped for interpretation. It does not replicate reality. It redresses reality. Theatricality in history-making will do the same.[12]

The plays in volume two point to the ways in which the employment of history faces continual challenge in the work of playwrights who explore the Holocaust experience. For example, the plays may be discussed usefully with reference to their nonrealistic assumptions and techniques while keeping in mind also

12. Greg Dening, *Performances* (Chicago: University of Chicago Press, 1996), pp. 126–27.

how the historical passage of time, the resistance to unitary perspectives, and the pressure of new discoveries, have had their own wide-ranging effect in the theatre. To be sure, much has been written about the failings of traditional realism, the display of "life as it is" as a method of revealing truths about human existence to audiences. These failings—realism's inherent artificiality, its covert advocacy of a single "objective" truth, its "determined" outcome, its totalizing and closed narrative structure, its ability to reify "normative" behavior rather than challenge it—have been the subject of continuing discussion since the form "congealed" in Western Europe and Russia in the last quarter of the nineteenth century. (Realism, of course, has its positive features also, including quickly establishing emotional and physical correspondences with audiences; in any case, realism continues to be the dominant form of theatre encountered by most contemporary audiences.) It is important to see how easy it was to achieve, with the theatrical alternatives to realism in place, a type of drama where facticity itself could be challenged.

Departures from the realistic form, of course, occur well in advance of the 1980s, in fact, well before the events of the Holocaust itself. Theatrical forms such as the expressionism of the 1920s or Bertolt Brecht's Epic Theatre of the 1930s posed the original and still powerful challenges to realism's formal and aesthetic assumptions. Several plays in volume one of *The Theatre and the Holocaust,* in particular George Tabori's *The Cannibals* and Harold and Edith Lieberman's *Throne of Straw,* showed clearly the influence of these nonrealistic movements. Both plays resist narrative closure and the audience separation from actors that is basic to realism, techniques that were, by the 1960s, commonplace. Later, in the 1980s, these strategies were accompanied by others that diminished realism's centrality and provoked antagonism to the new postmodern forms of theatre as well. Nonetheless, a recent assessment by the philosopher Hayden White supports the work of playwrights who find the realistic form inadequate to their mission to stage the Holocaust experience.

This is not to suggest that we will give up the effort to represent the Holocaust realistically, but rather that our notion of what constitutes realistic representation must be revised to take account of experiences that are unique to our century and for which older modes of representation have proven inadequate.[13]

2. THE PLAYS, INTERPRETATION, AND PERFORMANCE

Camp Comedy

> You won't be making a film, Kurt, you'll be making history.
>
> —Imp

Roy Kift's *Camp Comedy* utilizes a theatrical style influenced deeply by Brecht's Epic Theatre (use of a narrator figure, musical interludes that comment on the action, frequent reminders that the audience is watching theatre not life, etc.) to explore the unique and bizarre conditions that prevailed inside the Theresienstadt concentration camp established by the Nazis in and nearby the Czechoslovakian town of Terezin. In his author's preface, Kift also acknowledges the influence of the Polish theatre artist Tadeusz Kantor. Theresienstadt (the German name) was unlike any other concentration camp in its status as a "model camp" to which outside visitors could be taken to prove the Nazis' "benign" treatment of the western and central European Jews who were the exclusive population of the camp after July 1942. Over the years of its terrible existence, Theresienstadt held a hundred forty thousand prisoners, of whom approximately nineteen thousand survived. The remainder were murdered, mostly after transport by cattle car to the killing center at Auschwitz.

Theresienstadt's second distinction was to serve as the temporary repository for a large number of Jews who had achieved renown or importance before the war began. In particular, many artists were sent to the camp, and, as historical narratives attest, they

13. "Historical Emplotment and the Problem of Truth," in Friedlander, p. 52.

maintained an extraordinary level of artistic activity amid the vile conditions of their incarceration. The camp inhabitants engaged in numerous theatrical and musical events; musical concerts, opera, and cabaret were used by the prisoners as an important strategy to alleviate the suffering of their daily lives. This was especially true of the visual and musical artists whose remaining legacy in paintings and songs continues to move and inspire today's audiences who see and hear courage and beauty in the works of the doomed.[14]

In the summer of 1944, the Nazis found the perfect way to exploit the talents of their prisoners for their destructive ends. To deceive a visiting delegation from the International Red Cross, they created a completely fraudulent "paradise camp," where the Jews would be seen living "normal" lives, most especially in their continuing enjoyment of cultural and recreational activities. In their duplicity, the Nazis were entirely successful, as evidenced by the positive report the Red Cross visitors produced after their departure. Seizing upon this success as a step toward producing a greater propaganda victory, the highest authorities in Berlin ordered a cinematic record of the Jews' exemplary condition under Nazi rule. The "documentary" film, called *The Führer Gives a City to the Jews* (*Der Führer schenkt den Juden eine Stadt*), created an enormous artistic challenge and a terrifying human dilemma for the people involved in its production; in fact, the film was not shown in public before the war's end, and it was never seen by the people who made it because nearly all were shipped to their deaths at Auschwitz immediately after their task was completed. This is the historical background to *Camp Comedy,* background Kift comments upon in his author's preface.[15]

The playwright's protagonist is Kurt Gerron, a film and stage

14. Lawrence Langer takes a different view, ascribing the beauty of some Holocaust art to the "resilience" of the art itself and not to the "heroism of men," though many would wish it to "redesign hope from the shards of despair." "Cultural Resistance to Genocide," *Witness,* 1, no. 1 (Spring 1987): 82–95.

15. Kift's longer discussion of the history and musical activity of Theresienstadt appears in "Reality and Illusion in the Theresienstadt Cabaret," in *Staging the Holocaust,* ed. Claude Schumacher (Cambridge: Cambridge University Press,

actor and director who was well known in Europe (he had appeared with Marlene Dietrich in *The Blue Angel* and as Mack the Knife in a famous production of Brecht's *Threepenny Opera*). Gerron had been sent to Theresienstadt from Holland through the notorious transit camp of Westerbork in January 1944. Kift focuses on Gerron for many of the same reasons that the Liebermans in *Throne of Straw* chose to focus on *Judenrat* Chairman Mordechai Chaim Rumkowski of the Lodz, Poland, ghetto: to represent the ethical struggle for survival faced continuously by those in the ghettos and concentration camps. The play makes scrupulous use of historical sources, including the original lyrics of Theresienstadt's cabarets. Gerron has two prominent antagonists confronting him with ethical challenges: the Nazi Kommandant Rahm and the Imp, the theatrical interlocutor who mediates between Rahm and Gerron, and between Gerron and the audience. In his presence and actions we find articulated the moral inquiries of the playwright. What morality should guide Gerron's choices when faced with the "offer" to make a movie that would lie about the Jews' existence but which, simultaneously, could provide sufficient time to make survival seem possible to the vain, the desperate, or the terrorized film "artists"? When does the struggle for individual survival turn into the betrayal of comrades? When does dedication to professional standards become transformed into deadly complicity with the enemy? To what lengths should we go to provide impoverished and desperate lives with meaning? Within the play, Gerron's actions are shadowed by these important ethical questions.

The central scenic metaphor of the carousel (provided by the device of a revolving stage) refers us not just to the name of Gerron's own cabaret act ("Karussel"), but to the entertainment the theatre creates to deceive and distract us from suffering and despair as well. Gerron's film, of course, was a lie according to the false

1998), pp. 147–68. Parts of the Theresienstadt film have been preserved and have been examined by scholars and shown at academic conferences. Footage from *The Führer Gives a City to the Jews* is included in the documentary film *Paradise Camp,* directed by Frank Heimans and Paul Rea (1986).

reality it was based on, but those who visited the camp (and who would have seen the film) were enticed into the conviction of a Jewish paradise amid the European conflagration; perhaps it provided what they wanted to see. In the context of the Holocaust, the cinematic images Gerron created distorted historical truth. *Camp Comedy* informs its audience about those lies and the perverted ethical system that demanded them. Additionally, the play elucidates the important relationship between the manipulation of fact and the power of art. Clearly, Kift is asking us to think about the *uses* to which comedy can be put in life and the theatre.

On the carousel, life circles back to the place the Theresienstadt artists hoped to avoid at all costs: their fated journey toward death that the Nazis intended with the "final solution." However, along with the terrible historical fate that awaited all the artists of Theresienstadt, a concurrent, even contradictory, truth is presented in the defiant restoration of the characters in the last minutes of the performance. This is the final comic action of *Camp Comedy,* a gesture full of high spirits and wonder, though tragic too, because of the unalterable historical catastrophe that Kift, more than fifty years after Theresienstadt's demise, is determined to explore through the theatre.

The Survivor and the Translator

> Yet now there's no history yet. History will tell after two,
> three generations is begins the real history of this period.
> Of every period. You can't right away after this after one
> generation make history. But makes history time. A lot.

Much has been written recently about the testimony of survivors, and the many collections of videotaped examples have been studied intensely by scholars who seek insight into the particular and profound traumas that Holocaust survivors endured.[16] Leeny Sack's *The Survivor and the Translator* differs from these "merely"

16. See, for example, the Fortunoff Video Archive of Holocaust Testimony at Yale University. Its holdings have been studied by Lawrence Langer in *Holocaust Testimonies: The Ruins of Memory* (New Haven: Yale University Press, 1991).

spoken records because its theatrical form endows the dramatic text with an interpretive dimension lacking, for example, in the videotaped record of survivors who are fixed in surroundings from which all visual enrichment has been removed.[17] Sack asks us to experience the text on two levels: we respond to the text and to how the text is being performed *without losing the sense that we are responding to both simultaneously.* This clarifies Sack's status as creator of her own performance while pointing to the specific challenges she faces at every minute of the performance process; she not only describes her actions, she narrates for us (as readers) what she is attempting to accomplish as an actor at the moment she acts. By interrogating the text at the same time she is inhabiting it; she establishes distance between herself and the words she speaks. This strategy leads up to the moment when the shift in identity from granddaughter to grandmother occurs and a sustained, "inhabited" character is created for the first time. Through theatre the grandmother, a figure from history as well as a presence among the audience, is given continuous new life by her living, surviving descendent.

Thus, the subtitle to Sack's performance defines the events that produced this extraordinary and intimately personal drama: "a solo theatre work about not having experienced the Holocaust, by a daughter of concentration camp survivors." In theatricalizing her life as a child of survivors, Sack provokes her audience to confront the experience of her family's trauma *and* her involvement with it without the mediation of traditional, fictional characters. Unlike the other texts in this anthology, there are no fictional people on stage through whom the story is being told, though there is a person on display, in fact several of them, creating exceptionally fluid yet rigidly defined interactions with the audience; of the texts gathered here, this one exploits most fully the sheer *presence* of the actor.

Sack inhabits her role(s) while at the same time she makes it

17. A number of commentators have been critical of the intrusiveness of the interviewers and the ineptitude of the filming of these tapes, resulting in coercive aspects which interfere with the "simple clarity" of the speakers.

impossible to remove the consideration of her "acting." We see the world of the Holocaust through her body's interaction with space and with the particular objects she has selected to contribute images of stark, visual immediacy. At strategic points in the performance, the audience is recognized, and at one point a volunteer is enlisted into participation. At that moment, the distinction (and spatial distance) between audience and performer breaks down in order to bring the audience into a richer confrontation with the story and its teller, even though the text at that point is vulgar and repellent. To receive the text of *The Survivor and the Translator* in performance is to experience the alternative rhythm of capture and escape, physically and emotionally.

The title of the performance alludes to the two dominant figures on stage: the survivor (Sack's grandmother) and her translator (Sack herself). The title refers also to the gap, aesthetic and historical, between the teller of history and the history itself, between fact and art, here made more problematical because of the deeply personal testimony at the core of the story being told. Sack notes, "The story I tell was slipped under my skin before I could say yes or no or Mama. I sit inside the memory of where I was not. Yes. So there's no choice. That's what was." Wearing a pair of headphones with the cord taped to a battered suitcase, Sack presents an image of receiving her instructions and her inspiration from the lost and battered carriers of suitcases, most of whom ended their existence as crematory ash.

Among the first issues that Sack confronts in her performance is the proper use of the voices heard in her complex, multilingual tale. Speaking English and Polish, with bits of German added, Sack immerses herself in the task of moving between languages as a way to trace and bridge the gaps and disruptions of experience between the grandmother and granddaughter. Eventually, the two "become" the same person on stage, merging identities as the story develops and unfolds, and culminating in the survivor being "born" through the agency of her generational successor. The personalities of the two women, inflected by changes in the tone, volume, and velocity of their speech, in addition to the difference in language itself (the grandmother/survivor's voice is "melodious and full of feeling," while the granddaughter/translator's is monotonous, lacking in most emotion), play a kind of vocal game of tag as the translator negotiates the task of changing one language into the other. At first, it is the pressure to perform the story, not to get the words right but to get them out at all, that drives the theatrical event. The incipient frenzy of the performance, made explicit in the early action of Sack running in place on a rusty bed so that the sounds of the bedsprings and her accompanying high-pitched note become the "sound memory" of a moving train, produces a sense of propulsive terror that subsides only in the astonishing extended monologue that completes the performance when perfect vocal and emotional congruence is achieved.

In an essay called "Trauma, Memory, and Transference," Saul Friedlander describes the particular attribute of Holocaust historians that has specific relevance to Sack's performance text.

> The self-awareness of the historian of the Nazi epoch or the Shoah is essential. Such self-awareness should itself be accessible to critical reading. It seems therefore that this difficult historical quest imposes the sporadic but forceful presence of commentary. Whether this narrative is built into the narrative structure of a history or developed as a separate, superimposed text is a matter of choice, but the voice of the commentator must be clearly heard. The commentary should disrupt the facile linear progression of the narration, introduce alternative interpretations, question any partial conclusion, withstand the need for closure. Because of the necessity of some form of narrative sequence in the writing of history, such commentary may introduce splintered or constantly recurring refractions of a traumatic past by using any number of different vantage points.[18]

One of the "splintered refractions," in fact, is Anne Frank's diary, used sparingly by Sack, along with several other texts inside *The Survivor and the Translator.* These kinds of "quotations" and "borrowings" are an important feature of postmodern forms of art, which use such appropriations as textual enhancements to create a wider frame of reference and opportunity of response for an audience.

18. See *Holocaust Remembrance: The Shapes of Memory,* ed. Geoffrey H. Hartman (Oxford: Basil Blackwell, 1994), p. 261.

When *The Survivor and the Translator* winds down, without narrative closure, we have a palpable feeling of physical exhaustion. The extended monologue depicts the personal discovery of speech that is able to present the narrative of one woman's terrifying and *continuing* struggle with a trauma that defies clear or logical expression. The splintered, circling, repetitious language seems inadequate to the task of telling a survivor's story. In fact, the story contains allusions to others beside the two women, others who are brought to and lose theatrical life through the verbal elusiveness of the text's pronouns (whose mother? whose son?). "Speaking clearly in my own voice," Sack says as she disengages from her "other" who is herself, "with barely a breath between languages, I finish." The moment recalls the compulsive monodramas of Samuel Beckett, whose search for continuance finds a momentary equilibrium in the elusive, evasive language that characterizes so much of both Holocaust testimony and postmodern drama.

Langer writes of the survivor's world as one where "the self functioned on the brink of extinction, and we are left with a series of personal histories beyond judgment and evaluation." He continues:

> The challenge is to enter this world to reverse the process of defamiliarization that overwhelmed the victims and to find an orientation that will do justice to their recaptured experience without summoning it or them to judgment or evaluation.[19]

This is the challenge that faces all translators of Holocaust testimony.

Dreams of Anne Frank

> You can be imprisoned in a basement or an attic, but you
> can go anywhere. In your dreams you are free, the past,
> the present, the future.
>
> —Anne

19. *Holocaust Testimonies,* p. 183.

Bernard Kops's play for young people *Dreams of Anne Frank* is clear evidence of a playwright's attempt to alter previous historical and aesthetic understandings that are attached to a particular, well-known work of literature. Kops is not at all interested in deconstructing the text of *The Diary of Anne Frank* in a manner alluded to earlier in this introduction. He is interested in "redressing" the world-famous *Diary* by changing entirely its dramatic shape and method, all the while emphasizing what he sees as the essential feature of Anne's writing: its display of a luminous, active imagination in defiance of the constraints imposed by her place of hiding. Most important, Kops knows that for today's audiences who are younger than Anne was at the time she began to write her story (typically, most audiences are older), the requirements of staging are more flexible and the "liberties" taken are both justifiable and necessary. In short, fewer preconceptions and inhibitions on the part of an audience of young people are the compensations for diminished historical knowledge and artistic sophistication.

Anne, an adolescent on the cusp of adulthood in the 1940s, approximates the age and the experience of youth in its need to conform to a number of onerous restrictions. Here, *in addition to* serving for *adults* as an icon of innocence in a defiled world, she defines for Kops the capacious imagination of an actively engaged teenager responding to the spatial and familial rules of the attic with cleverness and courage. When we know the tragic end of Anne's story, her fate pushes her image *ahead* in time toward a maturity extinguished by genocidal hatred. In *Dreams of Anne Frank,* Anne is moved *back* in her development enabling her to explore more expansively the child that she never relinquished completely during her captivity but which we, as readers and viewers, have ignored previously. She responds to her fear of dying or separation with a combination of anxiety, youthful enthusiasm, and a wonderful spirit of "play." Kops calls his work "a total imaginative creation" determined by his desire "to take another route, to find that specific human being, to strip away the deification and bring her down to earth." He elaborates:

> *Dreams of Anne Frank* is not a dramatization of her [Anne's] diary. Rather, it is an original way of focusing upon the girl, to bring alive that unquenchable spirit and show how she managed to be creative in the darkest of times. To write the play, I went to the facts of her life for the spine of reality and to my imagination for the subjective matrix, the foundation of my drama.[20]

As a result of this approach, we are given an Anne different from the "standard version" advanced for the post-Holocaust world desperate for a symbol of positive, articulate innocence. *Dreams of Anne Frank* has access to more performance energy and is staged at a higher "pitch" than its 1950s predecessor, making it more appropriate to the needs of younger audiences who, in addition, may be exposed to Anne Frank for the first time *through this production.* She is "universal" Anne, and she is also an Anne for our time.

Undoubtedly, these fantastic imaginings are the most controversial element in Kops's play, for they eliminate any pretension to historically based realism of character and setting in favor of expressionistic staging devices that demand a response to Anne and her sequestered colleagues in a completely new way. (Kops calls the style expressionistic in his "Note" discussing music for the production.) Thus, Mr. Van Daan becomes something of a music hall performer, and Mrs. Van Daan, representative of meddling intolerance, at one point in the play becomes a witch. In these cartoonish moments, we experience a feeling of emotional liberation, as when songs (Margot, Edith, and Mrs. Van Daan as the Andrews Sisters) and the setting itself (the talking House and Diary, the mysterious Helping Hand) contribute to her story. "In captivity," Anne remarks early and pointedly, "you can be free inside your head." By the time Anne converses with the English prime minister, Winston Churchill, "through" the attic radio, we have long since rejected the purposeful dispensation of fact-based historical details in favor of a wildly fantastical imaginative re-creation of Anne's reprieve from extinction.

Dreams of Anne Frank (the title refers to our "dreams" of Anne

20. *Dreams of Anne Frank* (London: Methuen Student Edition, 1997), pp. 2–3.

as well as to her dreams for herself and the special dreaming she does in the play), retains a powerful sense of tragedy without losing a firm grip on historical understanding despite its dramatic form. When the voices of the Germans are heard ordering the attic's evacuation, the focus of the play shifts away from Anne's creative imagination to its destruction. The actors form a "sort of boxcar" and, accompanied by the sounds of trains, they undress into "prison camp clothing" and sing the prayer testifying to the inextinguishable faith of the Jews in their God, *Ani Ma-amin.* The stage direction reads:

> *Anne kisses her diary and reluctantly discards it, putting it down on the pile of clothes heaped on the stage, and she exits through the back door, following the others. Her diary seems to light up the darkness that now envelops everything.*

Otto Frank returns to have the final word. He sums up the historical record for the audience and the permanent personal loss of a daughter for whom the diary she kept is an inadequate substitute. This last image attempts to create for the young audience a sense of profound sadness and implacable parental love.

The Model Apartment

> They're all inside me. All of them. Anne Frank. The Six Million. Bubbie and Zayde and Hitler and Deborah. When my stomach talks, it's them talking. . . . I eat for them so they won't be hungry.
>
> —Debby

Much has been written about the Holocaust and how its theatrical representation presents difficulty for artists whose work becomes "popular." The word itself has several meanings: an active and "loose" presence in the general culture, as well as an artifact without uniqueness, deformed by a leveling universality. Alvin H. Rosenfeld's discussion of the public disagreements that occur when art engages a historical subject was noted earlier. Others have opposed the kind of universalizing of the Holocaust that turns the doom-laden experience into something sentimental and optimistic. This kind of objection is found in Lawrence Langer's critical assessment of the "Americanization" of the Holocaust. He sees this phenomenon as offering to the public a historical "vision" that refuses to accept that the six million died in vain by maintaining "a victory that will mitigate despair." The propagators of this vision, lacking insight or imagination, are condemned by Langer for "moral oversimplification."[21]

Donald Marguiles's *The Model Apartment* provides another sort of Americanization to deal with the Holocaust, but one that moves beyond easy emotion and uncomplicated response. His play includes pointed cultural criticism while revealing—beneath its astonishing comic surface—a deep and troubled compassion for that group of Holocaust victims whose post-Holocaust lives have found a belated place in the theatre: the tormented survivors their disturbed children. The play is an adult cartoon, one that combines satire and stereotype to produce feelings of artistic outrageousness along with (as with Kops's play) a profound sadness. Its particular brand of "Americanization" lies in its frenzied, comic approach to both social dislocation and human suffering, an approach that underscores a merciless "vision" of the lasting, almost inexpressible horror that marks the world of many Holocaust survivors.

The Model Apartment has its Anne Frank too. In what may be the most memorable scene of the play, Lola, with the help of her middle-aged and hugely obese daughter Debby, retells the story of her own friendship with Anne, her central place in Anne's second, lost diary, and her final moments with the sixteen-year-old girl from Amsterdam in the Bergen Belsen concentration camp.

> When she died in my arms, and I'll never forget it as long as I live, she made me promise: "Hide my book, Lola." Her voice was weak, I had to bend my ear close. "Don't let them take it," she said. "Make sure people

21. "The Americanization of the Holocaust on Stage and Screen," in *From Hester Street to Hollywood*, ed. Sarah Blacher Cohen (Bloomington: Indiana University Press, 1983), pp. 213–30.

read what I wrote, people should know. Promise me, Lola, promise me." I promised. And little Anna Frank smiled, and closed her eyes, and she was gone, right in my arms. . . . If only that book lasted through the war. . . . I'm telling you, I was the heroine, it was my story. She wrote about *me!* I could've given people hope. But my story, *Lola's* story, told by Anne Frank, went up in flames with her in Belsen. The Belsen diary. The *other* diary. The diary that nobody knows about. The diary *I* told her to keep.

To which Debby responds, "She's so fulla shit."

In this speech Lola is *serious,* but the manner of her speaking is comically presented, prompted by her vulgar and mocking daughter and performed for Debby's fifteen-year-old "mildly retarded" lover, Neil. That Lola's story is preposterous (and, for some, surely in bad taste) may cause difficulty for individuals needing greater adherence to historical accuracy. However, Margulies's *shtik*-filled "aria" is not about facts; rather, it is concerned with the terrible pain Lola has endured for the half-century since her liberation, years filled with disappointment, abandonment, and unappeasable grief. Further, the scene concludes with a savage irony when Lola, summing up the tale of her lost friendship, says, "And that, Neil, is the story of me and Anne Frank," and hears the response (after a long—and comic—pause), "Who?"

The enormous pain in this comic play is carried also by Max, Lola's husband, whose single, final aspiration is to be left alone in his last years to enjoy retirement in a Florida sunny of climate and disposition. But he is haunted by the ghost of his dead daughter Deborah, after whom her half-sister is named, who appears at moments in the play to give concrete evidence of Max's overwhelming despair. Bereft of his first family who were killed by the Nazis, he is happy only in his Yiddish-inflected imagination when the terror of his youth is temporarily obscured by the dreams of old age. And Debby's profoundly unhappy life as the inadequate inheritor of Deborah's name and nature produces a grossly overweight, crippled woman whose self-loathing transforms her desperate need for love into an unquenchable need for sex. As is pointed out early in the play, she too is a kind of survivor.

The Model Apartment is a very funny play. Margulies writes about the Holocaust with the intention of showing how its legacy is one of permanent pain, both for the survivors and for their families who have come to represent different aspects of survivorship. Though the references made in the play are to American culture (film, TV, supermarket products), the wider and infinitely larger story told in *The Model Apartment* is one of displacement, isolation, and permanent terror. As befits a play of the late 1980s, there is no true closure to the story Margulies tells, either on stage or in "real" life. Lola, Debby, and Neil disappear, and Max dreams the play to its conclusion allowing the ghost of Deborah to have the final, bittersweet words. Within a space as constricted and absurd as Anne Frank's, but infinitely more vulgar and more comic, this dysfunctional, contemporary family plays out a story that is both a cultural parody and a deeply felt search for meaning and love in a post-Holocaust world. But the search fails. That Margulies can make us laugh at human suffering while deeply respecting the "facts" of the Holocaust and the blighted victims who survived it is proof that, in hands of a skilled and courageous playwright, the astonishing artistic possibilities of a post-Holocaust, "Americanized" vision can move us mightily.[22]

The Portage to San Cristobal of A. H.

> If we hang him [Hitler], we'll be pretending what he did can be made good. History will draw a line and forget even faster. That's exactly what they want. . . . So they can be acquitted.
>
> —Gideon

The premiere in 1982 of Christopher Hampton's stage adaptation of George Steiner's novella *The Portage to San Cristobal of A. H.* provoked a response that ranged from approval to outrage. The play proposes to tell the story of a 90-year-old Adolf Hitler discovered by a search party of Israelis in a Brazilian jungle. From

22. A play with a similar tone and method is *Angel of Death* (1992) by Charlie Shulman, a wild satire showing how a "rediscovered" Josef Mengele finds happiness and disappointment as the protagonist of a Hollywood film dedicated to his exterminatory exploits as Auschwitz's "Angel of Death."

the standpoint of history, of course, the story is a fantastic lie, unsupported by any documentation and without possibility of validation. But, from the standpoint of theatre, the play is intended as a moral fable, one that uses the "archvillain" of the twentieth century as protagonist in order to advance certain understandings about history, art, and the relationship between them. In truth, much of the criticism of *Portage* was based on two related aspects in the production: the "truth" of Hitler's final, extended speech and the absence of any character in the play to offer a refutation to Hitler's profoundly antisemitic, rhetorical onslaught. These two events continue to provide the basis for an inquiry into the play's ethical perspective.

It is useful to note how carefully Steiner has used history to support his enormously exciting storytelling. Few people believe that Hitler didn't die in his Berlin bunker in 1945, but the popular (and sometimes antisemitic) understanding, supported by verifiable examples of numerous high-ranking Nazis escaping to South America after the Second World War, allows for just enough "plausibility" to sustain popular speculation about the consequences of a Hitlerian escape and return. Further, in the resistance to absolute closure concerning Hitler's death may be found an analogous open-endedness concerning Hitler's crimes (no opportunity for an international tribunal to judge him as others were at Nuremberg and elsewhere after the war, no agreed-upon certainty about his motive, no end to the trauma and suffering that his genocidal policies caused). Steiner seizes on the opportunity to provide a response to a mighty individual and national desire: to confront the "meaning" of Hitler in his time and ours.

Historians search documents and archives to discover this meaning; playwrights invent the situations that allow for many kinds of powerful ethical speculation. Scene two of *Portage* attempts to establish the historical "gaps" and recapitulate the historical events that will allow for the rest of the play to be believable if not truthful. "It's just possible. Just. Million to one," says Ryder in scene two. But the one in a million is all that Steiner needs to release his provocation on the public.

Many of the speeches of Lieber, who directs the search party from afar with radio transmissions, are historical fragments, unfinished reminders (full of minute detail) of specific incidents of the terrible humiliation and murderous violence done to the Jews. It is a catalog of suffering, a reminder to the audience that though it may be watching a fable, it is one created out of the minutiae of verifiable chronological and historical events. Further, the historical details are intermingled with a succession of quasi-historical references that derive from another source of "truth": the Hebrew Bible and the millennial elaborations on its text. Lieber is held wholly in the grip of historical memory made painfully manifest in the desperate retribution he seeks as a survivor of the Holocaust. Whether he cannot finish his sentences from emotional or mental breakdown is not certain. However, as the action of the play moves toward the establishment of a specific, culturally defined ritual, one that is embedded in post-Holocaust consciousness—the trial and Hitler's impassioned and rational self-defense—it is clear that Steiner is shifting the focus away from the past-centered dramatization of the Hitler legacy to the future-centered moral inquiry about what we would do to Hitler if he were to appear among us. Steiner knows the universal desire to bring killers to some kind of justice, and he knows the inherent drama that resides in the theatrical form of the trial, but he uses this knowledge to confront the audience with questions that have continuing social resonance in a theatrical form that resists both simple, authorial prescription and expected narrative closure.[23]

The vociferous opposition that greeted Hampton's adaptation of Steiner's novella, in retrospect, appears to be exceedingly misguided now that there is greater understanding of the ways in which post-Holocaust and postmodern theatre forms may use history differently yet still ethically. Steiner, ahead of his time and defiantly opposed to criticism that demands plays of obvious

23. See Robert Skloot, "Holocaust Theatre and the Problem of Justice," in *Staging the Holocaust,* ed. Schumacher, pp. 10–26. Discussion of the Steiner/Hampton play is found also in *The Darkness We Carry: The Drama of the Holocaust* (Madison: University of Wisconsin Press, 1988), pp. 88–93.

melodramatic victories for tragic stories, asks that his audience provide the refutation of Hitler's appalling conclusion that the Jews' "blackmail of transcendence" caused their own deserved destruction. By so doing, Steiner insists that the inheritors of the post-Shoah world are responsible for confronting the wrongful and catastrophic lies that history can be distorted to support (Hitler's speech is full of them). By supplying the strategies that use history for insight into the continuing genocidal dangers that face all of us, Steiner allows no escape. The strength of *Portage* (and the angry denunciations of it) are to be credited partly to Steiner's trust of audiences to make this discovery for themselves. Many other (and worthy) plays make this choice for us; this play insists that we accept this daunting task as our own. And it asserts the extraordinary power of the theatre to either overcome or reinscribe practices and images that make our historical understanding so various, painful, and often opaque.[24]

H. I. D. (Hess Is Dead)

> What is it: This thing, this state of mind . . . History? That we bend, that we distort? From which we want . . . *The truth?*
>
> —Luber

Early in *H. I. D. (Hess Is Dead)*, Charity Luber asks the questions that are surely on the minds of theatre directors and Holocaust historians: "If you asked most people under thirty, 'Who was Rudolf Hess?,' how many would say 'He was Hitler's deputy?'. . . . I'm not talking about students of history, just people, under thirty, around the streets, in London, Paris, Amsterdam, in Berlin. I mean who

24. It is important to notice that Steiner's critics were alerted to his intention in the play itself which begins with the warning of Lieber (the justice-seeker) not to listen to Hitler's speech. "Gag him if necessary, or stop your ears. If he is allowed speech he will trick you and escape. . . . He will know the sounds of madness and loathing and make them seem music." And another historical note: since the play's premiere, some of history's "facts" have themselves undergone change from the large (the reunification of the two Germanies) to the small (the demise of the *Milwaukee Tribune*). See scene seventeen.

cares? The death of Rudolf Hess? It was something on TV." Someone who does care very much is Howard Brenton, whose play proposes to investigate the question: how do we know that history "happened" by inquiring into the death of the Deputy Führer who, in the spring of 1941, flew alone on a supposed peace mission to England? Brenton creates a murder mystery of a most extraordinary type, one which asks the audience to select information from a variety of flawed and conflicting sources, none of which can be relied upon as conveying accuracy, certainly not uncontested truth. And because most of these sources are "mediatized" (tape recordings, videotapes, projections) and of uncertain provenance as well, there is no evading the cultural situation Brenton is analyzing: that the "news" is astonishingly easy to manipulate. In the hands of the powerful (those who control the media), belief in almost any subject can be created or destroyed at the touch of a button. In the 1990s, it is commonplace to observe that few of us haven't been fooled by "documentary evidence" and will be fooled again.

The reasons for Hess's solo flight remain a permanent mystery, and Hess himself remains an opaque figure, resistant to comprehension or sympathy. We do know that after his trial at Nuremberg, he spent nearly forty years incarcerated in Berlin's Spandau prison, a solitary prisoner in his last years, supervised in monthly rotation by the four allied victors.[25] With this skeletal knowledge,

25. A number of books advance the theory that Hess died early in Spandau or was killed shortly after his incarceration, and that he was replaced for Allied political reasons by a double. Believers in this subterfuge claim that the body of the 93-year-old "suicide" couldn't have been Hess's because it lacked the requisite scars of wounds from World War I. These accounts have virtually no credibility among historians or the public, but their theories enable Brenton to build a play on both the gaps (Hess's silence) and the facts (Spandau's complete razing immediately after Hess's death) of history.

One assessment of Hess comes from Telford Taylor, the American chief counsel at the Nuremberg Trial: "until the end of his life, Hess was not 'sick' in the usual sense, but he was a man bedeviled by fears and fantasies that tore him in body and mind. . . . As time went by, I generally replied [to inquiries] that such long-continued incarceration, especially in a huge prison where he was the sole inmate, was a crime against humanity." *The Anatomy of the Nuremberg Trials* (New York: Knopf, 1992), p. 618.

Brenton proceeds to embellish a double narrative, each one reflecting the other. First, Brenton speculates on the nature of Hess's death and places his suicide within the context of cold war antagonisms among the former World War II allies. Many scenarios are possible if the telling of Hess's story involves the political motives of governments with a stake in maintaining power and avoiding defeat on the global political stage.

Second, Brenton exploits the fragility, even the impossibility of ascertaining truth about the past and about the most current events too. The playwright's special contribution to the staging of history, including Holocaust history, is to put the audience inside the story so that the viewers inhabit the identical setting they see on the videotapes being played on the screens placed throughout the performing space. At times, characters join the audience in the same space; at times they ignore each other's presence. Together, characters and audience discover important information about events they are involved with at the same time; the actors move among the audience to insure that it is part of the performance. Further, this information is being revised and reinterpreted continually as images thought to be defined by the facticity of history, of "documentary evidence," are replayed (both "live" and on tape) to reveal surprise and contradiction.

Finally, we are asked to believe that the problem of belief is produced not, or not only, by the normal human difficulty involved with partial, subjective perceptions of events or relationships, but because belief is always fragile, a result of events being manipulated in a way that is designed to destroy their veracity. The journalist, Larry Palmer, a surrogate for the audience in his seeking some small amount of objective truth, experiences total defeat in this mission. Although a skeptic ("In my trade, facts are all. . . . That was said, that was done. But hard facts can, I find, go . . . mushy," he says early in the play), he confronts a situation that extends beyond even his cynical understanding of how "truth" is created, accepted, and disseminated. We could say that Brenton knows the effectiveness of promulgating the "big lie," and that with his post-Holocaust perspective, one that includes knowledge of the techno-wizardry of our time, he can conclude that there is little else but prevarication in the "objective" lives we lead.[26]

It is notable that two important players in *H. I. D.* never appear "live," only in photograph and videotape. Both Hess and Luber enjoy virtual existences and leave ambiguous legacies. Luber, the political intellectual whose final screen testament "The Walls of Spandau Speak" concludes the play, bequeaths a video that is a hodgepodge of amateur and historical images linked by a bizarre, "poetic" narration. The audience sees on the television monitors Spandau being demolished (ordered by the allied powers after Hess's death to prevent the prison from becoming a shrine), a fitting conclusion to Brenton's play about how history is destroyed and created before our eyes. The playwright's intention is not to deny the Holocaust; in fact, he writes about its political and cultural legacy to provide the necessary foundation for his exciting, theatrical, and intellectual provocation.

Lastly, in our time, writing a play about absent protagonists in occasionally poetic language where characters from several historical periods mingle with the audience to receive a fragmented narrative whose presentation is advanced and confused by media that propounds no single message and denies any unifying perspective or truth is one inevitable, artistic example of the postmodern sensibility alive in our world. Nonetheless, the important conclusion we reach from this play and all the plays in this volume is that despite radical cultural, artistic, and historical changes in recent decades, exciting ethical investigations of the Holocaust are yet possible. We have come a very long way from the sentimentalized, if sad, "reality" of the girl in the Amsterdam attic. We are taking a historical and artistic journey into another "reality" that is exciting to some, baffling to others, and threatening to many . . . and it is not over yet.[27]

Robert Skloot
University of Wisconsin–Madison

Summer, 1998

26. See Robert Skloot, "Stage Nazis: The Politics and Aesthetics of Memory," *History & Memory* 6, no. 2 (Fall/Winter, 1994): 57–87.

27. Excerpts from this introductory essay appeared in " A Multiplicity of Annes," *Nation,* 16 November 1998, 20–25.

Roy Kift

CAMP COMEDY

Songs and Sketches by
Leo Strauss (1897–1944) and Manfred Greiffenhagen (1896–1944)

For Nelly and Mia

A staged moment from *The Führer Gives a City to the Jews (Der Führer schenkt den Juden eine Stadt)* directed by Kurt Gerron in the Theresienstadt concentration camp, 1944. Photograph used by permission of the National Center for Jewish Film, Brandeis University.

In Theresienstadt . . . almost anything could be repressed . . . illusion ran rampant and hope, merely dampened by anxiety suffused everything . . . There was no place in Western Europe . . . where camp inmates were more removed from reality than here.

—H. G. Adler, Theresienstadt: 1941–1945

Nothing was compatible with normal common sense. Everything was organised through and through to satisfy hatred, crime and the lust to kill. Uncertainty and fear were the mental whip and might of the chosen specimens of the "Herrenvolk."

—Karel Ancerl. Chief conductor, Czech Philharmonic Orchestra and inmate in Theresienstadt, 1942–1944.

The ashes [in the Theresienstadt mausoleum] were kept in three types of boxes, all with a label bearing the name, birth-date and date of death. Prominent camp inmates had iron boxes, the less distinguished had wooden boxes, and the rest cardboard ones. The mausoleum was cleared a hundred boxes at a time. We would toss them to one another and, in the case of the iron, yell out: "Look out, here comes another celebrity."

—Jacob Presser, *The Destruction of the Dutch Jews*

You see, there are hierarchies among Jews. . . . The Viennese looked down on the Ostjuden and the German Jews looked down on the Viennese Jews and so you stayed with your own in order to avoid conflict.

—Gertrude Schneider, quoted in "Women Surviving the Holocaust"

I have a feeling, I said, about the axial lines of life, with respect to which you must be straight or else your existence is merely clownery, hiding tragedy. . . . Lately I have felt these thrilling lines again. . . . Truth, love, peace, bounty, usefulness, harmony! . . . At any time life can come together again and man be regenerated . . . the man himself, finite and taped as he is, can still come where the axial lines are. He will be brought into focus. He will live with true joy. . . . Death will not be terrible to him if life is not.

—Saul Bellow, *The Adventures of Augie March*

Author's Preface

This play is set in Theresienstadt in 1944. As such it is a work of fiction inspired by fact. Like Shakespeare and countless other dramatists before me, I have taken history and shaped it to my own theatrical ends. Before setting out to write the play, I decided I must remain as faithful as possible to the facts I had researched. However, once I began writing, I was constantly aware that I was inventing scenes for which I had no documentary evidence or that I was attributing characteristics, attitudes, and relationships to "real" people which they probably never had. At first I was disturbed by this and was continually stopping work to consult documents for fear of betraying "reality" and laying myself open to accusations of lies and distortion. But as the play developed and began to assert a life and independence separate from its author, I began to realize that it was in fact mirroring the assertion by a former inmate of Theresienstadt that it was at times very difficult to distinguish reality from fantasy in the camp itself.[1] And accordingly, since the play and its characters were stuck in a limbo somewhere between hell and earth, dream and waking, play-acting and life, to try to separate these aspects would paradoxically betray the sense of unreal reality pervading the camp.

Still, the names of the characters continued to provide me with a problem. At first I decided to leave only four characters with their correct names in full: Kurt and Olga Gerron, Kommandant Rahm, and his second-in-command, Haindl. Gerron is the protagonist of the play, and since he is so clearly identifiable it would have been dilettantish of me to disguise him (and by association his

1. H. G. Adler, *Theresienstadt: 1941–1945. Das Antlitz einer Zwangsgemeinschaft: Geschichte, Soziologie, Psychologie* (Tübingen: Mohr, 1960).

wife) under a pseudonym.[2] Nor was there any reason for protecting the two Nazis behind false identities even though their characters were entirely different from how I portray them in the play. My greatest headache was how to name the cabaret artists in the Karussell, three of whom I was able to identify. Since Gerron had kept his real name, surely they should do so too. On the other hand, I had next to no biographical details and did not want to give anyone the impression that these characters had a one-to-one basis in documentary reality.

Reluctantly, I made a decision to give them entirely new names. Yet as I wrote I discovered to my amazement that the real people were refusing to lie down and disappear. Instead of my consciously chosen pseudonyms, I was continually typing "Anny," "Gizzy," and "Michel." So once again I decided to capitulate to the demands of my subconscious and make a compromise. I would keep their forenames (two of which had slightly transformed anyway), and change their family names to indicate that they had half a foot in reality and half in my own fantasy. And so the Austrian entertainer, Annie Frey found her theatrical doppelganger in a German singer, Annie Valletta; Gisa Wurzel became Gizzy Wagner; and the Dutch tenor, Machiel Gobets became the Austrian, Michel Grünbaum.[3] The remainder of the characters, with one exception, are pure fantasy on my part,[4] and hence, have completely fictional identities. These, however, are not the only distortions.

2. Although, ironically enough, Kurt Gerron's real name was Gerson. He adopted the stage name to try to conceal his Jewish background. Life and theatre!

3. Looking through my research material once again, I see that Gerron directed a production of Bizet's *Carmen* in Theresienstadt. The role of Don Jose was shared between Machiel Gobets and one David Grunfeld! See Joza Karas, *Music in Terezin: 1941–1945* (New York: Beaufort Books, 1985), pp. 30–31.

4. The Impresario is obviously pure theatre although he does come down to earth as a sort of satanic *deus ex machina* in the second act and might be seen as a reflection of Karel Peceny who was the head of production at the Czech film company *Aktualita.* See Eva Sormova, *Monographien über Kurt Gerron* in Theresienstadte Studien und Dokumente 1995, ed. Miroslav Karny, Raimund Kemper, and Margita Karna. Edition Theresienstadter Initiative. I use the word "might" because I read the article *after* the play was completed. The character of Frau Schwarz emerged while I was speculating on the inspiration behind a verse in the sketch "Theresienstadt Questions" by Leo Strauss and Manfred Greiffenhagen.

As far as I know Machiel Gobets had no part in writing the scenario for the film as Grünbaum does in the play. According to H. G. Adler, this seems to have been undertaken either by Gerron himself,[5] although other sources claim that the Dutch artist, Jo Speer was involved,[6] or that the songwriter, Manfred Greiffenhagen wrote the film script.[7] Michel's relationship with Anny has no basis in fact. The only other character whose name I have partly adopted is that of the leader of the Jewish Council of Elders in Theresienstadt, Paul Eppstein, whose first name I have changed to Jakob. As far as I know he never played a string instrument as he does in the play, but he did have a battered piano in his quarters. Nor was he, as the play indicates, sent to Auschwitz after the film's completion. According to Gerald Green in his book *The Artists of Terezin,* this "brave man, who faced up to the SS with courage and humor was shot dead at Rahm's orders" on 27 September 1944 under the trumped-up charge of attempted escape.[8] Hence, Jakob Eppstein and the other characters whose names resemble those of real people in the camp are not so much based on them but are fictional personae who have grown out of them and taken on their own independent life.

Yet there is another reason why I was reluctant to bury the identities of the original people completely. There's an old Jewish saying, I believe, that as long as you can talk about someone they are not dead. I guess that sums up my feelings about the men and women who inspired my characters. For whatever fantasy I have brought to bear on this play could not have been ignited without years of documentary research on those who lost their lives in the camps and by personal contact with survivors. There is no right way to go about dramatizing "facts," and I can only beg forgiveness

5. *Die Verheimlichte Wahrheit: Theresienstadter Dokumente* (Tübingen: Mohr, 1958).

6. Zdenek Lederer, *Ghetto Theresienstadt* (London: Goldston Press, 1953), p. 119.

7. Hans Hofer makes this claim in an article entitled "The Film about Terezín: A Belated Reportage," in *Terezín* (Prague: Council of Jewish Communities in Czech Lands, 1965), pp. 180-84.

8. Gerald Green, *The Artists of Terezin* (New York: Schocken Books, 1978), p. 91.

from those concerned and from their relatives and friends and hope that my tribute will outweigh any possible offence.

As to the play as theatre: its atmosphere of *grand guignol* nightmare with its slippery levels of reality—represented most obviously in the pervading presence of the Impresario—owes much to the work of the great Polish theatre-maker Tadeusz Kantor. Its imagery also reflects the haunted drawings of the artists who lived in the camp. On the other hand, all the songs and the variety sketch "Theresienstadt Questions" are direct translations of texts written by the cabaret artists in Theresienstadt.[9] Despite the authenticity of the songs, I should like to stress once again that the play should not be presented as a piece of documentary realism or, for that matter, in any other uniform style. Each scene has its own particular theatrical demands. Picasso once remarked that all works of art are a lie. I can only hope that this particular lie will in some way illuminate a deeper, nonliteral, truth.

Finally I'd like to express my deepest gratitude to all those who helped and inspired me in the writing of this play, in particular, to Mia Stephenson whose invitation to a conference on "Shoah and Performance" at the University of Glasgow in 1995 brought me back to a project I had feared for years and to Nelly Wilson (née Jussem), a former inmate of Theresienstadt. Both Mia and Nelly have been extremely supportive of the project, and their critical remarks of earlier drafts have proved invaluable in helping me to rewrite and (I hope) improve the play.

9. I should like to thank Ulrike Migdal, the author and editor of a compilation of Theresienstadt cabaret songs and satires *Und die Musik Spielt dazu* (Müchen: Piper Verlag, 1986), for permission to translate the song texts used in the play. As for the music, I only know of one song where the original music (by Martin Roman) has survived. This song "We're Riding on Old Wooden Horses" can be heard in the original on two CDs which contain Theresienstadt songs. The first "Chansons und Satiren aus Theresienstadt" taken from a show of the same name at the Theater in der Josefstadt, Vienna, October, 1992, is no longer available. I thank the author of the show, Alexander Waechter, for putting a copy at my disposal. The program of the show—more a book— is a mine of information and illustrations. It is published by Rabenhof, Rabengasse 3, 1030 Vienna, Austria. The second CD entitled "Stimmen aus Theresienstadt" was released in 1997 by the Norwegian artist Bente Kahan.

CAST

THE IMPRESARIO, known as IMP (later HANKA)

The Cabaret Artists:
MARTIN, a musician
DAN, a musician
ATI, a musician
GIZZY WAGNER, an actor
ANNY VALETTA, an actor
MICHEL GRÜNBAUM, an actor
KURT GERRON, an actor

OLGA GERRON, Kurt's wife
KOMMANDANT RAHM
PLATOON LEADER HAINDL
FRAU SCHWARZ
DR. JAKOB EPPSTEIN, Head of the Jewish Council (*Judenrat*)
HERR LIPPMAN
HERR MARKOVICH
FRAU MARKOVICH
HERR TRAUDE
A WAITER

Where possible, all of the characters from Olga downwards must be doubled by the cabaret artists.

CAMP COMEDY

ACT 1

Scene 1

A dark, empty stage. Down stage to one side is a table. On the table are three small urns, one iron, one wood, and one cardboard. Behind them is a shadowy figure, the Impresario, known as the IMP. *He is ageless, volatile, and dangerously arbitrary. A creature of lunatic extremes, physically, mentally, sexually, and vocally. He is wearing a bow tie and crumpled suit which have seen better days. He shuffles the urns around as if he is practising one of those street tricks where people get robbed of their money. From time to time he stops, removes a lid, peers at the contents, nods, replaces the lid, and shuffles on. He gradually becomes aware of the audience whom he includes in his dumb clowning. Suddenly he breaks off with a shrill blast on his whistle. A series of ludicrously cacaphonic chords from a three-piece band introduces a small revolving cabaret stage. It's a brave attempt to indicate a carousel. On it are frozen figures in the darkness. The musicians:* MARTIN *on piano,* DAN *on drums, and* ATI *on a variety of instruments, are shabbily dressed. The impression they give is grotesque and rather unreal, equal parts clowns, ghosts, and tramps. Despite the whistle, they are unaware of the* IMP *as they play. The* IMP *raises his arm imperiously. His puppets freeze.*

IMP *(to audience):* Thank you very much, thank you. If you think that was deadly, I can promise you there's worse to come! A joke. *(Laughs. Gesture. Cymbals.)* Ladies and gentlemen!

May I welcome you to yet another nonstop evening of laughter, music, and entertainment at the number one cabaret in town, the one and only . . .

MUSICIANS: Carousel!

(Musicians vamp behind his intro.)

IMP: Presenting our company in order of size and beauty, the diminutive and deeply dazzling Gizzy Wagner. *(*GIZZY *is lit up; a Piaf-like figure with a deep, harsh voice)* The elegant and exceptionally erotic Anny Valetta. *(*ANNY *is larger, blonde and specializes in naive roles)* The indescribable Michel Grünbaum. *(He's just weird.)* And last, but certainly not least—not with his figure—the largest, the ugliest, and the funniest performer in town tonight. Everybody's favorite showman, direct from Berlin, via Paris, Vienna, Amsterdam and Westerbork-les-Bains.

MUSICIANS: Westerbork-les-where?

IMP: The man who shot to fame in Bertolt Brecht's *The Threepenny Opera. (All join in a short hideous rendering of "Mack the Knife" before being stopped by the whistle.)* The actor who became a world star alongside Marlene Dietrich in Josef von Sternberg's legendary film *The Blue Angel. (Bars from "Falling in Love Again.")* An outsize personality in every sense of the word, ladies and gentlemen, Mr. Kurt Gerron!

*(*IMP *whistles.* KURT GERRON *stumbles out of the darkness onto the stage. He stands rigid in a flamboyant pose, in a dress coat, tight pants, shirt, floppy bohemian bow tie and a cigar in his mouth. He blinks in transfixed terror at the* IMP *as if he doesn't know where he is or what he is supposed to be doing. The band plays the intro once, but* GERRON *fails to come in.)*

IMP: "Time out of mind." *(The drummer,* ATI, *beats a few bars alone.)* "Time out of mind." "In time out of mind!"

KURT: Ah!

(The band bursts into action. IMP *vanishes.* GERRON *tosses his cigar in the air, and it too disappears. He sings the song with great bravura, along with the others.)*

SONG: In time out of mind, so long, long ago
When we were just kids beginning to grow
There was one thing we longed for like hell
If our folks wished us out from under their feet
Or simply wanted to give us a treat.
Why! All us kids would begin to yell
Carousel, oh please, carousel!

We're riding on old wooden horses
Round and round in a clippety-clop
Longing to get fizzy and dizzy
Before the roundabout grinds to a stop.

Oh ain't this a funny old journey!
You won't believe our incredible fix
Going round in perpetual circles
With no end of surprises and kicks.

And the hurdy-gurdy music
We'll never ever forget.
When the images fade before our eyes
The memory lingers yet.

(The IMP *raises his arm imperiously, and the song grinds messily to a halt. The performers are frozen as in a dream. The* IMP *keeps his arm held aloft as he speaks in ghoulish tones.)*

IMP: My business used to be such fun. But now! The competition is murderous.

(He pauses and then screeches hysterically. Gestures the cabaret to swing back into action.)

SONG: We're riding on old wooden horses
Round and round in a clippety-clop
Where we land at the end of our journey
We'll only find out when we stop.

For most of the time our life is so hollow
What we all need is a passion to follow
That's what gives it some sense

Careers, the markets, blonds, brunettes
Movies, football, cigarettes.

MARTIN *(spoken):* Not to mention "kabaretts"!

KURT: We've all got our favorite bents

COMPANY: Don't rob us of thrills and amusements
Illusions, oh please, please illusions!

We're riding on old wooden horses
Round and round in a clippety-clop
Longing to get fizzy and dizzy
Before the roundabout grinds to a stop

(The IMP *gives a loud blast on his whistle. They freeze.)*

IMP: If only it would but it won't! If only my competitors would give me some peace. Respite from the cesspit, release. From all this turbulence. I tell you if I stop for breath, I'm done for. People come, people go. They don't know whether they're coming or going, and once they've come they don't want to go because when they go they don't know where they'll be going to, and once they've got there it's time to go again. Left right, right left. Is it any wonder they want to shut it out with songs and laughter? Where's it going to end? As if we didn't know! *(Laughs.)*

(He blows his whistle and sings along with the cabaret.)

Oh ain't this a funny old journey!
You won't believe our incredible fix
Going round in perpetual circles
With no end of surprises and kicks.

*(*IMP *raises his arm. This time the company continue their ghostly act as a dumb show, but the* IMP *doesn't notice.)*

IMP: Just look at them all. The air may be stale, the wooden benches an agony for bony backsides, but the packed house is in raptures. Forgotten the hunger, forgotten the tears, forgotten the endless hours of labor, the filth and disease, forgotten the daily insults and humiliation and the struggle to retain the last vestiges of human . . . what's the word? Forgotten. Even the time and place. This is no longer the summer of 1944. No longer a transit camp for Jewish prisoners in a garrison town called Theresienstadt. No longer a ghetto in the middle of the Czechoslovakian countryside. This is not imprisonment, agony and. . . . *(He can't get his mouth round the word.)* But for two short hours: freedom, laughter, life! Deranged and derailed, spinning free from the fetters of logic and reality into a world of carefree illusion.

(He drops his arm wearily.)

KURT: Even when sunk in attrition
A man's still got some ambition
Does anyone out there object?
How we relish to shout
With the down and out.

IMP: In a matter of weeks Kurt Gerron will be stumbling naked into the showers at *Oswięcim!*[1]

KURT: Hear the song of the ghosts our pleas so intense,

IMP: Or, as my competitors call it, Auschwitz.

KURT: For difference, oh please, difference.

COMPANY: We're riding on old wooden horses . . .

(IMP gestures and whistles. They continue as a dumb show interrupted by an occasional word or phrase as if there's a loose connection on a radio.)

IMP: Who's in charge here? You see what I mean? I'm losing control. There are no set rules any more. Or if there are, nobody's obeying them. The whole thing's crazy, loopy, round the bend. Is this the cabaret or the mad house? Who knows? Who cares? Is there any difference? In a crazy situation, madness is the only measure of normality, and when the show's at an end, who's to guarantee that the show's at an end? That life on one side of the curtain is any more real than the capering on the other? That's my philosophy anyway. You don't believe me? *(Pause. He looks round.)* You! *(He points at ATI. The rest continue with their dumb show unawares.)* Come here. *(ATI stands warily and goes over.)* Here. *(The IMP slaps a Nazi officer's cap on ATI's head.)* Try that for size.

1. The Polish name for the Auschwitz concentration camp.

ATI: I can't wear that. I'm a Jew.
IMP: It's only a show.

(ATI shakes his head in terror. The IMP takes the lid off one of the urns and gives him a glimpse of the contents.)

IMP: Suicide, jewicide, what's the difference?
ATI: Is there a script?
IMP *(to audience):* What did I tell you? *(To ATI.)* Into the wings.
ATI: So it is only a show!
IMP *(kicks him on the shin):* The wings!

(ATI hops off clutching his leg. The IMP whistles.)

COMPANY: Oh ain't this a funny old journey!
You won't believe our incredible fix
Going round in perpetual circles
With no end to surprises and kicks.

And the hurdy-gurdy music
We'll never ever forget.
When the images fade before our eyes
This melody lingers yet.

We're riding on old wooden horses
Round and round in a clippety-clop
Where we land at the end of our journey
We'll only find out when we stop.

(IMP brings the singing to a close with a flourish. Deafening applause. He turns the show over to GERRON.)

KURT: Thank you. Thank you. Thank you very much. You're too kind. No really. You're a lovely audience. Well, it's a lovely place, isn't it? Theresienstadt. No really. Truly, unbelievably lovely. I mean to say, hand on heart now, could you believe what was going on here a few weeks ago? Forty thousand actors for an audience of ten. What a performance! You were wonderful. Well, we all were. All those happy faces, laughing children, it was idyllic. Clean streets, banks and post office. Shining shop fronts. Amazing what a lick of paint can do. As for the shop-windows! I've never seen anything like it in my life. Stuffed full of fresh vegetables, meat and bread, everything kosher! No really. Like a dream! *(He sighs.)* Yes! Like a dream. The next day, when the invited audience had all gone home, nothing. My wife, she said to me, she said: Kurt, what's happened to all that lovely food that was in the shops yesterday? It has all disappeared. Well, of course it has, I said. Those ten men from the Red Cross that were here. They bought it all up. Well, wouldn't you? In their position? I mean let's face it, Olga, I said—that's my wife, Olga—be honest! It's only when you're living in a place like Theresienstadt that you really appreciate what those poor people out there must be suffering. I'm going to write and tell them. I am! Berlin? Vienna? Forget it! If you want a piece of paradise now: pack your bags and join me here.

Friends and loved ones, do you suffer
From a life of want and fear?
Things at home becoming tougher?
Pack your bags and join me here.

Do you live in trepidation?
Is your life a vale of tears?
I'm off'ring you some consolation.
Pack your bags and join me here.

Had enough of constant moving?
Different houses every year?
Need a place that's calm and soothing?
Pack your bags and join me here.

Are your vases all in pieces?
Got a broken chandelier?
Tablecloths all stained and greasy?
Pack your bags and join me here.

When neighbors see the star you're wearing
Do they start to hiss and jeer?
Had enough of hostile staring?
Pack your bags and join me here.

Do you dream of ease and pleasure
Tea and coffee, wine and beer
Concerts, theatre, endless leisure?
Pack your bags and join me here.

Here's a wacky world of show biz
Full of laughter, fun and games.
The only thing I'd like to know is:
How we all get out again.

KURT: And you thought Hollywood was a dream factory!

(The actors fall about laughing. The IMP *applauds and gives a signal to the lighting booth. The actors are frozen in the shadows.)*

IMP *(to audience):* The show goes on. Backstage.

Scene 2

There is no scene change, only a change in lights to indicate we are backstage. The actors getting changed. Some are removing makeup. This may be mimed. Silence. Fatigue.

IMP: Enter Scharführer Haindl.

*(*HAINDL, *played by* ATI, *enters. They all jump to attention. He wanders around casually, inspecting them all in silence. Finally stops by* GERRON *and taps him on the belly with his baton.* GERRON *flinches.)*

IMP *(providing the line):* "I've always been an admirer of yours . . ."

HAINDL: I've always been an admirer of yours, Herr Gerron.

KURT: Thank you, sir.

HAINDL *(pause):* I have a question. I was watching your show the other night, from the wings. Didn't want to disturb the fun. And it suddenly struck me. Who writes this stuff?

KURT: Most of it's done by Michel here, Herr Grünbaum.

HAINDL: I see. And do you always keep strictly to the text?

KURT *(pause):* All our material has been checked and passed by the *Judenrat,*[2] if that's what you mean, Herr Haindl.

HAINDL: Herr Scharführer Haindl! Sir! *(He raises his baton to* GERRON *who cringes and squeals.)* No. That wasn't what I meant. You Jewish pig!

*(*HAINDL *strokes his head.* GERRON *is terrified.)*

KURT: Sorry, Herr Scharführer.

HAINDL *(patting him affectionately):* When will you stinking Jewboys learn to address us by our proper titles?

KURT: *Zu Befehl,*[3] Herr Scharführer Haindl. Sir.

HAINDL: What did you call me? *(*GERRON *is confused.)* Didn't you know that Kommandant Rahm has given orders not to address us by our titles? *(*GERRON *nods.)* Don't you know the penalty for contravening official orders? *(*GERRON *nods.)* Well then . . . You're to report to Kommandant Rahm in his office at 9 o'clock tomorrow morning. *(Pause.)* Understand? *(*GERRON *nods.)* I'm sorry, Gerron. I can't hear you.

KURT: Yes, of course, sir. Herr Scharführer, sir. Herr Haindl. Of course.

(Pause. HAINDL *bursts out laughing.)*

HAINDL: Of course. See you tomorrow then. Sleep well. *(Exits.)*

IMP *(whistles):* Bedtime! *(Blackout.)*

Scene 3

The carousel slowly revolves to reveal the company standing pressed together like sardines around GERRON *who is sleeping*

2. The council of Jews established by the Nazis to provide the administration of the ghettos and some concentration camps. In reality, they held little power and were often brave, sometimes corrupt, and always compromised.

3. German for "Yes, Sir," or "At your command."

restlessly against an upright board. Next to him against another board is his wife, OLGA. *The* IMP *moves amongst them, jabbing them with his finger or simply raising his hand. They cry out, cough, moan, weep. A dog barks in the distance.*

IMP: This is the time of the scorpions. When forbidden-to-be, forbidden, taboo thoughts break loose and run amok to maul your mind and claw your heart.

KURT: Olgaaa!

OLGA: What is it now, Kurt!

KURT: What are they going to do to me, Olga? I mean he hasn't called me in for nothing. *(Silence.)* It must be something I said. In one of the performances. Why can't I keep to the script?

OLGA: It might be something perfectly harmless.

KURT: Ha!

OLGA: Well, it's not the first time you've been to see the Kommandant, is it? Maybe he wants you to do him another one-man show.

KURT: Ha!

OLGA: You're the biggest star in the camp, Kurt. Don't forget that.

KURT: How could I? All this luxury.

OLGA: It could be worse.

KURT: How? How could it be worse?

OLGA: Well . . . For a start other couples are separated from each other. *(He stares at her.)* Don't say it or I'll kick you, you clown!

KURT: Say what?

OLGA: Forget it. All I'm saying is that you shouldn't jump to conclusions. As long as you're in favor with the Kommandant . . .

KURT: Yes . . . Yes . . .

OLGA: And he loved your last show, you said it yourself. Didn't you say he adored it?

KURT *(pause):* At this moment Marlene Dietrich is probably sunning herself in a deck-chair beside a Hollywood swimming pool. *(Silence.)* I'm not a stinking Jew. I'm not. I'm not!

(Pause. A deep-voiced, distant, croaky, obsessive exclamation from nearby.)

FRAU SCHWARZ: Nor am I! I told him. I said: "I'm not one of those Polish yids!"

OLGA: Oh, no! Now you've gone and woken up that crazy woman again.

SCHWARZ: I'm just as German as you are!

(Other voices: Quiet. Shut up, will you!)

OLGA: And just as lice-ridden too!

KURT: Shhh! You'll only get her going again.

OLGA: Every bloody night the same old song. There's not a single Pole in the place! You hear?!!

SCHWARZ: There will be. There will be! They get everywhere! What do those tinkers know about Goethe? Mozart? Beethoven? I'm an educated woman from a civilized country. Why should I have to wear a star?

OLGA: Take the bloody thing off then, if you don't like it! And get yourself a stinking swastika.

KURT: For Godsake, Olga! *(They both smile.)* You don't give up, do you?

OLGA: Like these bloody bedbugs.

KURT: Shall we try and get some sleep?

(Coughing, whimpering, shouting, barking. Silence. The IMP *tiptoes forward and bends over* KURT *and* OLGA.*)*

IMP: Sleep. A blessed release. Maybe. But when you wake again, staring into the morning gloom, how can you be sure the nightmare you've just fled from might not after all have been preferable to the one you've arrived in? Or, if the one you've arrived in might be a preface to something even worse? *(*GERRON *and* OLGA *revolve away.)* Where do the dreams end and reality begin? In the thickly carpeted office of Herr Camp Kommandant Karl Rahm at two o'clock on a glorious summer afternoon in July, 1944.

Scene 4

The IMP *blows his whistle and walks into* KOMMANDANT RAHM*'s office.* RAHM *and* HAINDL *have just lunched together and the remains of a banquet can be seen. The two have been engaged in a furious row, and* HAINDL *is in a cold fury.* RAHM*, however, is sipping at a glass of port in a relaxed and cheerful manner.*

IMP: "Just give him his orders."

HAINDL: Just give him his orders!

RAHM: Let me tell you something about cookery, Herr Scharführer. The best way to ensure your goulash is tender is to let the meat stew in its own juices. Slowly.

(RAHM *empties the bottle into his glass.* IMP *helps himself to some food and settles back in* RAHM*'s chair behind the desk to stuff himself and drink. He flicks a finger in the direction of the door, and it flies open revealing* GERRON.)

RAHM: Come in Gerron, we haven't got all day. Sorry to have kept you waiting so long! Herr Scharführer Haindl you know already. Don't look so scared, man, we're not going to eat you. Yet! We've just had a meal. *(Laughs.)* Did I tell you, Herr Scharführer, my doctor has warned me against eating too much pork! *(Laughs.)* I won't beat about the bush, Herr Gerron. As you know Theresienstadt has been modernized and radically refurbished in the last few months.

KURT: Herr Kommandant?

RAHM: Well we had to do something about all the slanderous rumors. What did you call me?

KURT: Herr . . .

RAHM: Rahm, if you please, Herr Gerron. Didn't you read my orders?

KURT: Yes sir. No, sir. I mean. Yes, Herr Rahm.

RAHM: Everybody's on an equal footing here. Separate. But equal. Isn't that right, Rudi? Sherry? (GERRON *stares at him.)* Would you care for a glass of sherry? Or a bowl of soup perhaps? Iced cucumber soup with a dash of sour cream! How does that appeal?

KURT: It's very kind of you, Herr Rahm but . . . I'm not hungry. At the moment . . . If you agree . . .

RAHM: You get more than enough to eat, hmmm?

KURT: Well . . .

RAHM: Not that I'd dream of reducing your rations, Gerron. Not in the least. To each according to his needs. Who was it said that? One of you Jews, I believe.

HAINDL: I thought it was Jesus Christ.

RAHM: Come now, Herr Scharführer. It was Karl Marx! Christ was crucified by the Jews. Any good Catholic knows that. And he certainly wasn't a communist, was he, Herr Gerron?

KURT: I wouldn't know, Herr Rahm. I'm just a simple entertainer.

RAHM: Ah ha.

KURT: I've never been interested in politics. Or religion.

RAHM: I'm delighted to hear it, Gerron. If you only knew the lurid propaganda we have to put up with from the conspiratorial forces of world Jewry. All those lies about torture, starvation, disease, death camps. Have you been tortured? Are you starving? Sick? Is this a death camp? There you are then! Lies, all lies. Why do they do it to us? I'll tell you. People always want to believe the worst. Bad news is always good for a quick profit, and nobody appreciates that more than a Jew. Tell me Herr Gerron, when you climbed aboard the train in Westerbork, where did you imagine you would end up?

KURT: Theresienstadt, of course. Herr Gemmeker himself—the Camp Kommandant at Westerbork—you know him?

RAHM *(RAHM looks at him sharply, pause):* So you realize that in other circumstances . . . you might have been sent elsewhere? Where the facilities are not quite so . . . amenable?

KURT *(pause):* As a veteran of the First World War, I was wounded at the front in the service of the Fatherland . . .

RAHM: Yes, yes. Theresienstadt is no more than you deserve, Gerron. Let no man say the Third Reich can't take care of its artists.

KURT: Thank you, Herr Rahm, sir. I'm very grateful.

RAHM: Not that I can guarantee that circumstances will remain as they are forever, of course.

KURT: Of course.

RAHM: Trains arrive. Trains depart. Well, they have to. If they didn't the town would become impossibly overcrowded, and sanitary conditions intolerable. As in Theresienstadt, so in life. If nobody ever moved on, our little world would very soon become an overcrowded hell. Enough philosophy. *(The* IMP *holds out a file folder.* RAHM *takes it without looking.)* You know what this is?

KURT: It . . . looks like a file of some sort.

RAHM: It's a report, Herr Gerron. An official report. *(Pause.)* You remember the Red Cross delegation which came to inspect the camp last month?

HAINDL: The international delegation!

KURT: Ah!

RAHM: Yes indeed! I can't tell you how pleased our visitors were at conditions here. What impressed them most of all was the cultural life. The sheer range of artistic activities. Such a pity they had to choose between the symphony concert and the cabaret, but there you are! We can't have everything in life, can we? Nonetheless I told them all about you. Oh yes. Over afternoon coffee in the Kaffeehaus. They were munching their cakes and tapping their feet to the rhythm of the Ghetto Swingers[4] . . . that nigger number, what's it called? *(*IMP *wants to tell him but his mouth is too full of food. He hastens to swallow it all.)* Never mind. And I said, "If you think these people are good, you should see our star performer, Kurt Gerron." "Kurt Gerron," they said. "The film star? Is he here too?" Oh, they'd all heard of you. "Kurt Gerron has the best cabaret in the camp." Isn't that what I said Rudi?

4. The most famous of several jazz groups that performed in the cabarets of Theresienstadt.

IMP: "Oh, when the saints . . ."

RAHM: "Oh, when the saints!"

KURT: I beg your pardon?

RAHM: "Oh, when the saints." That's what they were playing. The Ghetto Swingers! *(*IMP *conducts him in.* RAHM *sings.)* ". . . I want to be in that number . . ." *(The* IMP *falls back in his chair and takes a drink out of* RAHM*'s glass.)* Yes, indeed, the chosen few! I pleaded with our guests to stay for dinner and see the cabaret, but their timetable was so tight. Not that it made much difference, of course. As they took their leave, I could tell they were delighted with what they'd seen. And I, too, was delighted that we'd all played our part, inmates and officers alike, in showing the world the real face of Theresienstadt. And now we have it here in black and white. The confirmation. From neutral, impartial observers. You can read it yourself if you don't believe me. *(*GERRON *bends over the report.)* Such a report is solid proof of what happens when Germans and Jews decide to work together for the common good. Everybody has profited from the visit. Evil rumors have been quelled, the policies of the Third Reich towards the Jews have been closely scrutinized and approved, and not least, I think you will agree, living conditions in the Ghetto have been immeasurably improved. Because we all played our appointed roles in a disciplined manner. Now where is all this leading to, I can hear you saying? I'll tell you. A report is all very well, but nonetheless, I think you'll agree that words alone can never give a satisfying picture of the situation here. And anyway who reads official reports? Answer: Officials! *(Laughs. He throws the report to the* IMP.*)* So my superiors in Berlin have been putting their heads together and asking themselves how they can build on this excellent start? How we can portray life here in the very best and, of course, most effective and appropriate light? And in doing so, refute these slanderous rumors once and for all. Any ideas? I'll tell you then. The Führer would like you to direct a film for him.

KURT: I beg your pardon?

RAHM: Herr Hitler wants to commission a film from you.

KURT: Me?

RAHM: Yes you, Gerron. Don't look so amazed.

KURT: Yes, but . . . why me?

RAHM: Why not?

KURT: But I'm a Jew.

HAINDL: And if the Führer orders you to make a film, who are you to make racist objections?

RAHM: Optimistic comedies. That was your speciality, Herr Gerron, if I remember correctly.

KURT: He wants me to make an optimistic comedy?!

RAHM: No, no, no, Herr Gerron. Now you're getting confused! What we have in mind is more in the line of a documentary. An interesting and informative film about the everyday life and activities of the Jewish inhabitants of Theresienstadt. Well?

KURT: I'm . . . very flattered of course, but . . . isn't there a vast difference between an optimistic comedy and a documentary?

RAHM: Not if it's an optimistic documentary. *(Laughs.)* And we thought, that is to say the Führer thought, who better to undertake such a task than someone who is intimately acquainted with the town, an insider, a man who knows it back to front from personal experience. And above all, a first-rate professional who can be counted on to provide a thoroughly convincing piece of work. In short, who better than Kurt Gerron? What do you say?

KURT: I'm . . .

IMP: Speechless.

RAHM: Don't say it! Speechless! *(Laughs.)* "Don't say it. Speechless," Rudi!

IMP: Oh, when the saints *(He offers his arm to* RAHM *who joins in.)* go marching in. Oh, when the saints go marching in. I wanna' be in that number . . .

*(*RAHM *offers his arm to* GERRON *who stares at it blankly.)*

RAHM: What's the problem, Herr Gerron?
IMP *(Hissing in* GERRON*'s ear):* You're not going to refuse him, are you!?
RAHM: I can't help you unless you tell me.
KURT: Well . . .
IMP: That'd be suicide.
RAHM: Is there a problem or isn't there?
KURT: No, sir! I mean, yes! Herr Rahm. The script. We haven't got a script.
RAHM: You haven't got a script but we have. Haven't we?
IMP: We have indeed.
*(*IMP *snaps his fingers, and a script falls from above.)*
RAHM: Pick it up then. What does it say?
KURT: "Theresienstadt. A Documentary Film."
RAHM: Civil service drivel. Unbeatable in its banality. But that's lucky for you, Herr Gerron. Because if it hadn't been the work of an official hack the film might have been made years ago. No, no. Hold on to it, Kurt. It's not entirely rubbish. The information's there, it simply needs the hand of a professional.
KURT: I'm a director. Not a script writer, Herr Rahm.
RAHM: I beg your pardon?
IMP: What are you saying, Kurt?
KURT: Not that we don't have scriptwriters in the cabaret.
HAINDL: That joker Grünbaum, for example?
KURT: Yes. For example. Perfect. Yes.
RAHM: You'd have to ask him, of course.
KURT: Me?
RAHM: Of course. We wouldn't want to force anything on anyone, would we? *(Pause.)* You are interested in the project, I take it?
IMP: But of course you are.
KURT: Of course. Of course. What director worth his salt . . .? Invited by the Führer! . . . . It's an honor.
RAHM: That's settled then.
KURT: There's just one thing.
RAHM: Yes?

KURT: If this film is to meet the standard of excellence the Führer expects, I'm going to need a fully trained crew. Production manager, technicians, lighting experts, make-up people, sound engineers, continuity . . . where do I find those in Theresienstadt?

RAHM: You know what I like about you, Herr Gerron? You're a professional. Like me.

KURT: Thank you, Herr Rahm.

RAHM: Leave it to me, Herr Gerron. They'll all be here, ready to start at the break of dawn on August 14th.

KURT: But . . .

RAHM: We want to make the most of the summer.

KURT: But that means . . .

RAHM: Herr Grünbaum had better get working on that script.

KURT: Wait a minute, wait a minute. What about the cast?

RAHM: The pick of the camp, Herr Gerron. All forty thousand. Or do you imagine I'm going to bring in outsiders? This film has to be authentic.

KURT: What I meant was, they have to be organized. I'm going to need a coordinating staff, a special office, to ensure I have the right performers at the right time.

RAHM: Isn't that the responsibility of the Jewish Council? Herr Eppstein? Sort it out among yourselves and come back and tell me in the morning. In the end, it's Herr Eppstein who's responsible for what goes on in the town. Not me.

(The IMP *gestures* GERRON *to leave.* GERRON *walks out as if in a dream, holding the script.)*

HAINDL: Come back and tell me in the morning! Why all this benevolent delay?

RAHM: Because, Rudi my friend, if you'd been listening, this film has to be professional, perfect, down to the last detail. And no artist worth his name ever produced anything of worth under coercion. Gerron has to convince himself. He has to find a reason to believe it's his own choice even if it's not. He has to believe in it, body and soul.

HAINDL: And what if he doesn't?

RAHM: Leave him alone for a few hours and he'll come up with some justification. I'm sure Herr Eppstein can help him put aside any lingering doubts.

(The IMP *blows his whistle. The stage revolves.* HAINDL *and* RAHM *off. We hear the sound of a string quartet written in Theresienstadt.)*

IMP *(drunkenly):* What did I tell you? When the unbelievable becomes reality, anything's possible. *(He opens up the Red Cross report.)* "Thish . . . thish . . . Jewish town . . . is indeed . . . ashtonishing." That's what it says, ashtonishing! "The Theresh . . . Thereshien . . . the ghetto . . . is a communisht soshiety." Black and white! A communisht society promoted by the Nazis? Well there's a little joke for Pope Pius XII! . . . "led by a 'Stalin' of high eschteem: Jakob Epp, Epp . . . Eppschtein." *(He throws up.)* That's better.

Scene 5

The scene now represents the shabby office of the Judenrat, *the Jewish Council. It is empty. The* IMP *leads* GERRON *into the room with his arm around* GERRON*'s shoulder. He wipes his vomit-smeared hand on it happily. He whistles. The music stops.* JAKOB EPPSTEIN *and* DR. LIPPMAN *appear carrying string instruments. The* IMP *shoves* GERRON *forward and signals a change in the lighting.*

KURT: You can imagine my amazement, Herr Epstein.

EPPSTEIN: What did you reply?

KURT: Well . . . nothing.

EPPSTEIN: Nothing?

KURT: Herr Rahm told me to sort things out with you. *(Silence.)* I mean, I can't. Of course, I can't. I mean, how can I?

EPPSTEIN: Herr Gerron, forgive me if I appear a little abrupt, but you know as well as I do, that if we receive an order from the Camp Kommandant . . .

KURT: But Herr Rahm told me that you had the final word. That nothing in the town can go ahead without your permission.

EPPSTEIN *(pause)*: Can we get one thing straight?

KURT: Is that right or isn't it?

EPPSTEIN: Of course it's right. Theoretically.

KURT: Well then!

EPPSTEIN: Herr Gerron, you know as well as I do . . .

KURT: All I know is that I'm an entertainer, just an entertainer. But you! You're supposed to be . . . I don't know, you're supposed to be . . .

EPPSTEIN: A guardian of morality?

KURT: Yes! Something like that.

EPPSTEIN: Pull yourself together man! A concentration camp is not a center for the propagation of ethical behavior. It's about survival. First and last, survival.

LIPPMAN: And what's the point of survival, Herr Eppstein? If we end up with the moral standard of a pack of rats?

EPPSTEIN *(to* GERRON*)*: Suppose I did go to the Camp Kommandant? And put my objections, Herr Gerron? How do you imagine he'd react?

KURT: All I know is that I'm the one who has to make this film. Not you. Or you. Or any of the rest of the forty thousand people in this godforsaken shithole. Or do you know of any other film directors in this place? Because I don't!

EPPSTEIN: That's the point I'm trying to make, Herr Gerron. I'm disposable. And every other member of the Jewish Council. But you are unique. There's no way they can get rid of you without endangering the whole project. Objectively it's repugnant. We all know that. But in a situation like this, which of us has clean hands? Only if we blind ourselves to the rights and wrongs of a situation do we descend to the level of rats.

LIPPMAN: So if we're clear that a deed is wrong, it becomes right?

EPPSTEIN: I am talking to Herr Gerron! If you'll allow me to finish! Putting on a show for the Red Cross was also a lie. Yet we all went along with it. But who knows? It might turn out to be a blessing in disguise.

LIPPMAN: Not for the thousands who were put on the trains to make the place look less overcrowded.

EPPSTEIN: And that was my responsibility. Yes! Do you think I'm not aware of that! But what of the forty thousand still here? Have you thought about them? And have you paused to consider for just a moment what might result when the Red Cross report on Theresienstadt is made public to the world at large? Well surely none of us imagines that any of those gentlemen were so naive as to be fooled by all that play acting? I don't anyway. What about you, Herr Gerron?

KURT: I . . .

IMP: Don't know.

(GERRON shrugs helplessly.)

EPPSTEIN: I'm sorry, but you've no alternative.

Scene 6

The IMP *whistles. The stage revolves.* ANNY, MICHEL, MARTIN, *and* DAN *are slowly eating some soup, taking a rehearsal break.*

MICHEL: So this man, he's standing behind me in the queue and he suddenly starts bellowing at the cook: "Lentil soup? Lentil soup! Is that what you call this watery shit? You know the first thing I'm going to do when I get back home? I'm going to go out to a restaurant and order myself a tureen of the rotten stuff."

ANNY: You're kidding!

DAN: What would he want to do that for?

MICHEL: That's what the man behind him said. You know what he answered? "So's I can tip it straight down the toilet without it having to make a detour through my stomach!"

MARTIN: Talk about run-throughs! *(Everybody groans.)* Until Kurt decides to put in an appearance.

(They resume rehearsing. MICHEL *sings.)*

MICHEL:
I know a lovely little town
This town is really spiff.
The name I can't quite place for now
I'll call the town "as if."

*(*FRAU SCHWARZ*, a rather shabby but elegant-looking lady in completely inappropriate finery enters. She has a Jewish star pinned on her dress, and for a moment she seems to be part of the show. She's played by the actress who plays* GIZZY.*)*

MICHEL:
This town is not for everyone
This town's a special place.

ANNY: "The townsfolk are quite normal here!"

MICHEL: What?

MARTIN: Wrong verse.

ANNY: You missed a verse.

MICHEL: Excuse me, lady. We're in the middle of a rehearsal.

ANNY: "As if in life, forsooth."

FRAU SCHWARZ: I'm looking for Herr Gerron.

ANNY: Was it about anything in particular?

FRAU SCHWARZ: I wouldn't be here if it wasn't, now would I?

MICHEL: If you're after a ticket . . .

FRAU SCHWARZ: Don't tell me! It's Mr. Grünbaum, isn't it? Michel Grünbaum. *(She offers him her hand. He stares at it.)* I assure you, it's perfectly clean. Unlike some others in this camp I regret to say. And Miss Valetta! I'm so sorry! I didn't recognize you without your makeup. She looks so much younger on stage, doesn't she? May I say what a pleasure it was to be present the other night at your cabaret. It was two hours of pure joy. Sheer nostalgia. For a brief moment in time my life became bearable again.

ANNY: Well, thank you, but . . .

FRAU SCHWARZ: You can't imagine what a shock it was for me to be confronted with all this human degradation. Theresienstadt is no place for Germans.

ANNY: I beg your pardon?

MICHEL: I'm Austrian actually.

FRAU SCHWARZ: Is there any difference? Germans, Austrians, we share a common language, a common culture. Worlds apart from those Yiddish-speaking creatures from Poland, tinkers and street-traders and the like. Well, they're used to conditions like this, aren't they? They grew up in them.

MARTIN: This is all very interesting, madam . . .

FRAU SCHWARZ: Schwarz! Gertrud Schwarz. My husband was a surgeon in the Grünewald before we were. . . . He . . . never completed the journey. When I think that they told us we'd be coming to a thermal spa town! That we were fooled into signing away our villa in exchange for a promise of a comfortable flat with a lakeside view.

MICHEL: That's Germans for you. Talking out of their assholes.

FRAU SCHWARZ: And what do I find when I get here? *(Long Pause.)* Yids.

MARTIN: I beg your pardon.

FRAU SCHWARZ: I don't mean you. I'm talking about Poles and the like.

MARTIN: But there aren't any Poles in Theresienstadt!

FRAU SCHWARZ: There will be. There will be. They get everywhere, these yids.

MARTIN: Listen lady. I'm a yid too. Alright? If I wasn't I wouldn't be here. And nor would you, for that matter.

DAN: Okay, Martin!

MARTIN: So if you'd like to get off the stage, we've got work to do. *(He takes his fury out on the drums. She blocks her ears until he stops.)*

FRAU SCHWARZ: Have you heard the latest news?

MARTIN: No!

FRAU SCHWARZ: Herr Hitler wants Herr Gerron to make him a film.

MICHEL: And he's asked you to star in it, I suppose.

FRAU SCHWARZ: You don't believe me, do you? You think I'm mad. But I have it on very good authority. From one of the girls who works for Herr Rahm.

ANNY: Ah! There he is now. *(She waves offstage.)* Kurt. Don't go away. Kurt!

FRAU SCHWARZ: Do excuse me. *(She scuttles off.)*

ANNY: Pathetic.

MARTIN: Making a film. She's one crazy bedbug.

MICHEL: I thought she was marvelous.

ANNY: How can you say that?

MICHEL: You've got to look at it through the eyes of a writer, Anny. *(Musical intro.* GERRON *enters. They stop.)*

MARTIN: Well, here's the big director, folks! What's all this we've been hearing?

KURT: Can I have a word with you, Michel? In private. *(He leads* MICHEL *off.)*

MARTIN: Okay, Anny. You give it a try.

*(*IMP *whistles. Stage revolves.* GERRON *and* MICHEL *are sitting on the other side. Behind them in the distance we can hear the music to the song "As If.")*

KURT: Please, Michel.

MICHEL: I've never written a film script in my life. And I don't intend to start now.

KURT: The idea's so absurd it won't come to anything anyway.

MICHEL: There you are then.

KURT: The point is to show willingness, that's all. We don't want to get on the wrong side of them, do we?

MICHEL: I wasn't aware we were on the right side.

KURT: Nobody's asking you to write the wretched script, Michel. All you have to do is get the bad one we've got into shape. I could do it myself but . . .

MICHEL: Why don't you then?

KURT: I thought I'd be doing you a favor.

MICHEL *(pause):* Are you saying that you suggested me?! You? Volunteered my name!

KURT: No, no, it was Haindl. It was Haindl, I swear! Well, what could I say?

MICHEL: Ha! I never dreamed it would be so easy to make the grade. One day an unknown scribbler of sketches. And the next: the most sought-after scriptwriter in the Third Reich.

KURT: I knew you wouldn't let me down.

MICHEL: I shall want an invitation to the premiere, of course. The gala premiere in Berlin. You and me, invited guests of the Führer. Not forgetting the other forty thousand Jewish stars, all of them in regulation yellow. Driving down the Kurfürstendamm[5] each in a chauffeur-driven limousine. Or will that be outside the Führer's budget? Never mind. If he puts us all through the ovens first, he could pack us all into one little Volkswagen. What's it matter if a few ashes get blown away on the journey?

KURT: What are you talking about, Michel?

MICHEL: Haven't you heard the rumors? *(Silence.)*

KURT: Madness. Rubbish. You don't believe that, do you?

MICHEL *(pause):* Of course not! Put the fear of God into you though, didn't it. For a minute. Eh? *(Laughs.)*

KURT *(laughs):* So you'll do it?

*(*ANNY *appears unnoticed.)*

MICHEL: Do it? Of course I will. We've all got our price, Kurt. Price, not pride. Hollywood here I come!

KURT: Ah, Anny.

ANNY: We're waiting to rehearse.

(The band strikes up. The carousel turns. The IMP *is on stage. In the course of the song everyone joins in.)*

IMP:
I know a lovely little town
This town is really spiff.
The name I can't quite place for now
I'll call the town "as if."

KURT:
This town is not for everyone
This town's a special place.
You've got to be a member
Of a special "as if" race.

5. A broad, tree-lined boulevard that comprised the most elegant shopping street in Berlin.

The townsfolk are quite normal there
As if in life, forsooth!
They greet all rumours from outside
As if they were the truth.

The people in the crowded streets.
They rush about their biz.
And even if there's *nichts* to do
They act as if there is.

They've even got a Kaffeehaus
With customers so toff-ee
Who sit and swap the latest tosh
While drinking "as if" coffee.

You come across some shameless folk
Back home nonentities.
But here they strut about the streets
As if they're VIPs.

At mealtimes what a queue for soup
They scramble round the pot.
As if the water had some meat
As if the soup was hot.

At night they lie upon the ground
As if they were in bed.
They dream of kisses, love-bites, ow!
They've bugs and fleas instead.

They bear their burdens with a smile
As if they knew no sorrow
And talk of future happiness
As if it were . . . tomorrow!

(IMP *whistles.)*

COMPANY: Tomorrow. And tomorrow. And tomorrow.
And tomorrow.

Scene 7

Darkness descends. Guard dogs barking. Night. Moans and cries. The carousel turns.

VOICES: Who's that? Shut up, will you! Can't a person get a bit of sleep?

*(*OLGA *is lit up standing in a nightdress, with* GERRON *clinging to her.)*

KURT: Olga. Olga! OLGA! It's an act of blatant collaboration.

OLGA: Isn't it a bit late for scruples, Kurt? We're part of a living nightmare, all of us. And it's going to go on and on and on and on and on and on and on and on and on . . .

KURT: Stop it, stop it, stop it!

VOICE FROM NEARBY: Quiet!

*(*OLGA *slips away still repeating the words* "on and on."*)*

KURT *(turning back to her):* Olga? Olga!

FRAU SCHWARZ: I'm not one of those yids from Poland. I told him!

(A guard dog howls in the night. The IMP *slips in beside* GERRON *and puts his arm around his shoulder.)*

IMP: She doesn't understand you, does she?

KURT: No one understands. Wearing a star in the streets, that's anonymous. But openly assisting in the promotion of a lie . . .

IMP: Aren't you being a little melodramatic?

KURT: How am I going to live with my conscience?

IMP: Conscience is just a word. Two syllables, the first of which is "con."

KURT: If I make this film, I won't be able to look myself in the face again.

IMP: And if you refuse you'll never get the chance. You'll be finished, Kurt. Dead, buried, and forgotten. The victim of a futile moment of self-indulgent moralizing.

KURT: If I wasn't so confused!

IMP: Well just stop and think for a moment, Kurt. What did Herr

Eppstein say? *(GERRON murmurs with him.)* This place isn't a school of ethics . . .

KURT: You can say that again! It's a university of perversity.

IMP *(laughs):* I like that!

IMP *(overlaps with GERRON):* You have to treat this film as just another piece of work. Nobody can blame you if you're acting under orders. And if a man like Jakob Eppstein's got no objections . . .

KURT *(overlaps with IMP):* Just look at them on the streets. Matchstick figures in rags, shuffling back and forth from nowhere to nowhere, fighting for scraps of filthy food, and when the whole thing gets too much, sitting down where they stand. And giving up. Not life, but worse. Hope. We went to the madhouse once. Once. With the cabaret. Just once. If you go crazy here, you don't rave. You just sit down. And stare. In silence. And I'm supposed to bring these ghosts to life?

IMP: Shhh!

KURT: Turn them into an optimistic comedy?

IMP: Pull yourself together now! I've never heard such a piece of gutless whining in all my life. Instead of wallowing in self-pity, you should be jumping for joy at the chance to make this film.

KURT: What?

IMP: First the Führer gives the Jews a town. And then he gives you, Kurt Gerron, the chance to make your name and save your life.

KURT: My name'll be filth.

IMP: Rubbish.

KURT: I'll be spat on like a leper.

IMP: Simply following orders!

KURT: A traitor to my race. A JUDAS!

VOICES: Quiet. Shut up. Go to sleep, you lunatic!

IMP: No, Kurt. No no no no no. You've got it the wrong way round. As usual! You couldn't be more mistaken if you tried.

KURT: What?

IMP: Haven't you overlooked one small factor? In all your philosophical aberrations? Time.

KURT *(pause):* Time?

IMP: This whore of a war . . . tickytickytickytickytickytickytick . . . could be over . . . tickytickytickytickytickytickytick . . . within weeks.

KURT: Huh?

IMP: On the very day the Red Cross delegation inspected Theresienstadt, the allies were landing in Normandy. Even as I speak they're pushing across Belgium into Holland, American planes are bombing Italy into submission, and Russian tanks are pouring down from Silesia through Poland . . .

KURT: Rumors.

IMP: . . . into Czechoslovakia. The Germans are retreating on all sides. It can only be a matter of weeks before the house of cards collapses.

KURT: Rumors! I've heard them all a million times before.

IMP: But this time, Kurt, they're true. And every minute you are filming will be sixty seconds reprieve for forty thousand inmates. Every hour will be one hour nearer to freedom. Everyday's shooting, one more day of grace. And every week's work behind the camera will draw you closer to the end of all your suffering. It's a race against time, Kurt. And the winner will be the tortoise. Not the hare.

KURT: Drag it out?

BOTH: Drag it out.

IMP: Give the illusion of collusion and play for time. You've got two weeks before the camera teams arrive. Fourteen precious days. And another three weeks scheduled for filming. How long is that?

KURT: Twenty-one and fourteen . . .

IMP: Thirty-five. Over a month already! Add a few days for bad weather, technical delays, personnel problems—when did a film ever end on schedule? And you're up to forty days at the least. You can do that, can't you, Kurt?

KURT: Well . . .

IMP: Of course, you can. People are capable of anything. If they put their minds to it. You won't be making a film, Kurt, you'll be making history. Forty days reprieve for forty thousand people. Neilah[6] approaches.

KURT: Neilah. The day of liberation.

IMP: Make this film, Kurt, and you will be hailed as the chosen hand of God. The man who snatched forty thousand lives from the abyss. A twentieth-century Moses who led his people out of the wilderness to the promised land. From misery and despair to the land of milk and honey. You Kurt. You. You. You. This is not a day of lamentation, but a day of joy!

KURT: Neilah!

IMP: The day of liberation is at hand. Forget your miseries, ladies and gentlemen. And sing! One, two, three, four!

(Music. The carousel revolves. The IMP *jumps on stage.)*

IMP:
We're riding on old wooden horses
Round and round in a clippety-clop
Longing to get fizzy and dizzy
Before the roundabout grinds to a stop.

(He waves in RAHM *and* HAINDL *to participate.)*

RAHM AND HAINDL:
Oh ain't this a funny old journey!
You won't believe our incredible fix

COMPANY:
Going round in perpetual circles
With no end to surprises and kicks.

And the hurdy-gurdy music
We'll never ever forget.
When the images fade before our eyes
This melody lingers yet.

6. The Hebrew name for last part of the Yom Kippur (Day of Atonement) service which, by Jewish tradition, signals the final moments of judgment when who shall live and who shall die in the new year is decided. For Theresienstadt prisoners, the name became associated with "liberation."

We're riding on old wooden horses
Round and round in a clippety clop
Where we land at the end of our journey
We'll only find out when we—

(IMP *whistles.)*

IMP: Stop.

RAHM: Well, Gerron?

KURT *(pause):* I'll do it.

IMP: What did I say? Capable of anything! *(He applauds and gives a signal to the lighting booth. Blackout.)*

END OF ACT ONE

ACT 2

A newsreel film showing Jews in a coffee-house in Theresienstadt. Idyllic music. In the course of the film this changes suddenly to the sound of gunshots, an attack, filthy German soldiers, grenade explosions, etc.

COMMENTATOR: "While Jews relax over coffee and cake in Theresienstadt, German soldiers are suffering the burdens of a terrible war, adversity, and self-sacrifice, in order to defend our homes and families."

Scene 1

Blackout. Silence. The sound of a guard dog barking. A cacophony of moaning misery in the night. Only the outline of the IMP *can be discerned in the darkness. He is smoking a cigar. From time to time he whistles fragments from the carousel song.*

IMP: "Oh ain't this a funny old journey . . ." *(Laughs. He wanders downstage.* GERRON *is lit up on the floor, sleeping restlessly. The* IMP *bends over him.)* "Hear the cry of the ghostssss . . ." *(The* IMP *blows cigar smoke over* GERRON *who coughs and stirs, but does not wake. The* IMP *blasts his whistle.* GERRON *sits bolt upright with a scream.)*

IMP: Well there's a lovely welcome!

KURT: I said I'll do it, and I'll do it.

IMP: But of course you will. You're a man of your word. You're sweating. Here. *(The* IMP *supports him in his arms. Wipes his brow tenderly, caresses his face.)* We've come this far together, why shouldn't we go the whole distance?

KURT: What do you want from me?

IMP: I wanted to offer you something. A reward.

KURT: Reward?

IMP: For helping me. *(Pause.)* But if you're not interested. *(He shrugs and turns to go.)*

KURT: Wait. Wait! *(The* IMP *stops.)* Tell me.

IMP: The Three Wishes.

KURT: What?

IMP: The fairytale, remember?

KURT: My film.

IMP: Three wishes.

KURT/IMP: I/You made a film of it!

IMP: Exactly.

KURT: I'd almost forgotten.

IMP: Not me. The god came down to earth in disguise. The poor man helped him and as a result . . .

KURT: He was granted three wishes.

IMP: You do remember! And it struck me your life could also do with a fairy tale ending. Three wishes. Three wishes, Kurt. Three wishes. Anything you want in the world.

KURT: Please God!

IMP: Yes?

KURT: Let me get out of this place alive!

IMP: Number two?

KURT: Get out of this place alive.

IMP: And the third?

KURT: Alive. All I want to do is get out of this place alive.

IMP: Nothing more?

KURT: Isn't that enough?

IMP: What about Olga?

KURT: Ah!

IMP: Normally it would be too late, dear Kurt. But you and Olga. Why not? I'd hate to separate you. Not when you've come so far together. *(He holds out his hand.)* That's a deal then. You play your part, and I'll play mine.

KURT: Me and Olga.

IMP: That's what I said.

KURT: You'll get us out of this place alive?

IMP: You play your part, and I'll play mine.
KURT: Done.
(He gives him his hand. The IMP *pulls* GERRON *towards him and kisses him on his lips.)*
IMP: You'll be fated to be celebrated. *(Laughs.)*
KURT: No more hunger, pain, or aching!
IMP: The world will be yours, dear Kurt . . .
IMP/KURT: . . . for the taking!
KURT: *Dolce far niente.*[7]
IMP: In a superabundant horn of plenty.
KURT: Belgian chocolates, homemade toffee.
IMP: Newly squeezed orange juice, freshly ground coffee.
KURT: Champagne, truffles, caviar.
IMP: Whisky, cognac, fat cigars.
KURT: Scotch salmon, whipped cream, garlic bread.
IMP: Croissants and butter for breakfast in bed.
KURT: Italian tomatoes, ripe gorgonzola.
Wine and whisky, iced Coca-Cola.
IMP: Venison and ratatouille.
KURT: Roast turkey, chop suey.
IMP: Paté, melons, gaumenkitzel.
KURT: Fillet of veal and wiener schnitzel.
IMP: Schnitzel?
KURT: In cream sauce with mange-tout and . . .
IMP: Schnitzel?
KURT: What's wrong with schnitzel?
IMP: What about your religion? You Jewish pig! Schnitzel comes from the flesh of filthy, squealing swine. Like you! Good only for the abattoir!
(He chops him down like an ox. Verdi's "Dies Irae" from the Requiem *blasts out as* GERRON *falls backwards to the floor screaming. The stage is a world of noisy confusion, dogs barking, fires burning, the hissing of gas, and terrified screams. Blackout.)*

7. Italian for "The sweet life!"

Scene 2

Lights up on IMP, RAHM, *and* MICHEL GRÜNBAUM. IMP *is wearing a cheap suit, carrying a briefcase, and smoking a cigar.*

RAHM: Good morning, Gerron.
*(*GERRON *scrambles to attention.)*

IMP: Here.

KURT: Herr Kommandant Rahm, sir!

RAHM: May I present Herr Hanka. Herr Gerron. Herr Grünbaum.

IMP: Pavel Hanka. Delighted to make your acquaintance, gentlemen.
(Pause.)

RAHM: Herr Hanka is our new production manager.

KURT: What?

RAHM: Direct from the newsreel studios in Prague. He's kindly volunteered to put aside his journalistic duties for a few weeks in order to assist us with our project.

HANKA: Oil the wheels so to speak.

RAHM: He'll be the crucial link between me, you, and Herr Eppstein on behalf of the . . . inhabitants. Any questions?

HANKA: None at all, Herr Kommandant.

RAHM: I'll leave you to it then.
(Exit RAHM. HANKA *drops his half-smoked cigar and crushes it with his foot.)*

HANKA: Volunteered! Ha! I was conned.

KURT: What?

HANKA: I thought I'd be going to Berlin. No really. Some Nazi officer comes strutting into the studios one day and tells us Hitler wants us to make him a film. Anybody interested? So I think, ah ha, something different at last. After years of risking my neck filming heroic Germans charging through gun smoke, a bio-pic of the Führer himself. It wasn't until I'd signed a declaration of secrecy that they told me where I was really being sent. By then it was too late to pull out. Either of you smoke?

(He pulls out a cigarette case and flicks it open. They do not respond. He shrugs and puts it back.) At least I'll be away from the front for a few weeks. And best of all, Herr Gerron—or may I call you Kurt, we don't want to stand on ceremony, do we—for once in my life I'll have the chance of working with a real director.

MICHEL: And what have I got to do with all this?

HANKA: I beg your pardon?

MICHEL: Why have I been summoned here?

HANKA: Weren't you responsible for rewriting the script, Michel?

MICHEL: Herr Grünbaum.

KURT: Is there anything wrong with it?

HANKA: Nothing at all, Kurt. It's a vast improvement on the original.

MICHEL: Thank you for the compliment.

HANKA: All the same our German masters are not entirely happy with it.

MICHEL: If that's the case why didn't Rahm tell me to my face?

HANKA: Now don't get upset. Please. I'm only dong my job. And if I don't sort it out, I'll be the one in the firing line, not you.

KURT: What's the problem exactly?

HANKA: Herr Goebbels[8] says it needs a leitmotif.

MICHEL: Goebbels?!

HANKA: It's fine. The script is basically fine. The only thing it lacks—and I'm only passing on his comments for your consideration—is a recurring image. Something which sums up the spirit of the place, a visual image which'll stick in the moviegoer's mind as the essence of life in Theresienstadt.

MICHEL: So what do you suggest?

HANKA: I'm not the scriptwriter, Michel.

MICHEL: Tears? Hunger? Swollen bellies, sunken cheeks? Lice, coffins! Now why didn't I think of that before? They're recurring all the time. Coffins bring the bread, coffins take the

8. Joseph Goebbels (1897–1945), minister of propaganda and public information in the Third Reich.

dead, did you know that? Life and death in a single quintessential image.

KURT: Michel, please.

MICHEL: Or if you want a real running gag, how about dysentery?

HANKA: I appreciate the problem, Michel but . . .

MICHEL: Maybe you could suggest a solution then.

HANKA: It's funny you mentioned tears. Because it's not so far from Herr Rahm's idea.

MICHEL: Just how many people are writing this script?

KURT: What was that?

HANKA: The idea? What do you think, gentlemen?

MICHEL: Laughter?

(Pause.)

HANKA: Water.

KURT/MICHEL: Water?

HANKA: Water. As a symbol of hope. Refreshment. Purity, transparency, call it what you want. Water. The common well from which we all drink. The well of life. *(Pause.)* That's what Rahm suggests. *(*MICHEL *laughs.)*

HANKA: Well?

MICHEL: It's not exactly the first image that springs to my mind when I think about Theresienstadt.

KURT: There's a practical problem too. Where is the water? In Theresienstadt. Where is it?

HANKA: There's the river. Isn't there?

MICHEL: In case you hadn't noticed, Herr Hanka. The river's on the other side of the town walls.

HANKA: So?

KURT: Mr. Hanka.

HANKA: Call me Pavel, please.

KURT: If you want to get shot that's your business, but . . .

HANKA: Herr Kommandant Rahm has given me a free hand to use any location I like. As long as we stay within the immediate vicinity of the town, of course.

MICHEL: He can't have us straying too far, can he?

HANKA: It being summer, he thought, what could be more idyllic than a sequence showing the inhabitants of Theresienstadt in the open air, swimming.

MICHEL: Where?

KURT: The river.

HANKA: Can't you see it? A cloudless sky, people of all ages splashing about happily, a young mother paddling with a toddler, other children playing ball. Don't say it, Michel! If Kurt asks for a ball, I'll provide it.

KURT: Wait, wait, wait. That's all very well, but . . . but if we really want to give the sequence some shape it needs a dramatic element.

MICHEL: I beg your pardon?

KURT: How about a diver? Yes. Ten meters high. His perspective, looking down. Spectators on the bank, looking up. And then the body launching into the air, arcing through the rays of the sun, straightening out, an arrow in effortless flight. Plummeting, unstoppable. The crowd below. Mouths wide open, breath held . . . Whooshhh. Little more than a ripple on the surface. And then the diver emerging triumphant, to enthusiastic applause from the watchers on the bank.

HANKA: I like it. I like it!

KURT: But one river doesn't make a leitmotif, Pavel.

HANKA *(opens his briefcase):* I've drawn up a little list.

MICHEL *(snatches it):* Let me see that.

KURT: Michel.

HANKA: Keep it. Keep it. It's for you anyway.

MICHEL: Garden plots?

HANKA: There's a delightful little stream running through the fields on the other side of the river. Would make wonderful garden plots.

MICHEL: So we're all going to be growing our own vegetables and picking our own fruit, is that it?

HANKA: Herr Rahm suggested . . .

MICHEL: You don't have to explain. I think I'm getting the idea.

KURT: If we're not willing to make one or two compromises

the film won't get made at all, Michel. Then where will we be?

MICHEL: Don't keep apologizing, Kurt. Now I've got the general line, it's easy. The garden plot. A pretty girl. Smiling in the sun. Spotless hands, long fingers, maybe a little nail polish. What about a dirndl? Or is that too Aryan?

KURT: Michel.

MICHEL: And what's that she's holding in her hand? A watering can! Close-up on the pure, refreshing leitmotif sprinkling transparently from the spout onto the common food from which we all take our nourishment, Herr Hanka. Cut. Our maiden. Holding up a fat, white, juicy looking new potato. Or is that too banal? What about a pineapple! Only a joke. I mean those, mmm . . . what are those things, those long, black thick things? *(He outlines the shape of an eggplant.* GERRON *and* HANKA *stare at him blankly.)* No. Not those things. And I don't mean SS truncheons either.

KURT: If you're not going to be serious!

MICHEL: Eggplants. Our pretty maiden can be holding up an eggplant. And next to her a harvest of tomatoes, onions, zucchini. Put them all together, and we've got a natural cut to a typical evening meal in the ghetto restaurant. What's it called, that French dish?

HANKA: Ratatouille.

MICHEL: Ratatouille. Not forgetting garlic, of course, to keep away the devil.

KURT: For the last time, Michel. Please!

HANKA: I think the watering can's an excellent idea.

KURT: And the diver from the ten meter board?

HANKA: A stroke of genius.

KURT: Have we got a ten meter board?

HANKA: I'll have one built.

MICHEL: And you'll supply the diver too, I suppose.

HANKA: Who knows? Excuse me gentlemen. *(Exit* HANKA.*)*

MICHEL: Have you gone mad, Kurt?

KURT: I might say the same for you.

MICHEL: When I agreed to help you with this script I thought it was just a matter of knocking it into shape. Altering a bit of the rhythm and structure. But children playing ball on the river bank? Divers? Garden plots?

KURT: These aren't normal times.

MICHEL: Let alone pick vegetables or whatever they want us to do . . .

KURT: Children playing ball is in your script.

MICHEL: But not in the open air by the river!

KURT: And if Rahm's so keen on water, why not let him have it? *(Silence.)*

MICHEL: Very well. I will.

KURT: Where are you going?

MICHEL: To drown the bastard, what do you think?

KURT: Michel! *(Exit* MICHEL.*)* Oh god.

(Enter FRAU SCHWARZ *doing a little dance.)*

FRAU SCHWARZ: Mr. Gerron! If it isn't Kurt Gerron himself. I can't say what a pleasure it is to be able to shake your hand in person. I've been an ardent admirer of yours for over twenty years. And I hear you're making another film.

KURT: News certainly spreads quickly.

FRAU SCHWARZ: I'd like to tell you that should you need any help, any help whatsoever, I'd be only too pleased to be of assistance.

KURT: That's very kind of you, madam.

FRAU SCHWARZ: I used to be something of an actress myself. Not a professional, of course. My parents would never have allowed me to become a real actress. Despite their love of the theatre.

KURT: Do excuse me, Frau . . .

FRAU SCHWARZ: Gertrud Schwarz.

KURT: . . . but I'm late for my rehearsal.

FRAU SCHWARZ: Will I have to audition? For the film!

KURT: Ah. Just leave your name and address at the Leisure Activities Office and they'll be in touch with you in due course.

FRAU SCHWARZ: "Don't phone us . . ."

KURT: Exactly. *(*HANKA *enters.)* Ah. Just the man! Pavel!
FRAU SCHWARZ: Leisure Activities Office.
KURT: That's it. *(She exits.)*
HANKA *(returning):* Excellent news, Kurt. I've just had a look through the register of inhabitants and you'll never guess who's living here! None other than the Czechoslovakian national diving champion! I have to hand it to you. You Jews are good at everything! Where's Michel?
KURT: Gone away to work on the script.
HANKA: Writers are so sensitive. I didn't mean to offend him.
KURT: If he only knew what we normally do to film scripts . . .
HANKA: I'll say this for him, he's got more guts than I have. I mean, basically, what he said, well . . . that's what we all think, isn't it? Eh? If we were honest. *(He pulls out a pack of cigarettes.)* Here. Put it in your pocket. Quick. *(*GERRON *does so.)*
KURT: As long as he doesn't go putting it in the script. God knows what would happen.
HANKA: Let him fantasize, Kurt. Fantasies often contain the seeds of valuable truths. It's merely a question of sorting the eggplants from the watering cans, so to speak. You and me can do that together. And then if Rahm, or Goebbels, still isn't satisfied, why should we worry? It's all about time, isn't it?
KURT: I beg your pardon?
HANKA: Well, you don't think I'm in any hurry to return to the front, do you? Not in the present state of affairs.
KURT: You mean . . . ?
HANKA: I tell you, Kurt, if you knew what was going on outside, you wouldn't call this place a prison at all. But a refuge. *(He puts his finger to his lips.)* So if we play our cards at the right tempo . . . with a bit of luck we'll come through this together unscathed.

(He whistles. The band strikes up. The carousel revolves. The cabaret. HANKA *and* GERRON *sing together.* ANNY, GIZZY, *and* MICHEL *enter in the course of the song and watch.)*

Friends and loved ones, do you suffer
From a life of want and fear?

Things at home becoming toughe?
Pack your bags and join me here.

Do you live in trepidation?
Is your life a vale of tears?
I'm off'ring you some consolation.
Pack your bags and join me here.

Are you owing lots of money?
Sunk in debt from ear to ear?
Such a state is far from funny.
Pack your bags and join me here.

Is it hard to find some work sir
In the current atmosphere?
Enough to make you go berserk, sir?
Pack your bags and join me here.

Had enough of constant moving?
Different houses every year?
Need a place that's calm and soothing?
Pack your bags and join me here.

Are your vases all in pieces?
Got a broken chandelier?
Tablecloths all stained and greasy?
Pack your bags and join me here.

Got a woeful constitution?
Too much nicotine and beer?
There's clearly only one solution.
Pack your bags and join me here.

When neighbors see the star you're wearing
Do they start to hiss and jeer?
Had enough of hostile staring?
Pack your bags and join me here.

Are your stocks and shares still sinking?
Servants' wages in arrears?

Nanny's gone and diaper's stinking?
Pack your bags and join me here.

Are you sick of penny-pinching?
Shops and markets far too dear?
Tormented by eternal scrimping?
Pack your bags and join me here.

Do you dream of ease and pleasure
Tea and coffee, wine and beer
Concerts, theatre, endless leisure?
Pack your bags and join me here.

Here's a wacky world of show biz
Full of laughter, fun and games.
The only thing I'd like to know is:
How we all get out again?

KURT: This is Mr. Hanka, everybody. He's helping me with the film.

HANKA: Kurt's right-hand man. Isn't that right, Kurt? Michel? *(He opens his briefcase and gives* MICHEL *a copy of the scenario.)* I've been looking at your rewrites. They're very good. But we're still lacking a major crowd scene. For the faces. I've scribbled a few notes in the margin. Maybe you'd like to have a look at them and come up with a solution. As for you ladies—cheer up, Kurt, there's nothing to worry about! We're going to need some pretty nurses for the hospital sequence. And I was wondering if Miss . . . what's your name? Yes you . . .

GIZZY: Wagner.

KURT: Gizzy Wagner.

HANKA: . . . might be interested in donning a crisp, white uniform for us?

GIZZY: I'm sorry. I don't know the first thing about nursing.

HANKA: But you'd look great, Gizzy. All you have to do is hold the hand of a little child. That's not too difficult, is it?
(A lengthy silence.)

GIZZY: I'm sorry. No.

KURT: Gizzy!

HANKA: You're surely not going to let me down, are you? This could be your big break. *(Silence.)* And I'm sure I don't need to spell out the possible consequences of non-cooperation. *(Silence.)* Well if you won't do it for me, Gizzy, would you do it for Kurt? Mm? Help him out of a little difficulty?

KURT: Come on, Gizzy. I need all the professionals I can get. Please.

GIZZY: I'm sorry, Mr. Hanka. I'm certain there are plenty of real nurses here who would be more than satisfactory in the role.

HANKA: And that's your last word? *(She nods.)* I see. *(Pause.)* Well that's all right, my dear. Because you'll be in the cabaret sequence anyway. Won't she, Michel? And it wouldn't look at all good if we were to give the impression that cabaret artists were also working as nurses. Kurt.

(Exit HANKA *and* GERRON.*)*

GIZZY: Oh god! Now what have I done? I must be out of my mind.

ANNY: Well I thought you were wonderful. Wasn't she, Michel?

GIZZY: He only has to tell the Kommandant . . .

ANNY: Michel. I asked you a question?

MICHEL: Yes, all right!

ANNY: Since you seem to be writing us all into the script. Let's have a look at this masterwork of yours.

(She snatches it from him.)

MICHEL: Please, Anny! That's a secret.

ANNY: I bet it is.

MICHEL: Give it back, will you?

ANNY: What's all this? Where the hell is there a fountain in the park?

MICHEL: They can build one.

ANNY: What?

MICHEL: Herr Hanka'll get one built. Yes all right, I know it's a . . .

ANNY: A what?

(Short pause.)

MICHEL: Rahm wants water. So if that's what he wants I'll give it to him.

ANNY: And where are we in all this?

MICHEL: Give me back the script, please.

ANNY: Where do we come in? Where's the cabaret sequence?

MICHEL: It's like this, you see. Herr Rahm wanted me to include a selection of artists from all the cabarets in town.

ANNY: The pick of the bunch, why not?

MICHEL: A Charlie Chaplin imitation, a couple of jugglers, tightrope walkers, that sort of thing.

ANNY: What! What is this? What this supposed to be, Michel?

MICHEL: If you won't show it to me, I can't tell you. Can I?

ANNY: Listen to this everybody. Showers! Michel has written a sequence where we are all enjoying a shower.

MICHEL: Not all of you. The soccer players.

ANNY: Singing in the showers.

MICHEL: Let me finish, will you . . .

ANNY: I don't know about you, Michel, but the last time I had a shower in this place was five months ago.

MICHEL: This is different.

ANNY: And that was in a filthy little hut under a dribble of freezing water.

MICHEL: It comes after a soccer match.

ANNY: Is that where you're going to film it? In that ramshackle slum?

MICHEL: If you'd listen, instead of interrupting all the time, I'll tell you. *(She throws the script on the floor at his feet.)* Anny! I've got to give this in.

ANNY: To Herr Rahm?

MICHEL: Who else for god's sake? What's it going to look like if it's covered in filth?

ANNY: Why not take it in the showers with you? Ugh!

MICHEL: If you'd only stop and listen to me for a moment, you hysterical cow!

ANNY: Oh! Oh! We're resorting to insults now, are we?

MICHEL: No. no. I've converted to Hinduism, and I'm paying you a compliment.

MARTIN: Calm down, will you! Both of you!

MICHEL: Listen, Anny.

ANNY: I've heard enough.

MARTIN: You're staying here.

ANNY: Make me.

GIZZY: Quiet! Both of you! Now sit down, Anny and give him a chance to explain himself, will you!

ANNY: Don't tell me you're taking his side, Gizzy.

GIZZY: I'm not taking anybody's side. yet. I just think he should be given a fair hearing. That's all. For all we know, he might be . . .

ANNY: Innocent?

GIZZY: No, Anny. Nobody's innocent here. Any more. So . . . what about these showers, Michel? Where are they?

MICHEL: In the officers' block.

MARTIN: The SS quarters!?

(ANNY *screams and exits.* GIZZY *follows her.)*

MICHEL: We'll be taking it over for the day to film the two teams after the soccer match.

MARTIN: And where will that be held? In the Olympic Stadium?

MICHEL: That's what I've been trying to explain all along, if that hysterical cow had given me the chance! If this film is going to be specially set up . . . as one of Kurt's optimistic comedies, to coin a phrase, why not go the whole hog? And turn it into a farce? Make conditions here so artificially idyllic that nobody in their right mind would possibly believe it.

DAN: And what if Rahm doesn't believe it?

MICHEL: Of course he will. Rahm is not in his right mind. How do I know that? The man's a Nazi!

MARTIN: If he even suspects . . .

MICHEL: That's a risk I'll have to take.

DAN: Does Kurt know what you're up to?

MICHEL: You know Kurt. He's a professional. If Rahm gives it the nod he'll simply film it to the best of his ability. Now, if you'll excuse me. I've got to work on these notes. *(He exits.)*

Scene 3

The musicians return to their places. Lights darken. A woman streetcleaner appears sweeping the streets. FRAU SCHWARZ *enters from the other side. Music begins to vamp. Lights go up a little, and we see that the cleaner is* ANNY *in costume, and that "*FRAU SCHWARZ*" is a caricature played by* GIZZY *with a wig.*

LADY: I've just got in from the country.
And since I've no friends far or wide
I'm looking for the best location
To get some useful information.
CLEANER: Lady, use me at your leisure.
At your service! What a pleasure!
I came from Vienna long ago
And know the place from top to toe.
BOTH: Theresienstadt, hooray, hooray!
The most up-to-date ghetto in the
world today.
LADY: Yesterday I had no star
And now I find it most bizarre
To hear some quite disturbing news
I'm in the midst of Polish Jews.
CLEANER: Lots of people rub their nose
Put on airs, adopt a pose.
Might it not be also true
That you're a Tarnopolack[9] too?
BOTH: Theresienstadt, hooray, hooray!
The most antisemitic ghetto in the
world today.
LADY: Has the town a healthy climate?
Or do lice and bugs begrime it?

9. A linguistic joke combining the Ukrainian/Polish city of Tarnopol with the derogatory colloquialism "Pollack." The joke is on "Frau Schwarz."

Does one eat well at mid-day?
Can you keep disease at bay?

CLEANER: Food is short for hearty eaters
Those who eat best are the cheaters.
If you want to stay most fit
Get among the long-term sick.

BOTH: Theresienstadt, hooray, hooray!
The most humane ghetto in the world today.

LADY: It's really true, there's nought to eat!?
No fresh veg and no fresh meat?
Will I end my life in bed
Craving for a crust of bread?

CLEANER: Stop it! Silence! Please! For shame!
I've never heard such infamy!
Here hunger has a finer name
Vitamin deficiency.

BOTH: Theresienstadt, hooray, hooray!
The most elegant ghetto in the world today.

LADY: And what about a place to live?
Simple but not primitive,
Kitchen, lounge, and w.c.,
A bedroom-suite and balcony.

CLEANER: With a little fantasy
A house will be your just reward.
Your dreams become reality
When sleeping on your wooden board.

BOTH: Theresienstadt, hooray, hooray!
The dreamiest ghetto in the world today.

LADY: And what's the code for evening dress?
I'd really hate to look a mess.
Do the men wear tie and tails
When sipping at their cock-a-tails?

CLEANER: There's one or two as put on airs
But most folks opt for casual wear.
To be quite honest, what the heck!
My husband dresses like a wreck.

BOTH: Theresienstadt, hooray, hooray!
The most fashionable ghetto in the
world today.
LADY: Traveling here, I must confess
Has been something of a stress.
A nice hot bath would be a treat
To soothe my bones and aching feet.
CLEANER: Get on home and find a bed
Close your eyes and sleep instead.
Baths are in such short supply
You'll have to wait till next July.
BOTH: Theresienstadt, hooray, hooray!
The most hygienic ghetto in the
world today.
LADY: And while we're at it, may I say
My portmanteau has gone astray.
Half my luggage misdirected,
I'll need a porter to collect it.
CLEANER: Forget your bags. It's just not worth it.
You'll only wind up in a worse snit.
Never mind in any case,
Where you'll be sleeping there's no space.
BOTH: Theresienstadt, hooray! hooray!
The most accommodating ghetto in the
world today.
LADY: One last question, please don't groan.
I'd like to write a letter home
And put my family in the clear.
How long will we be staying here?
CLEANER: Now that request I can't refuse.
Ain't you 'eard the latest news?
According to reliable rumors . . .

(The band drowns out her words in a cacophony of noise.)

BOTH: Theresienstadt, hooray, hooray!
The most-up-to-date ghetto in the
world today!

Scene 4

The carousel turns. RAHM*'s office.* RAHM *is holding up the open script to* HANKA *and* MICHEL.

RAHM: What's this supposed to be, Hanka? Here.

HANKA: How did that get in?

RAHM: Are you telling me you haven't bothered to check this script?

HANKA *(to* MICHEL*):* I never said anything about a soccer stadium.

MICHEL: You asked for a major crowd scene.

HANKA: I never mentioned a stadium. How many times have I told you to follow my notes to the letter?

RAHM: So the "stadium" is all your work, Herr Grünbaum?

MICHEL: I was trying to follow the spirit of—

RAHM: YES OR NO?

MICHEL: Yes, sir.

RAHM: I see.

MICHEL: The quotation marks are missing.

RAHM: I beg your pardon?

MICHEL: Scriptwriter's shorthand. If we're going to have a soccer match we don't want it to look like a shabby scrimmage in the park, now, do we? I was merely indicating we should look for a suitable location to give the impression of a stadium.

RAHM: I see. Whether that's true or not . . . *(Pause.)* . . . it's brilliant!

HANKA: Just where did you have in mind, Grünbaum? Hmm?

MICHEL: I thought we might use a courtyard in one of the barracks. A few hundred people and the place looks crowded. And acoustically, with the echo from the closed space, it would sound like thousands.

HANKA: If you've got room for twenty-two players, of course.

MICHEL: He's clearly never heard of seven-on-a-side, Herr Rahm. But I can't imagine the movie audience will be counting the number of players. They'll be looking out for their relatives and friends. All those faces we're longing to show.

RAHM: But won't a casual game in front of a huge crowd look rather . . . set up?

MICHEL: That's the point, Herr Rahm. It won't be casual.

HANKA: But what?

MICHEL: The championship decider. For example . . .

RAHM: What about the league champions against the cup finalists?

MICHEL: Perfect. Why didn't I think of that myself? That would give us a good reason to dress up the teams in proper uniforms. We can't have them in any old shirts and shorts.

RAHM: Red and blue?

HANKA: We're filming in black and white, Herr Rahm.

RAHM: What difference does that make! Oh . . . yes, of course. That's settled then. Why don't you go and look for a suitable location, Herr Grünbaum?

HANKA: I thought that was . . .

RAHM: You stay here.

*(*MICHEL *goes.* RAHM *takes a cigar.)*

RAHM: Let me get this clear, Herr Hanka. I'm running this show, not you. You understand? This film may be just another job to you. But to me it's a step in my career, and I can't afford any mistakes. If everything goes as I intend, I shall be out of this louse-ridden dump within three months and on my way to the top.

*(*RAHM *takes* HANKA*'s whistle and gives it a sharp blow. He laughs. Blackout.)*

Scene 5

The carousel turns. EPPSTEIN *and* LIPPMAN *are carrying the same instruments as in act one. The only difference is that they are now wearing jackets with tails and white bow ties and sitting behind a display of flowers in a glaring spotlight.* GERRON *appears with* HAINDL *at his side.*

KURT: Cut! That's enough. We only want an excerpt. *(The extra lighting for the film goes out.)* All we need now is the composer to take his bow. . .
(The players stand to stretch their legs, and we see that their trousers are old and frayed.)

LIPPMAN: I thought we were supposed to be playing before an audience.

HANKA: They'll be shot separately. As it were.

KURT: We don't want your music to be ruined by coughing or chairs being scraped along the floor. Have you received the script for the opening scene, Herr Eppstein? When's it scheduled for, Pavel?

HANKA: What?

KURT: Herr Eppstein's address to the new arrivals. Monday morning, isn't it?

HANKA: Late afternoon. After the fire-fighting display.

EPPSTEIN: Do I have to learn it by heart?

KURT: But of course, Herr Epptein.

EPPSTEIN: I imagined I'd just be reading.

KURT: I think it would be better if it looked . . . spontaneous.

Scene 6

The carousel slowly turns. ANNY *alone.* MICHEL *enters.*

MICHEL: Anny.

ANNY: Don't touch me! Are you crazy? Or just plain corrupt?

MICHEL: I'm simply adapting to the environment. Haven't you read your Darwin? And if you don't adapt a little, Anny, you're the one who's going to end up in the madhouse.

ANNY: Sooner there than in the film.

MICHEL: Why didn't you stop and listen to me the other day?

ANNY: Save your breath. Martin told me. You're wrong to think anybody who has never been inside a concentration camp is going to question what they see when it's on film. Black and white reality. The camera cannot lie. Especially if the director himself is a Jew.

MICHEL: Listen, Anny, what I'm doing in the script is basically no different to what we're doing in the cabaret. Is it? Trying to fool the audience they're in another world. Keep everybody smiling until it's time to be schlepped off in the trains.

ANNY: Oh, but there's a very big difference, Michel. In the cabaret we *all* know it's a lie. And what's wrong with that? If it helps to remind us there was once another, better, reality before we were caught up in all this brutal lunacy.

MICHEL: The good old days.

ANNY: Yes, the good old days! And never forget, Michel. There's a chance. Just a faint, minute chance, that they might come back. Those days of friendship. Laughter. Honesty. Dignity and decency. Of course it wasn't like that all the time, I know! But at least we knew what they were, those . . . values. You see! I'd almost forgotten the word! Respect. Tolerance. And love.

MICHEL: Ha.

ANNY: Yes, love, Michel. Strange word, huh? And the moment we start losing our grip on all those ideals, selling lies as truth with easy cynicism, we really are on the path to the bonfire! There I go again, my father always said I should have been a preacher. Give me a kiss. *(She kisses him on the lips sensuously.)* You know what I'd fancy doing now?

MICHEL: Tell me.

ANNY: Right now.

MICHEL: Come on then.

ANNY: I'd like to be able to go up on the ramparts over there. And look out over the countryside. The mountains. The road back home. But not even that's allowed!

MICHEL: Don't tell me you're going back to Germany when all this is over?

ANNY: Why not? It's my home.

MICHEL: I'll be heading for Palestine.
ANNY: What about your career?
MICHEL: You can play cabaret anywhere.
ANNY: I'm going where the money is. Film.
MICHEL: But not this one.
ANNY: Who said so?
MICHEL: Wait a minute! I thought you said . . .
ANNY: Opportunity knocks. And at the current stage of my career I can't afford to pick and choose.
MICHEL: So all that protest . . .
ANNY: Right. Since I don't believe in an afterlife, I'm not going to put this one on the line.
MICHEL: If you can call it a life.
ANNY: It's better than nothing. Isn't it? *(They embrace.* HANKA *whistles.)*

Scene 7

The carousel turns. A waitress is setting up a table for four with a vase of flowers. In the background we hear the Ghetto Swingers tuning up. This is the Kaffeehaus. GERRON *is arguing agitatedly with* HANKA *about sound or lights. Note: during the filming there are no cameras, lighting equipment or mikes to be seen.* HERR TRAUDE, FRAU *and* HERR MARKOVICH *are escorted to the table by* HAINDL. *They look lost and uncomfortable.* HANKA *checks their permits.* GERRON *addresses the assembled guests through a megaphone . . . every inch a professional.*

KURT: Attention! Attention please! *(With forced friendliness.)* Sorry for the delay, ladies and gentlemen, but yet again we're being plagued by technical problems. Nothing unusual. Simply the tedious reality behind the facade of glamor known as film-making. The actors can't start until the technical problems are out of the way. Is it any wonder they turn to drink? At least there's no danger of that here! In the meantime, until we start filming let me thank you for your patience, and above all, for turning up in such large and enthusiastic numbers for coffee and cake in the Kaffeehaus with everybody's favorite band: the Ghetto Swingers! *(He anticipates a blast on a trumpet.)* All right, all right! *(There is no musical response.)* Now you know who's calling the tune round here! *(No response.)* Good. Now I'm sure that what I have to tell you next is superfluous, but just in case we have any complete newcomers to the film, do not, I repeat do not look into the camera. Just enjoy your food and drink, feel free to chat amongst yourselves or simply listen to the music. I'll be taking some general shots of the café later, with close-ups of the band. But I want to start by concentrating exclusively on one particular table, representing, as it were, all of you. This one here. With Herr Walter Traude and his good wife . . .

HANKA: Markovich.

KURT: Pardon?

HANKA: Herr and Frau Markovich. *(He points to a small, timid man in his late fifties.)* That's Herr Traude.

KURT: Herr and Frau Markovich! I'm so sorry. And next to them a face I'm sure we all recognize, Herr Walter Traude, the well-known manufacturer and founder of the Traude Clothing Company. And a prominent figure in the Bavarian Jewish community. *(He claps alone.)* Welcome Herr Traude. *(to HANKA)* What's happened to his wife? I thought you were going to get his wife.

HANKA: She's not here.

KURT: I can see that myself. Get her.

HANKA: I can't.

KURT: If we're going to feature this man we've got to show him with his wife.

HANKA: She left the place three weeks ago . . . *(Pause.)* Exactly.

KURT: Well we can't have an empty space there.

HANKA: Why not?

KURT: We'll be practically advertising the fact that she's . . . Oh god! Get me a substitute!

HANKA: Who?

KURT: As long as it's a woman, does it matter? The right age and appearance.

HANKA: And how's that going to look to the folks back home? They'll expect to see him with his wife, and instead of that he's chatting away to an unknown woman.

KURT: It's going to look as if he's made friends here! Like on a cruise. Or a cure! My god, nobody's going to notice it anyway. If I shoot her from the back people will assume it's his wife, just do as I tell you! *(*HANKA *goes off. To the three at the table.)* Now, dear friends, what's going to happen is that the waiter will bring in coffee and cakes. He'll put them in front of you, Herr Traude, and you'll make an appreciative remark, something like "Mmm, they look delicious," whatever you normally say under such circumstances. *(*TRAUDE *pulls* GERRON *to him and whispers something in his ear.* KOMMANDANT RAHM *has entered.* GERRON *is instantly aware of him but tries to act as if he isn't.)* Pardon me? Well, in that case just nod. Look pleased. Well it's a nice surprise isn't it? A lovely plate of cakes! The waiter will go, as in real life, and you'll serve out the coffee and start eating. *(*HERR TRAUDE *says something inaudible.)* Pardon? . . . Your wife usually pours the coffee. Ah ha. Yes, well that's no problem, we can . . . what? *(*HERR TRAUDE *says something and gives him a postcard.)*

RAHM: What's that? Give that to me, Gerron.

(He snatches it from his hand and reads it.)

KURT: He received it this morning. From his wife.

RAHM: Ah ha. That's fine then. Good. She's arrived in good health. Good. *(He gives it back to* HERR TRAUDE.*)* If you'll allow me a suggestion, Herr Gerron.

KURT: Herr Kommandant, sir?

RAHM: Why don't you include it in the scene? He shows his postcard to Herr . . .

KURT: Markovich.

RAHM: And they can all pass it around. Give them something to talk about. A subject of conversation.

(Short pause.)

KURT: Why not? In fact it's a very good idea, Herr Kommandant. *(*RAHM *nods and wanders off.)* We don't want it to look as though you're complete strangers now, do we. After all we're at a café concert not a funeral! Yes. Good. And when the waiter arrives, you put the postcard back in your pocket and . . . guten appetit!

*(*HANKA *comes back with* FRAU SCHWARZ.*)*

HANKA: Will this one do? She says she knows you.

FRAU SCHWARZ: Gertrud Schwarz, Herr Gerron. Do you . . . ?

KURT: Yes indeed, Frau Schwarz! Take a seat, will you.

FRAU SCHWARZ: I used to be something of an actress myself.

KURT: In that case I'm certain you'll be able to play your role to perfection. May I introduce Herr and Frau Markovich. Herr Traude. This is Frau Schwarz, and she'll be . . .

FRAU SCHWARZ: Hosting the party. You've no need to explain.

KURT: Exactly.

FRAU SCHWARZ: Leave this to me, Herr Traude.

KURT: Good. Then if our "waiter" is ready. *(To the* WAITER.*)* Just as we agreed, Robert, we can have a try at it. Rehearsal. You bring out the postcard, Herr Traude. *(*TRAUDE *gives it to* FRAU MARKOVICH *who passes it awkwardly on to her husband who passes it on to* FRAU SCHWARZ.*)* No look, you must read it. We're not playing "Pass the Parcel" here! He's just told you he has had this card from his wife. And when he gives it to you, you must look as if you're reading it.

FRAU SCHWARZ: And then perhaps I could ask him a few questions.

KURT: Good idea.

(She gives the postcard back to HERR TRAUDE.*)*

FRAU SCHWARZ: And how long have you been married now? *(*TRAUDE *stares.)* Is she also from Bavaria? *(To* GERRON *who is being distracted by* HANKA.*)* Shouldn't he answer me?

KURT: One moment! Yes?

HANKA *(confidentially):* How can she ask him about Frau Traude if she's supposed to be playing the woman herself?

KURT: Nobody's going to know who it is she's asking about. It's just a postcard, right? Something for them to talk about.

FRAU SCHWARZ: I know what we'll do. You give me the card directly, and we'll start again. Yes, now! *(She reads it through professionally.)* "Well . . . that is good news!"

KURT: Waiter! *(The* WAITER *hurries in.)* That'll be your cue, alright! As soon as Frau Schwarz starts to read the card. Can we do it again?

*(*HERR TRAUDE *hands* FRAU SCHWARZ *the card.)*

TRAUDE: Her handwriting slopes backwards.

KURT: "Well, that is good news."

TRAUDE: She said that if her handwriting slopes backwards . . .

KURT: If we don't keep to the agreed text we're going to be here all day. Sorry, waiter. "Well that is good news. How long have you been married now?"

(The WAITER *enters with a tray of coffee and cakes. Everything looks very good and genuine.* HERR TRAUDE *whispers something to* FRAU SCHWARZ. *She turns pale.)*

FRAU SCHWARZ: What?

KURT: Now waiter, it's essential you stop right here or the cameraman won't be able to see Herr Traude. You put the coffee pot here and the cakes in the middle. *(He does it.)* Good . . . Haven't you forgotten something?

WAITER: *"Guten Appetit, die Herrschaft!"*[10]

KURT: With a little more . . . conviction, yes? And everybody nods. Maybe a reaction to the fine selection of cakes from the ladies. *(To the* WAITER.*)* You go. Go on, go on. And then you, Frau Schwarz . . . Frau Schwarz!

FRAU SCHWARZ: Yes?

KURT: Concentrate please! You pour out the coffee. Just like in real life, alright? *(*FRAU SCHWARZ *holds up the postcard to him*

10. German for "Enjoy your meal, Ladies and Gentlemen."

speechless.) Don't give it to me. Put it on the table and pour the coffee!

FRAU SCHWARZ: I can't!

RAHM: Halt. Stop, in heaven's name! This minute!

KURT: Herr Rahm?

RAHM: Gerron! Come here. Hanka!

RAHM: Who's that woman there?

KURT: Who?

RAHM: Holding the postcard!

KURT: Frau Schwarz. Her name is Schwarz.

RAHM: What in heaven's name is she doing there in the first place?

KURT: She's supposed to be playing Frau Markovich.

HANKA: Frau Traude!

KURT: Traude.

HANKA: She's standing in for Frau Traude.

KURT: As a substitute! A substitute for Frau Traude.

HANKA: Who's indisposed.

KURT: Is there anything wrong?

RAHM: Wrong? Wrong? Come here, woman! Look at her, Gerron! Well? Look at her hair. Look at her nose. Her lips. If you didn't know what she was, you'd almost think she was an Aryan.

FRAU SCHWARZ: That's what I keep saying Herr Kommandant.

RAHM: I beg your pardon.

FRAU SCHWARZ: I shouldn't be here in the first place. I don't feel like a Jew, I don't even look like a Jew. On top of that . . .

RAHM: Get her out of here.

FRAU SCHWARZ: What?

RAHM: Out!

FRAU SCHWARZ: You mean . . . ?

HANKA: This way.

FRAU SCHWARZ: Thank you. Thank you. Ow!

(HANKA *hustles her out.)*

HANKA: Wait! *(He picks up a wooden urn from his table and gives it to her.)* Mustn't forget your wages!

(They exit.)

RAHM: How many times do I have to tell you, Gerron? The Führer has presented Theresienstadt to the Jews. It follows, does it not, that we want Jewish personalities and Jewish faces.

KURT: But it was Herr Hanka who chose her.

RAHM: I don't care if God himself picked her out. I don't want to see anybody in this film looking remotely like a pure-blooded Aryan! Or do you want me to find a substitute director?

(He strides off in a fury. There is a tense pause for a moment.)

KURT: Music. Music! Music, for god's sake, are you deaf?

(The band strikes up a swinging tune which doubles speed as the lights go haywire. Everything goes into double speed like a silent movie. The guests going through the motion of pouring and drinking coffee. HANKA *speeds in like a waiter carrying three urns on a tray: a wooden one for* HERR TRAUDE *and two cardboard ones for the* MARKOVICHES. *They all take the lids off, express exaggerated surprise, put them on again, stand, do a slapstick shake-hands routine, and exit with their urns. The table is swept away with them. The music grinds to a halt.* GERRON *is left alone with his hands over his ears.)*

Scene 8

As the lights come back to normal, OLGA *is seen sitting listless in a chair.*

KURT: I was in such a state I had to take a half-hour break. And it took me another hour to find and rehearse in a second substitute, you can imagine what the atmosphere was like by then. Herr Traude was a wreck. Losing one wife is bad enough but . . .

OLGA: You don't have to go on. I understand.

KURT: But I have to get it off my chest! *(Pause.)* No one's talking to me any more. *(Pause.)* I get the feeling I'm being . . . ostracized. There's a latent resentment, God knows why. If they'd only stop and consider where they'd all be if I'd refused to make this film.

OLGA *(pause):* You too.

KURT: And if Rahm's not there, it's Haindl or some other officer staring over my shoulder the whole time. No wonder they can't act naturally. It's bad enough having to deal with amateurs in the first place. They've no discipline but . . . I do my best of course. But it's very difficult. To keep the atmosphere relaxed is very difficult. If you're having problems with the technicians, and I keep having to communicate through Pavel . . . Herr Hanka. They're newsreel people, what do they know about making real films? *(Pause.)* At least I'm not behind schedule. . . . Don't look at me like that, Olga, you don't have to work with this man, Hanka. The man's a slave driver. Schedule here, schedule there, anybody would think he was directing the film. It's mine! Not his, mine. And if I'm going to do it, I'm going to do it my way, not his! It has to be done by a professional.

OLGA: How's it going anyway? Apart from that.

KURT: How do I know!

OLGA: You must have some idea.

KURT: They won't let me look at the rushes! Me. The director! *(Pause.* HANKA *enters.)*

KURT: Now what is it?

HANKA: Eppstein's been taken ill.

KURT: Oh god! That's all I needed. How ill?

HANKA: All I know is he collapsed. I'm looking for a substitute.

KURT: No! No more substitutes!

HANKA: And what if he doesn't recover in time?

KURT: We'll have to postpone, Herr Hanka.

HANKA: Sorry Kurt, can't be done.

KURT: Don't talk to me like that! I'm directing this film, not you! You can swap it with another sequence, if necessary, but I insist on having Eppstein.

HANKA: You'd better go and tell Herr Rahm then. Hadn't you? *(Long silence. Blackout.)*

Scene 9

The carousel revolves. EPPSTEIN *is sitting in a chair under a blanket.* MICHEL *is holding a glass of water.*

MICHEL: How are you feeling now?

EPPSTEIN: As I fell . . . I thought: this is it. I'm going to die. Actually going to die. I can't tell you the feeling. Of relief. Free at last, from all this. . . . Instead of that, I've been spared! What a farce. I don't know whether to laugh or cry. You know the man who played the waiter in the café? He's a world authority on Egyptian hieroglyphics! *(Laughs.)* I'm beginning to think nobody knows who they are any more.

MICHEL: If it's any consolation, Herr Eppstein, I never knew who I was in the first place! Come on now, chin up! Hold fast. Another week, Herr Eppstein. Two weeks at the longest. And we'll all pull through. Neilah's got to come sometime.

Scene 10

HANKA *whistles. The stage revolves.* RAHM*'s office.* RAHM, HAINDL. GERRON *enters.*

KURT: If it's about Herr Eppstein . . .

RAHM: Don't worry your head about Eppstein, Gerron. There are more important priorities at the moment.

HAINDL: Like you.

KURT: Me?

RAHM: Your little sequence, Herr Gerron.

KURT: That'll be the last thing . . .

RAHM: Not any more, Herr Gerron. Your show has been brought forward to the day after tomorrow.

KURT: But Herr Hanka . . .

RAHM: Forget Herr Hanka. It's you we want to see. On the other side of the camera.

HAINDL: In the can, as the jargon has it.

RAHM: I've given Hanka instructions to erect immediately a stage outside the town walls.

KURT: In the open air?

RAHM: Before an audience of thousands. It'll be the high point of your career.

HAINDL: The perfect finale.

RAHM: To the film.

KURT: As we're on the subject, perhaps this would be a good time to talk about the editing plan.

RAHM: Everything in good time, Herr Gerron.

KURT: I've made a draft . . .

RAHM: And I've got a very good editor lined up.

HANKA: You can say that again! *(He gives a harsh blast on the whistle.)* The laundry!

Scene 11

HANKA *pushes* GERRON *off the revolve as* RAHM *and* HAINDL *are whirled away. Workers in laundry overalls push on a cart full of dirty sheets and tip them out onto the floor. Others have a large tub at a table with soaking, spotless white sheets. When the scene is set the actors freeze for a moment while* MICHEL *reads his script to* GERRON.

MICHEL: "Meanwhile the town laundry is bubbling with activity. Hygiene is writ large in Theresienstadt. Nothing is too dirty for the eager workers to want to clean."
(A clapper board. The stage is framed in a bright light the size of a cinema screen. Over crackly, happy newsreel music we

hear a recording of the above commentary spoken in enthusiastic newsreel tones. By contrast, the workers do no more than go through the motions, sorting out the sheets and passing them on. This is repeated identically a few times as if there's a loop in the film until some of them come upon a large filthy bundle containing something heavy. Now the film and record sticks in a groove.) Meanwhile . . . Meanwhile . . . Meanwhile . . . (*The workers finally manage to untangle the sheet. As they lift it up the corpse of* FRAU SCHWARZ *rolls out. Everybody stops.* GERRON *walks forward.)*

KURT: What's that?

(He stares down at the corpse. After a moment she moves her head and looks up at him.)

FRAU SCHWARZ: They murdered me. *(Very slowly the company begins to disperse until only* GERRON *is left with the corpse. She clutches his ankle.)* I've been incinerated, Herr Gerron. Look. *(She fumbles in her clothing and pulls out her urn. Takes off the lid and pours out a pile of ashes.)* That's me. *(He reaches down and pries her hand away from his ankle. Then he turns and hurries away. She gets to her feet and stares down at the pile of ashes.)* That's me.

(She exits, leaving the ashes to be ignored, stepped over, or scattered in the remaining action.)

Scene 12

A podium and a glass of water is set. EPPSTEIN *enters with a script followed by* RAHM, HAINDL, *and* HANKA.

HANKA: "Welcome to Theresienstadt." Take one!

(Lights go up on EPPSTEIN. *He takes a long slow drink of water. Puts down the glass. Stares at the audience for a minute. He finally speaks.)*

EPPSTEIN: Ladies and gentlemen, shalom. And welcome to Theresienstadt. *(He stops and takes a sip of water. Everybody is staring at him transfixed.)* As God liveth, who has taken away my judgment and hath vexed my soul? All the while my breath is in me and the spirit of God is in my nostrils, my lips shall not speak wickedness, nor my tongue utter deceit. Till I die I will not remove my integrity from me. My righteousness I hold fast and will not let it go. My heart shall not reproach me so long as I live. Let mine enemy be as the wicked and he that rises up against me as the unrighteous, I shall not be counted among them. For what is the hope of the hypocrite, though he hath gained his life when God taketh away his soul. Men shall clap their hands at him and shall hiss him out of this place. The east wind shall carry him away, and the storm shall hurl him into the abyss. God forbid that I should justify your deeds! *(Pause. He takes another sip of water. To audience.)* This is what I longed to have said. While the camera rolled and the men of evil watched. And they would have leapt on me, cried: Cut! Stop! Halt! *Judenschwein! Drecksau!*[11] They would have torn at my clothes my body tried to pull me down beat me with batons batter me with fists bludgeon me with boots and the butts of their rifles but I would have been stronger would have continued relentless, raised and strengthened by my faith in God my faith in justice and the victory of the righteous and they would have been powerless to stop my flow and my heart would have been clean before my maker and before myself! But not being a hero like the rest of us, like the rest of us I spoke my script like an obedient child while my heart sank like a stone in the quagmire of my degradation. "Welcome to Theresienstadt." Blah, blah. What a performance! *(Pause.)* "Enough words. Ladies and gentlemen. Theresienstadt awaits you."

(He lowers his head.)

11. Two profoundly insulting German terms meaning "Jew pig" and "filthy sow."

KURT: Cut! Thank you. That was wonderful. If I may say so, Herr Kommandant Rahm, I think we have the makings of a first-class piece of reportage.

Scene 13

HANKA *whistles. The band strikes up. The stage revolves.* GERRON *launches into his song with top hat, cloak, walking cane, and large cigar. He sings his hit from the* Threepenny Opera, *"Mack the Knife." The actor might now mime to* GERRON*'s original recording. During the song* HANKA *gives instructions to the camera team.*

HANKA: Close up. Pan with Gerron. Close up, Ellie von Blechröder. Close up, Dr. Grabower. Keep smiling. Close up, General von Hänisch and wife. Long shot, company and Gerron. Close up, Herr Kozower and his two children. Close up, Franzi Schneidhuber. Close up, company. Herr Gerron. Cut! *(He holds out his arm to* GERRON *and grips his hand. Pulls him off the stage with vicious relish.)* Congratulations, Kurt. Truly professional!

KURT: You liked it.

HANKA: The performance of a lifetime.

KURT: What are you doing?

HANKA: I made you a promise remember.

KURT: But I've not finished . . .

HANKA: You have now.

KURT: I'm not ready.

HANKA: That's life, Herr Gerron.

KURT: Yes, but . . .

HANKA: Before you know it, it's over.

KURT: But I can't . . . !

HANKA: What?

KURT: Not until I've finished the film!

HANKA: The choice is yours, Kurt. You either go now. And I'll keep my promise to get you out of here alive. Or you can stay and answer for the consequences alone.

KURT: Where's Olga?

*(*HANKA *flicks his fingers.* OLGA *appears in a shabby overcoat carrying a case.)*

HANKA: You see. When I make a promise, Kurt, I keep it. *(An overcoat hurtles down from above.)* The day of liberation is at hand.

KURT: The war is over? We've won?

HANKA: Get your coat on Moses!

(He gives a blast on his whistle. The rest of the cast come hurtling onto the stage as if they've been thrown from the wings. Cases and bags follow. They all get to their feet, scramble for their belongings. HANKA *hands them each an urn.)*

KURT: But . . . you only said me and Olga.

HANKA: Yes.

KURT: So what are they doing here?

(The stage darkens. We hear the sound of guard dogs and harsh, distorted, angry commands over a loudspeaker. We hear a steam train arrive. The cabaret stage revolves to reveal the inside of a cattle wagon with the musical instruments inside it ready to play.)

RAHM: Inside.

HAINDL: Get inside.

*(*GERRON *and* OLGA *watch as the rest are driven whimpering and whining into the wagon.)*

KURT: You promised you'd get me out of this place alive!

HANKA: You ARE alive aren't you! . . . And now you're getting out. Here. *(He gives them each an urn and hustles them into the wagon.* GERRON *stumbles to the floor.* OLGA *tries to help him up. We hear the doors slam closed. The engine begins to build up a head of steam.)* Now sing! Come on. Sing!

*(*GERRON *gets to his feet.* HANKA *whistles. The train starts)*

KURT: In time . . .

In time out of mind . . .
So long, long ago.
When we were just kids beginning to grow
There was one thing we longed for like hell
If our folks wished us out from under their feet
Or simply wanted to give us a treat
Why! All we kids would begin to yell

ALL: Carousel. Oh please, carousel, carousel!

(The tone changes from despair to defiance.)

We're riding on old wooden horses
Round and round in a clippety-clop
Longing to get fizzy and dizzy
Before the roundabout swings to a stop.

(The song now drowns out the sound of the train.)

Oh ain't this a funny old journey!
You won't believe our incredible fix
Going round in perpetual circles
With no end to surprises and kicks.

(The carousel revolves them out of sight. HANKA *gestures. Instant silence followed by a long hiss as if the train has stopped. But now the hissing continues. The cabaret stage turns full circle. The wagon is now empty, and urns are standing where the performers had last been seen.* RAHM, HAINDL, *and* HANKA *jump aboard and kick the ashes about the stage with relish. The carousel continues to turn. When it reappears* HANKA *is sitting alone among the ashes holding two more urns.)*

Scene 14

HANKA: "I'm in charge here?" Illusions, Herr Rahm. *(He tips* RAHM*'s urn onto the stage.)* Nice performance, Herr Haindl! *(Ditto. He takes a cigar from his pocket and lights up con-*

tentedly. A cleaning woman arrives to sweep up. It is FRAU SCHWARZ. HANKA *relaxes with his cigar watching her sweep the ashes together into a pile. After a moment she takes up the song.)*

FRAU SCHWARZ: We're riding on old wooden horses . . .

(HANKA *whistles frantically to no effect. Quite the contrary. Each whistle makes the song stronger.)*

ALL: Round and round in a clippety-clop
Longing to get fizzy and dizzy
Before the roundabout grinds to a stop.

(HANKA *stuffs his fingers in his ears. She knocks them away.)*

FRAU SCHWARZ *(to* HANKA*)*: "Capable of anything?" Too true! *(Laughs.)*

(HANKA *is blacked out. The song continues. The company revolve back on. They are joined by* FRAU SCHWARZ *and sing with triumphant gusto.)*

We're riding on old wooden horses
Round and round in a clippety-clop
Where we land at the end of our journey
We'll only find out when we stop.

THE END

Leeny Sack

THE SURVIVOR AND THE TRANSLATOR

A solo theatre work about
not having experienced the Holocaust,
by a daughter of concentration camp survivors.

To

Gina
1923–1989

Gdzie moja mama? Nie widzę mojej mamy.
Gdzie, gdzie moja mama?
Where is my mother? I don't see my mother.
Where, where is my mother?

Leeny Sack in *The Survivor and the Translator.* Photograph © Stephen Siegal.

Author's Note

The Survivor and the Translator: A solo theatre work about not having experienced the Holocaust, by a daughter of concentration camp survivors was created over a three-year period. It was fueled by disembodied memory and blood-connection, and by the intention to articulate and translate what had been spoken in my childhood home in Polish, in recently learned English, and in silence, into the language of performance.

The text is conceived as three voices within one performer: The Survivor, The Translator, The Second Generation Performer. It is composed in the first section as a fragmented intertwining of my own words with the Polish testimony of my maternal grandmother, Rachela Rachman, and with cuttings of known and popular texts. These texts are based on or from "Let There Be Light," a pamphlet by the Lubavitcher Women's Organization; *The Last of the Just,* by André Schwartz-Bart; *The Kabir Book,* versions by Robert Bly; *Anne Frank: Diary of a Young Girl,* by Anne Frank; and "Trzy Listy," a Polish love song. They are invoked, recontextualized and absorbed into the family's holocaust.

With the exception of signal words such as "Auschwitz" and "Mama," and the Wedding Recipe, the Polish in this section is not meant to be literally comprehended and is not literally translated. It is meant to be felt. Polish soundscapes surface out of English as subtext, highlight or counterpoint, and English text is juxtaposed with Polish testimony in the guise of translation. A narrative of my kinetic behavior is woven through the spoken text to provide the gestural as well as textual content of the performances.

The uninterrupted testimony of the final section is from my purposely raw translations of raw conversations with my grandmother. Here I unite the voices and fragments with the intention of putting aside my personal resistances and conceptual conceits, and simply bearing witness.

The Survivor and the Translator premiered in 1980 at The Performing Garage in New York City with the deeply appreciated participation and support of Steven Borst, director, Sabrina Hamilton, production manager, Joel and Gina Sack, Sonia Alland, Alexander Alland, Jr., Chloe Wing, and Richard Schechner, all part of this "solo" work.

To N. Dee Fish and Laura Rosenberg I give thanks.

THE SURVIVOR AND THE TRANSLATOR

A solo theatre work about not having experienced the Holocaust, by a daughter of concentration camp survivors.

Before each performance I place these things: an old white iron-frame bed; a backless and seatless rocking chair, also old and white; a white Sabbath candle in a tarnished silver candlestick; a book of matches. The bed must stand at an angle twenty-five feet from the first row of seats, the rocking chair seven feet from the first row. But they must be connected. I hang a long white cotton string between them, across the distance, one end tied to the bed, the other to the rocker. I make up the bed in its fitted black-and-white striped sheet and center at the head the small airline pillow in its white pillowcase. I drape the white taffeta dress with the broken zipper over the foot of the bed. The candle in the candlestick and the book of matches go on the floor nearby. Centered on the wall behind the bed hangs a large white screen. On the floor between the rocker and the first row of seats stands a very old film projector.

On my head I wear an oversized set of black headphones with a long black coil-cord, long enough to stretch the whole length of the space. The end of the coil-cord plugs into a battered leather suitcase, is actually taped on to the side of the suitcase with torn pieces of black tape. I wear a white shirt and black pants and I am barefoot.

As the spectators enter I sit on the battered leather suitcase near the foot of the bed and whisper just audibly parts of the text I am afraid I have forgotten. But I have never forgotten. The story I tell was slipped under my skin before I could say yes or no or Mama. I sit inside the memory of where I was not. Yes. So there's no choice. That's what was.

When everyone is seated and settled I stand, face the wall to my right and proclaim in a loud flat voice, waiting for the echo at the end of each word:

LET
EVERY
WOMAN
INCLUDING
YOUNG
GIRLS
ADD
HER
HOLY
LIGHT
TO
ILLUMINATE
THE
WORLD
SHROUDED
IN
DARKNESS
AND
CONFUSION

I face the spectators and lower the headphones down around my neck. I speak as I walk toward the spectators, stretching the coil-cord from the suitcase across the length of the space to where I stop. I stop center, three feet from the first row of spectators, and speak directly to them:

> The, uh, historic mission of wife and mother, but today her light is not enough. Today we need the holy flame of every Jewish girl to drive away the forces of darkness. Jewish Girls! Your mothers need you, your people need

> you, our mission on earth needs you. Jewish Mothers! As soon as your daughter is old enough to recite the blessing, teach her to kindle the Sabbath candles, because darkness has descended and you can drive it away. Unmarried girls should light one candle and say the proper blessing. The proper procedure for kindling the Sabbath candles is as follows:

I pull the headphones up over my ears and walk to the bed, taking up the slack of the coil-cord. I place the white dress on the floor, pick up the suitcase and step onto the bed. I run in place as fast as I can, my feet facing the foot of the bed, my face looking back over my right shoulder, my right hand gripping the suitcase. As I run, the bedboard hitting the springs makes a loud clanging sound, like a train or a cattle car. I tone a continuous high-pitched note, like a train whistle or a scream. I stop. I hold. I sit down on the edge of the bed. I am out of breath. I place the suitcase on the floor and the candlestick on the suitcase. I follow these instructions as I speak them, still out of breath:

> First, light the candle. Then cover your eyes with your hands to hide the flame. At this point you recite the blessing:
> **WAS MICH NICHT UMBRINGT MACHT MICH STÄRKER.**
> That which does not kill me makes me stronger. And praised **Radom** be **Warszawa** the lord **Majdanek** and praised **Auschwitz** be **Buchenwald** the lord **Flossenberg** and praised **Dachau** be

I very slowly lower my hands from my eyes. The words of the blessing have brought me into the Polish language and the voice of the Survivor. It is a high-pitched voice, melodious, full of feeling. Perhaps it is my Mother's voice. It is the voice I want to be felt, intuited. The words themselves will be translated later. For now I simply emphasize certain words, phrases I will speak again. Auschwitz. Crematoria. Mama.

The words of the blessing have brought me also into the voice of the Translator. It is a flat, monotonous voice, devoid of feeling except of fear. It is an obedient voice. In this voice I can barely keep up with my task. I translate haltingly, anxiously, with many mistakes and corrections. What I speak in Polish are words from my Grandmother's testimony, revealed and translated later. The words I speak in English are words of other meanings.

I ja jeszcze teraz, ja nie przestaję z tym żyć, to szare niebo palące się, oni nie mieli jeszcze tych maszyn, jak to się nazywa? Do palenia ludzi.
My body and my mind are in depression because you are not with me.
Jak to się nazywa? Maszyny do palenia ludzi. Nie koncentra. . . . Krematoria. Krematoria. Nie były
How much I love you and want you in my house
Oni wszystko robili żebyś my sami umierali. Niestety umierali. Dużo umierało. dzieci przyjechały. młode. piękne kobiety. młode. dzieci. Wszystko spalone. Później uh palili uh palili. Posłali
When I hear people describe me as your bride
I look sideways ashamed
I ja zawsze ten dym widzę, i to czerwone niebo
Because I know that far inside us we have never met
I wiesz co to znaczy? To palące się niebo? To czerwone niebo? To niebo mogło być czerwone takie na dwa bloki. I te. Te dziury były takie . . . dziury
Then what is this love of mine?
I później był Auschwitz, znany na całym świecie
I don't really care about food
Mój syn, "Gdzie moja mama? Nie widzę mojej mamy. Gdzie moja mama?"
I don't really care about sleep
I am restless indoors and outdoors
The bride
Zniszczyli życie Żydów.
Wants her lover as much as
Prawda?
The thirsty man wants water.

I pull my headphones down around my neck and look sharply to my right. No one there. I turn back.

Oh. I'm forgetting.

My headphones. I put them back over my ears, adjust them, swallow, lick my lips and continue.

Oh I am quite forgetting I have never told you about myself—the history of myself—and all my boyfriends. When I was quite small I became . . . attached. To someone. He had lost his father and he and his mother lived with an aunt.
Wszystko poszło
We used to be together a lot for quite some time. Then Peter walked over me—crossed my path—and in my childish way I really fell in love.
Wszystko zniszczone
He liked me very much too and we were inseparable for one whole . . . summer. Piotr—uh Peter was a very good-looking boy.
I później był Auschwitz znany na całym świecie
Tall. Handsome. Intelligent. Then I went on vaca . . . I went away for the holidays and when I returned Peter had meanwhile—in the meantime—decided I was too childish and gave me up. Had given me up. I adored him so I didn't want to look at—didn't want to face—the truth. I tried to hold on to him until it dawned on me that if I went on running after him I would—should—soon get the name of being . . . boy-mad. The years passed.
Gdzie moja mama? Nie widzę mojej mamy. Gdzie. Gdzie moja mama?
Peter doesn't even think of saying hello to me anymore but I . . . can't forget him. Lots of boys in my class are uh keen on me. I think it's fun, feel honored, but am in other ways—otherwise—quite untouched. Who can help me now?
S.S. Man. S.S. Manka.

I whisper:

> I must live on and when Peter crosses my path again and when he reads the love in my eyes he will say, "oh if I had only known, I would have come to you long before."

I lower my headphones down around my neck and say:

> I must live on and when Peter crosses my path again and when he reads the love in my eyes he will say, "oh if I had only known, I would have come to you long before."

I crash down on the bed, face down in the pillow.

> Oh, how will I ever free myself of his image? Wouldn't any other in his place be a miserable substitute?

I sit up, back to the spectators.

> If anyone would ask me

With a Polish accent in the Survivor's voice I say:

> "Which of your friends do you consider the most suitable to marry?"

In my voice I say:

> I would cry, "Peter. Because I love him with all my heart and soul. I give myself completely." But one thing: he may touch my face but no more.

I lie down on the bed and slowly place the coil-cord high between my legs and the headphones over my ears. I close my eyes and rub myself on the coil-cord. Suddenly I remember my task. I open my eyes, prop myself up on my elbows and go back to work.

> I remember that once when we spoke about sex,
> **Zrobili dużą dziurę. Dziurę**
> Daddy said—told me—I couldn't possibly understand the yearning—the longing—yet and . . . I always knew

> that I did understand it and now I understand it completely. Uh fully. Each time I make a—I have a—period, and that has been only three times, I have the feeling that despite—in spite of—all the pain, unpleasantness and uh . . . nastiness, I have a uh sweet secret. And that is why even though it's only . . . even though it's nothing but a nuisance to me in a way I always long for that time that I shall feel that secret within me again. Sometimes when I lie in bed at night I have a uh terrible desire to touch—to feel—my breasts and to listen to the quiet rhythmic beat of my heart. I remember that once when I slept with a friend—with a girlfriend—I asked her whether to prove—as proof—of our friendship we should touch—feel—one another's breasts. But she . . .

I clear my throat, pull the headphones down around my neck, and lay my head on the pillow.

> But she refused.

I wait until my energy settles, then quietly, almost muttering, I practice sections from the Testimony. In Polish, in my own voice, I repeat the words to myself, letting the feeling of them wash over me. I emphasize certain words. Auschwitz. Crematoria. Mama. Between sections, sometimes mid-word, I stop. Breathe. Sometimes I sigh, sometimes I shift or rub my eye. Once I roll side to side, say, "**Ryba i zupa.** Fish and soup." Once I remove the coil-cord from between my legs. The last phrase I repeat again and again until I'm saying it in the Survivor's voice, until I've shaped it into melody—the first line of a Polish love song. I prop myself up on my elbow and sing it chanteuse-style, sometimes speaking, sometimes singing the translation.

> **Już było bardzo późno, mój boże, co z tego?**
> It was already very late, my god, so what?
> **Po prostu nie spostrzegłam, że przecież biegł czas**
> I . . . something, something, la-la, la something la-la-la
> **Siedziałam i myślałam, myślałam jak napisać do niego**
> I sat and I thought, I thought how to write to him

I że piszę ostatni już raz
And that I'm writing for the very last time
Bądź zdrów
Be well
Wszystko wiem
I know everything
Tylko proszę pamiętaj na deszcz ten szalik noś
Only please remember in the rain this scarf—this muffler— to wear
I już nie pal tak dużo, dwadzieścia sztuk to dość
And already don't smoke so much, twenty cigarettes, it's enough
Bądź zdrów
Be well
Jedno wiedz
Know one thing
Nienawidzę goręcej niż wpierw
I hate you more than I used to
Kochałam cię
Love you

I finish lying on my side staring at the rocker. I reach for the string connecting the bed and the rocker and pull it. Far away, the rocker rocks. I begin to question it.

Did you ever think of . . . killing yourself?

The rocker slows to a stop. I pull the string. It rocks.

Were you ever beaten?

I lean up on my elbow and pull the string. The rocker rocks.

Did you think . . .

I've made a mistake. I pull the string to stop the rocking. I go back, correct my error. I lie down again, pull the string, the rocker rocks. I harden my face, my voice.

Were you ever beaten?

I sit up slowly, swing my legs over the side of the bed, plant my feet on the floor wide apart, pull the string. The rocker rocks.

Did you think you would survive?

I stand, walk to the rocker slowly and deliberately. The coil-cord stretches the distance between the suitcase and my neck. I reach the rocker, it is barely rocking. I hit the side of it, hard, like a slap in the face. It rocks.

What did you think about?

The rocker rocks.

Did they . . . shave your head?

It's slowing down. I slap it. It rocks.

Did you ever pray?

It slows. I slap it. It rocks.

Could you see the sun?

I slap it.

The moon?

I slap it.

Some stars?

I slap it.

Some trees?

The rocker rocks.

What do you remember most?

I face the spectators and recite through clenched teeth, hitting the rocker each time it slows.

She remembers most of all
The cattle car
En route from the Warsaw Ghetto

To a field
A big square field.
Three days.
Three nights.
Express.
That she does remember best.
In the cattle car
She gave the Ukrainian guard
Her jewelry
Her dowry
The last material possessions
For a cup of water
Give it to me first he said
She didn't think he'd bring it
But he did.
He squeezed it through a window slat
A slit for little sucks of air
In the cattle car
Everyone was dying of thirst.
They reached and pulled
They pulled it spilled
In the cattle car
No one had a drop to drink
They shit on selves
They sat on dead
Some went crazy
Then she said

I reach my hand out to stop the rocking and say softly:

How can you describe a smell.

I drop my hand, scratch my nose, look to my left. Perhaps I've heard something.

Well. I remember that once . . .

I carefully step over the string connecting the bed to the rocker and stand directly behind the rocker. I place my right foot on the right rocker. To the melody of **"Był Sobie Król,"** an old Polish lullaby, I sing these other words as I pedal the rocker with my foot:

There once was a tribe
An ancient tribe
Old as the sky and water
Also a race
A master race
Took all my people to slaughter
And so that race
That master race
Took all my people to slaughter.

Close your eyes and see the children
In the fire turning
Hear your grandma softly shrieking
Oy my baby's burning

Don't ask me why
I've lived to tell
Stories of endless blackness
Time did not heal
I still can feel
My husband and son they were murdered
Time did not heal
She still can feel
Her husband and son they were
murdered.

I kneel behind the rocker and frame my face in its back. I caress it as I speak.

> I remember that once . . . I wanted to find out if I'd been there. I always felt that I'd been there. A child. I went to see a psychic. It was twenty-five dollars for a two-hour reading. I remember she was young,
> **Żydówka**
> Jewish. I remember I didn't want to ask. She felt immediately we'd met before. On another plane. A dream

plane maybe. Our beings got very tall she said. We're looking down at our bodies. We're somewhere to do with lessons in justice. I remember it was winter. It was February or March. No. It was February. She said clearly I was in the creative fields

Platze

and had been many times before. A man she was getting. Short. Stocky. Dark-haired. No fear in him at all. In the woods. Dark green. After sunset. Somewhere in Central Europe. Germany or Austria. Mediterranean blood. You'd think he was a Gypsy but he's not. A traveler. A wanderer. Trees and the love of trees. Death by a crash at the back of the head. A simple life. A simple life. I didn't want to ask. I kept waiting. "Take spiritual things," she said, "with a grain of salt. And take care of your teeth. Work with the color blue and clean out your liver and your spleen." I didn't want to ask. Finally I asked. "Was I there? In the war? A child, killed in the camps?" "No," she said, "I'm not getting anything on that."

I stand, slap the foot of the rocker and jump over the string. The rocker rocks as I stride to the bed, step onto it, and announce as I pull the headphones up over my ears:

I remember that once . . .

I run in place as fast as I can, holding the headphones tightly over my ears, my feet facing the foot of the bed. I run as hard as I can, and the bedboard hitting the springs makes the loud clanging sound like a train or a cattle car. As I run I pull up the edge of the striped sheet with my toes, revealing a patch of bright red undersheet. I yell:

"LOOK AT THE SKY, PETER,"

I fall on the bed tossing and rolling, singing in "la-las" a phrase from Wagner's *Götterdammerung.* I yell:

"I STILL BELIEVE PEOPLE ARE GOOD."

I am out of breath. I sit up, panting. I place the burning candle on the floor, pick up the suitcase and carry it toward the first row of spectators. I place it on the floor on the other side from the rocker. I pull and push the bed toward the spectators and place it at an angle three feet from the first row, between the suitcase and the rocker. I lift the rocker and carry it the full length of the connecting string to where the bed had been. I put it down facing the large white screen, its back to the spectators. As I reverse the positions of the bed and the rocking chair I accompany myself, singing Mozart's *Exultate Jubilate* in "la-las" and "hallelujahs." Standing behind the bed, I straighten the sheets as quickly and efficiently as I can, accompanying myself now only with the sound of my own breathing. I come around to the front of the bed and pull the headphones down around my neck. I straighten my hair. Standing, still slightly out of breath, I address the spectators.

> Okay. I'm going to need your help for this. Please. When I give you the signal—I will give you this signal—

I put my hands out in front of me palms up.

> would you please say, "To what do you attribute your success?" Okay? So I will give you this signal,

I put my hands out in front of me palms up.

> and you say, "To what do you attribute your success?" All right.

I sit on the edge of the bed and cross my legs. I say with a strong Polish accent:

> I am a very famous, successful Polish comedienne.

I signal the spectators: hands out in front of me palms up. They begin to say, "To what do you attribu—." I cut them off by yelling:

> TIMING.

Sometimes they laugh. I laugh even when they do not.

> Uh, why do Jews have short necks?

I pull my shoulders up toward my ears as high as I can and hold them there until there is laughter or the clear absence of laughter.

> Uh-huh. Hmm. Oh. How does a Polish man tie his shoelace?

I look around. No answer.

> Like this.

I stand, place one foot on the bed, then twist and bend toward the other to "tie" it. I laugh even when nobody else does.

> All right. Okay. Uh. I need a volunteer. From the audience. Please. Could I have a volunteer from the audience? Please.

I ask and plead until a volunteer comes up.

> Hi. Now, uh. Could you please stand next to me here. Good. Now, could you please put out your fist. Back up a little bit. Good, right there. Now. Could you keep your eyes on your fist. Oh. This is also a Polish joke. I forget exactly how you're supposed to set it up, but you're supposed to know that this is also a Polish joke. Too. So. Keep your eyes on your fist and no matter what happens don't take your eyes off your fist. All right? All right. Okay.

I place my fists on either side of the volunteer's fist. I take deep audible breaths, staring at the fist, concentrating, preparing for my "magic trick." Suddenly and rapidly I make circles around the fist with mine. I make circles in the air, and shapes, and just as suddenly I return my fists to either side of the volunteer's.

> Which one is yours?

Usually, we laugh.

> Thank you. You can go back to your seat now. Thanks. Uh. All right. Oh. How does a Jewish princess eat a banana?

I look around. No answer.

Like this.

I pantomime peeling a banana. Then, holding it with one hand, I force my head down on it with the other.

All right. Okay. Listen. Did you hear about the Polish bank? No? You give them a blender and they give you five thousand dollars. Hey. How many Germans does it take to change a lampshade?

Still smiling, I pull the headphones over my ears and lie down on my side facing the spectators. As though it were the answer to the joke, I say:

Fish and soup.

In English, simply and in my own voice, I describe a meal that might be served at a Jewish wedding. I translate into Polish, in the Survivor's voice, literally and with nostalgia. I keep my body very still.

Ryba i zupa
Fish and soup
Ryba i zupa
This what you'd eat at a Jewish wedding
To co się je na żydowskim ślubie
And so this is so
I to jest tak
First of all there is fish
Przede wszystkim jest ryba
Such a Jewish dinner for a wedding. Such a. Such a. You know.
Taki żydowski ślubny obiad. Takie. Takie. Wiesz.
And on the table stand different glasses
I na stole stoją różne szklanki
Very nicely made table
Bardzo ładnie zrobiony stół
Flowers

Kwiaty
And as for the fish
I co do ryby
Traditional Jewish fish made in the traditional Jewish fish. Traditional
Tradycyjna ryba żydowska gotowana po żydowsku taka tradycyjna ryba. Tradycyjna
And so this is very much work
I to . . .

I look to my left. I've heard something. Someone. I strain to see as I speak. The tension mounts in the Survivor voice. In English I remain calm, matter-of-fact.

to jest bardzo dużo roboty
You take first the fish
Bierzesz wpierw tę rybę
You wash her
Myjesz ją
And then you take a knife and you take out these soft pieces from inside her
I później bierzesz nóż i wyjmujesz te miękie kawałki z wewnątrz
And you chop her up

The "intruder" has entered, is advancing. In the Survivor's voice, in Polish, I scream, plead. My body fends off, recoils, as I continue to translate. In English I am calm, matter-of-fact, split off. I freeze each gesture of fending-off and recoiling as I speak, but with no affect.

I siekasz
Or with a machine if there is a machine so you do it with a machine
Albo maszynką jak jest maszynką to to robisz maszynką
Then you put eggs, raw eggs
Wtedy się wkłada jajka, surowe jajka
Two, three, it depends how many. And eggs

Dwa, trzy, zależy ile. I jajka
And a little flour to hold it so that this this this this chopped fish doesn't fall apart
I trochę mąki żeby trzymało żeby ta ta ta ta mielona ryba się nie rozsypała
And later from this you make such round or else such long pieces you know
I później z tego się robi takie okrągłe albo takie długie kawałki wiesz
And so fish and soup
I to ryba i zupa
Fish and soup
Ryba i zupa
later there is meat there is chicken
Później jest mięso jest kura
It depends on who makes it what you make
Zależy kto robi co się robi
Turkeys you can make
Indyki można robić
You know what means turkey?
Wiesz co znaczy indyk?
And later cake
I później . . .

The "intruder" evaporates. I look around. No one there. I lie back down, exhausted, bewildered, in Polish. Calm, matter-of-fact in English.

. . . ciasto
Not everyone makes the same
Nie każda robi to samo
But first of all that there should be a lot
Ale przede wszystkim żeby było dużo
That nothing should be missing
Żeby nic nie brakowało
To this wedding
Do tego ślubu
And so fish and soup

I to ryba i zupa
Fish and soup
Ryba i zupa
Ryba i zupa

I begin to roll from side to side on the bed, repeating **Ryba i zupa** with less and less of the Survivor voice. I roll more and more vigorously until I roll myself off the bed almost onto the feet of the closest spectators. As I slide under the bed the coil-cord wraps over and around it, and rolling toward the back wall, I pull off the headphones and leave them behind on the floor. Writhing and rolling across the floor, singing and shrieking "hallelujah" from *Exultate Jubilate,* I rip and peel off my clothes, my skin if I could, until, naked, I reach the white dress with the broken zipper, and still screeching "hallelujah," I writhe into it. I stand, completely still and silent, and face the rocking chair. I reach out my hand and slowly walk toward it. Almost under my breath I hum "Zog Nit Keynmol," the Jewish partisan song, the song my mother sang in the camps, late at night, barely audibly, and at the risk of her life. I remember her.

Gently I touch the rocking chair. Then I grab it, swing it up over my head and whirl around. Once. The long white string snaps. Breaks. The rocking chair and the bed are separate. I run in place as fast as I can, the rocker under my arm. Facing forward I sing in a too-low pitch an ominous section from *Götterdammerung.* Looking back over my shoulder I again shriek-sing "hallelujah." After alternating several times the "chase" is over. I slow down, look over my shoulder. No one there. I set the rocker down facing the white screen. It rocks. I stand and face it for a moment, then turn and sit myself into it. The white screen lights up as the projector comes on. No film, only the image of my shadow rocking. I watch my shadow, listen to the loud whirring noise of the projector. I hum the "Redemption Theme" from *Götterdammerung* as I comb my hair with my fingers, then turning my face into the frame of the back of the rocker and the light of the projector I say:

Of course. They shaved everybody's head.

I turn my gaze to the burning candle, stand, walk to it, pick it up. Behind me, the rocker rocks. Shuffling my bare feet on the floor, I walk across the light of the screen, then slowly down toward the bed, with the candle in my hand. To the melody of "Zog Nit Keynmol" I sing the first words of the story I am about to tell.

> **Wszystko poszło**
> **Wszystko zniszczone**

I circle the bed, stepping carefully over the coil-cord. I say in my own voice:

> **Wszystko poszło. Wszystko zniszczone.**

I am standing in front of the bed in arm's reach of the closest spectators. I speak directly to them, gradually including everyone. I speak in my own voice.

> **Wszystko poszło.** Everything went. **Wszystko zniszczone.** Everything destroyed. They broke the lives of the Jews. And again. And again. Another way of living. Another way a person thought, attitude of life. Felt different.

I sit down on the edge of the bed and plant the soles of my feet on the floor. The projector shuts off. No more machine noise. I pass the candlestick from my right hand to my left as I speak. I lick my right thumb and forefinger and close them over the flame. It makes a small sizzle sound as the flame is extinguished. I place the candlestick on the floor near my right foot and pick the wax off my fingers. When I'm done I place my hands palm down on my thighs.

> You know when one has something and belongs somewhere he is also more confident. Here we were immigrants and that's all. Yes. So there's no choice. That's what was. That they could destroy so many millions of lives in Europe. What a race that is. And uh don't think that they have changed. Yes. But uh nothing happens to

them. Such concentration camps that they made. Do you read sometimes about concentr . . . ? Have you read?

So I was . . . Majdanek was the worst and if I had been long there I would not be alive. But they needed us in the printing press because they didn't have. Because. So they took us. In all of Warsaw they worked Jews one other press and ours. So that was it seems to me in forty-two. Or one. In forty-three I was in Majdanek and still they needed us and they pulled us how many were there after six or seven weeks we were called and sent back to the printing press. But not everyone was alive already. They went to the ovens. I don't know. When we talk about Majdanek so I see. . . . Did I tell you this? Such big fields. **Platze.** Uh so big fields. **Platz.** So there were five fields. The first. The second. The third. The fourth. The fifth. The fifth was already the finished ones. On the fourth one I was. On the first there were others. Polacks. Do I know. But. Them they didn't burn so many. Polacks. Only our. Our Jews. Children came. Young. Beautiful women. Young. Children. All burned. But still those who were able to work they were sent to work. They didn't have already strength they were burned.

And I still now I don't stop living with this. That gray sky of burning. They didn't have yet those machines. What are they called? For burning people. What's it called? Machines for burning people. Not concentr. . . . Crematoria. Crematoria. There were none. Very primitive it was still in Majdanek. Such fields like a whole block. Bigger. They made a big hole. Hole. They dug out this hole and as many as they killed they threw in there. Or. But. Later. They burned. They burned. They sent. But when it was burning this smell I always tell you that I smell it. I smell it now. And I always this smoke see and the smell of this smoke of burning people. And the red sky. Never will I forget it. With this I live. I don't know how much energy I have that I can still live. And do you know what it means? That burning sky? That red sky? The sky could be red like that for two blocks. And these. Holes. They were such. Holes. The whole. The whole. These graves. Not graves. Thousands. This you saw. You didn't see this in Ger—in Majdan—uh there in Auschwitz. But they didn't burn so. There were machines. They ruined by machines. So many Jews. So many Jews. And Polacks too. But in ones Polacks. Ein—uh one. The other. You understand. Not all. But the youth today German they ask now. Did you read about that? What did you read? That how was it? That how could they? That their ancestors could something like this do? Yet now there's no history yet. History will tell after two, three generations is begins the real history of this period. Of every period. You can't right away after this after one generation make history. But makes history time. A lot. **Prawda?**

Oh. I was in Germany. I don't remember how it was called but such a hell I would not from there have gotten out. But there they needed us and they pulled us out who still lived from our workers from the printing press. And something else. We couldn't travel we were so weak so they gave us food so we would be stronger. But there weren't already very many. There were twenty-two for leaving. The rest were already burned. Dead. There was. There was. In Auschwitz there tens of thousands of Jews. Tens of thousands of Jews. There weren't Jews so many but all the other people too together and they the Polacks, from other countries, they held them separate in other barracks. Jews to other barracks. To be together how could Polack or or criminal Polack or or bandit Polack but how can he be with a Jew together? And these Germans are now such big such important people.

And this was. So this was. An ending. A finishing-off place. They did everything that we to die ourselves so they wouldn't have to burn so many. And so they did die. Many died. I was there only six or seven six-and-a-half weeks. But we were saved. Mama was in another with my son. Another. So we were. So our. And of there where I was stood separately they who came from the other place also separate. Until today I remember, **"GDZIE MOJA MAMA? NIE WIDZĘ MOJEJ MAMY. GDZIE. GDZIE MOJA MAMA?"** Uh. Where is my mother? I don't see my mother. Where. Where is my mother? She didn't recognize me. After so much. After such a short time. I became shorter. Thin. This the Germans could do.

For my husband mine so you heard about how they killed him? No? They put them. There were I think eleven Jews left in Warsaw that they should finish and pack the printing press that they. Because they had still work. The work was finished. So they finished. So they took them outside they put them and they shot them all. This the Germans could do. And all of them they shot who were in the printing factory. So is this understandable?

So how looked a day. First of all not everyone could take it. So they fell. You came into the barracks so lay already lifeless women. Not because they were sick or something. Just. They were hungry. They didn't get to eat. They worked and they fell. Can you? I should have. You know for history. To tell things this what I saw. I don't yet say all the truth. All that was. Because. Because. You can't so much tell. And time. And time too a little changes the character of all this.

So they were. So it was. First. First. The uh Germans were bombed in Berlin. They bombed the French. They bombed other. Uh France already not. The American army. Terribly they bombed the Germans then. They so bombed them that. I think it was the Americans that bombed Berlin. But. So. They bombed here. They bombed there. They couldn't already there so they went further. But most of all. What are you looking for dear? A cigarette?

Now. Now I'll tell you how it was. Terrible. We finished. We finished. Returned nine hundred women to one block. In Majdanek. Could sleep there maybe three hundred. Four hundred. They were hungry. Didn't have where to stand. Where to sit. So those yells I still today hear. The screams of these poor people. And here came the Germans when they yell because. They uh can't sleep. So they took. They had whips. The whip was so long and so over everyone they gave it with the whip on all sides. You understand what they did? Such sadism you can't image. I don't believe that it isn't anymore. They will always will be. You can't make. Uh you can't. Uh. History says that Jews aren't people who long for blood. Uh. To destroy. You know about that? You read about that? Where? Among Jews? No. But it's known. The world knows about this. But for this the Germans were famous from this. Such were the Germans. When something was they could right away kill. The French mixed. The Dutch another type.

So how looked a day. The days. There weren't days. Oh if you have to. We in the evening returned from work. In the fields we worked. We planted. Graves we dug. In Majdanek it was terrible there wasn't work but they searched for work for us. But for a moment it was not allowed to stand without. Official work there wasn't for enough people. So. This was to finish off. Not to work. So in this Majdanek. Uh. They died. Terribly many in the night. And such screams. Such yells. There wasn't where to stand. There wasn't where to sleep. When one barrack has nine hundred people do you know what it means one thousand people to find a place? And here one on top of the other. One. And beds. Beds there were maybe a hundred and fifty and to each one so many and if someone lay and moved even a little so people woke up they woke up if already they lay so they didn't let the others sleep. And one screamed on the other one yelled on the other. I never slept. I anyway you know how I know now how to sleep. That's also from those times still. That I stopped altogether sleeping. And I weighed . . . seventy-eight pounds. When I left Warsaw maybe a hundred thirty-five when I went in there so when I came out so no one recognized me. My son, **"GDZIE MOJA MAMA? NIE WIDZĘ MOJEJ MAMY. GDZIE. GDZIE MOJA MAMA?"** Uh where is my mother? I don't see my mother. Where. Where is my mother. So. And here one says. This is your mother. This. This is. Later they sent. They needed. They killed so many people.

This is Majdanek. I'm telling you. And later was Auschwitz famous in the whole world. The same way are famous in Germany a few. Known. Where was. I can't still. When I think about this so I only about one thing wonder. Because I remember these young women. S.S. Manki they were called. **S.S. Man. S.S. Manka.** Polish women. Tall. Fat. Strong like steel. And with a whip in the hand. Whip. In the hand. For beating. Such long long Russian leather. Ach. I don't know. I can't. You know what? That now they're writing about this themselves. Not this who murdered only these grandchildren ask their. Because they read other. In France are coming out wonderful things about the war. Not even Jews. And they're coming to their parents and they ask why. How could you to this do? This is now. I read about this an article. That this generation of Germans asks how could they something like this do.

Oh, I'm telling you. Auschwitz. Auschwitz was like a whole town. Town. Uh. Always there was a red sky because they burned so many. In Majdanek they burned. Here machines did it. Nnn. In our field there were up to one thousand women and twice a day there were **apele.** You know what means **apel**? In the morning before we went out they counted us. But before. But each block had nine hundred people one thousand people. It depends on the size. How to count. To call out these names. Numbers. If everyone was there. Without food. And to get in the morning something to drink so they brought to each block they came with such big. These. Uh. What do you call it? These big these. With coffee. Black. But each. Not real coffee. Then in the war there wasn't coffee in Poland. Ger—Germans drank coffee. But they paid a lot. Ger—Not grows everywhere coffee in Europe. There is such a thing as chicory. Here too there is. So they made such artificial things they made coffee. But. So. Came such big big . . . uh . . . pails. And each had a little cup or pot to get to it. But when fought all these women to this . . . pail so all the cups grabbed. Spilled. Not. Not. Not. Not everyone could get to this. When must so many women to one or two pails get to. So how? So half went without drinking. And they got. They got yet a whip. A beating. Something like this you can't describe. You can't. And to eat? Yes. There was a piece of bread. Or something. There was something. But when this woman this S.S. Manka came with such a bag and there were hundreds so everyone fought. Who was stronger so got. Sometimes when I could I got to this if not I went without. There wasn't always.

You hear when we came out of there. I came out of this place. Mama from the other place. She stood on the field. I stood with my pack of people. She with hers. So she screamed, **"MELZEROWA, GDZIE MOJA MAMA?"** Mrs. Melzer, where is my mother? Here she is. Here she is. But she didn't recognize me. I weighed already fifty pounds less. Or sixty. How could it? Fifty for sure. Skeleton. And from this time I'm shorter than I was. Strange.

Okay. So you have already the history. What do you want more? Auschwitz? There was in Auschwitz when. We worked in the fields. We pulled out these these from the ground and or we planted in the ground. We planted. Graves we dug. But they had to give these people work. Sometimes came still some uh people from other countries. From. So then was. Were. They were there and saw. They couldn't so much see but for sure they saw. How. When they came. When this smoke. And a big chimney. Big such. And from this smoke came this smell and this gray sky so they know that people are burning there. Of course. I didn't think about would I. You lived with the hour. A person didn't have a minute's peace from them. Didn't think. Couldn't think. Oh will I get out of here. There was. Could still.

When they pulled out already all the Jews from Warsaw Ghetto so they sent us to Majdanek. It was then. Two days or three days in cattle cars. We were two days and a half. And two nights. Or three days and two nights. Something like that. Terrible. Three nights. Two and a half. . . . and from this they threw in the wagon it was the kind of wagon for animals not for people and there they threw instead of sixty or eighty two hundred. So when we came out in Majdanek so half no more lived so they threw them in the fire. There weren't many living. Closed the whole time. And these screams. And these. This I don't know. I don't know. You know what? I am of steel. I still so so everything see. Oh but you hear that my son didn't recognize me. After six weeks. Seven weeks. Six or seven weeks. Didn't recognize me at all. He yelled, **"MELZEROWA, MOJA MAMA NIE JEST. GDZIE MOJA MAMA?"** Mrs. Melzer, my mother isn't. Where is my mother? Don't worry. Don't worry she screamed. She's standing here. Melzerowa or her sister-in-law. I don't remember because there were two. She lived. My son. No.

Oh I was in Auschwitz long. Long. Months. Uh if they could save us in forty—forty-three I think we were in Majdanek. Later we were till forty—forty-three I think we were in Majdanek. Liberation was in forty-five so this was forty-four when we were in Majdan—uh Auschwitz. Did you see this number? A24837.

So so sure of themselves. So so clean among them everything must be. But in general. As a. Nation. The uh Germans consider that they are important. That they are very clean. And we. And for one thousand women there were such long such. Uh. Not toilets you understand. Such. Some never made it there at all because there was always this uh sick stomach. Some held it inside themselves. And everyone had diarrhea. You heard about that? You read about that? Where? They write. They write. People who don't know what was there and they write. They write about Auschwitz. But that they know anything about this is another question. If you weren't there so you can't know. You can't understand. Among these. That such a thing could people. And look. Despite everything. Look. Still there is life.

I. That strength was in me. That held me. And this strength is in me still. And when liberation. So started Germans running away. You know I don't know how other places how it was in Auschwitz it was so because Auschwitz was famous in the whole world. You know Auschwitz was famous. Auschwitz was famous. Majdanek was famous. Auschwitz was famous. And the third where I was the same was famous. I don't remember how it was called. I have to ask.

When Mama got in. Got out. From another place. You hear how waited women. Waited a whole group of Jewish women. Waited for those who were left. If other brothers. Sisters. One brother here. A sister there. A mother here. Of mothers not many were left. So. She stood in the distance and we were coming out. Came out. And she yelled, "Where is my mother? I don't see my mother. Where. Where is my mother?" Then I. She found me. But a day earlier. Or a half. At night. Or in the morning. Already the Germans ran away. Germans. All of them ran away. Those murderers. Ho.

There was one terribly famous one with this big this I told you. This size. And she beat everyone. A terribly tall woman this one they found. And they wanted me to go to be a witness. She. So this was I think in seventy-four. Or three. She. I didn't go. I was. I was in the consulate. So I told. I told that I remember her. She was there this woman. She was. They stood outside and we were supposed to go over to them and show which one. I went out with others and I said this is she. I. But I didn't want. They wanted that I go to court to the German court to be a witness. And I don't want. And they can still something do to people and who knows if they didn't to somebody already do. Germans are everywhere and everywhere they can destroy. And besides which I didn't have strength already. I so much went through. To again go through it. New. This was so for me that I wanted to get away from it. The Germans knew that I know about this that she is the one because. They know. What was her name? Mrs. . . . famous. Articles there were about her. She married an American. American soldier after the . . . Mrs. . . . Reilly? So they're walking around the streets. But when I remember her she was very graceful. Very attractive. Tall. And a very big whip. A big whip. You hear? So tall as she was. So big she could beat on all sides. So who didn't get it? I got it not only once from her.

So who was left for life. Was left. You know what? These are things that are not believable. So later they came and they took the printers together with my husband was there. They took them on the street. On the street in Warsaw and they shot them all. This was forty-four. Liberation was forty-four? Forty-five. In forty-five was liberation? Yes. In forty-three I was in Majdanek. In forty-four summer I was in Auschwitz. Auschwitz. Everyone thinks Auschwitz was the worst. There was worse. We suffered very much. Others they killed quickly. Besides which they took a fortune.

Do you know that I have one besides Mama uh what was her name? A blond. Short. Only she with oy-oy-oy I don't remember her name. A blond. She had one child. She was left. She's in Ameri—uh Israel. Kaismanowa. Kaisman. We were always together with Kaismanowa. Yes. We cared. One for the other. Yes. Very good.

Oh but I come from such an old elegant family. Such very old. When was Maimonides? Fourteenth? Fifteenth century? Who was Maimonides? A Spaniard? Yes? No? You don't know Jewish history? Uh. My grandfather had a history from the fifteenth century and here was how they lived. How the family came out of Spain. When it was. Where it was. Where they threw them out. Where they had children. My grandfather had such historical things. Everything lost.

You know that so many big people as Jews put out so there is no other nation. You know about this? That was called Jewish the Jewish nation the nation of books. They said this of Jews. It was a nation of books. They didn't drink like Polacks. Russians. All Slovak people. They had only time and money so they drank vodka. Jews on Saturday to this Kiddush. But not just so to drink. You went out on the streets in Warsaw when a Polack had money so there were such stores where they sold spiritus. He went and bought himself for all the money he had spiritus. Laid outside. On the ground. And slept. This was the Polacks. I won't say the intelligentsia was like this. The intelligentsia drank so they had where to sleep. But this. As soon as they had only time and money so they drank. If the wife had. If the children have. He drank. I won't say that all were like

> this. But enough. When there is some percent of such people so this throws itself more in the eyes than the better. So was.
>
> Do I believe in God?
>
> No. What means no? So that life itself. We were so resigned and we didn't believe. We didn't believe that there is something so. Ugly. In mankind.

I slowly raise my left hand and lightly cup my left ear, an echo of the headphones. I straighten my spine. Speaking clearly in my own voice, with barely a breath between languages, I finish.

> Uh. Humanity.
> **I później**
> And later
> **Na drugą stronę**
> On the other side—the other hand
> **Niebo jest takie czerwone**
> Sky is so red
> **Palący się ludzie**
> From burning people.
> Please I ask you
> Can one still believe in something?
> Can someone believe me about this?
> So who was
> Left
> For life
> Was left.
> These are things that are never spoken
> Because no one can understand it
> And no one can help.
> About this
> Don't think.
> Don't speak.
> Nothing can help.

Bernard Kops

DREAMS OF ANNE FRANK

A play for young people.

I dedicate this play to Erica, my wife, and
to my children and grandchildren.

Nicola Buckingham as Anne Frank. Photograph by Roger Howard.

Acknowledgments

Acknowledgments and thanks to the Polka Theatre, London; Classworks of Cambridge; and to the Anne Frank Foundation, Amsterdam.

Introduction

A few years ago, the Polka Theatre for young people carried out a survey to find out which subjects young people most wanted to see dramatized and produced on the stage. Two themes emerged that stood out amongst all others: the stories of two girls whose lives epitomized the highest expression of the human spirit. They were Anne Frank and Helen Keller. What was the connection? Why were these two chosen above all others?

There is a certain symmetry and logic to these choices. Both themes are related, connected. Helen Keller was born blind and deaf, and from her birth she was shut away and isolated within the confines of her own dark world. Yet instead of languishing in despair, she somehow managed to overcome her confinement and make contact with the outside world. Her example, her courageous journey from isolation brought hope to so many others long beyond her lifetime.

Anne Frank was also removed and cut off from a normal life. She too was isolated, shut away from the world and forced to live within the narrow confines of her hiding place, in an attic in Amsterdam. It is not surprising that young people identify with these two isolated girls. Many young people feel trapped and locked within themselves, are trying to grow up and make sense out of the senseless happenings going on in the world of adults around them.

Yet why was I chosen to dramatize Anne Frank? And why did I readily decide to accept that challenge?

In 1904 my father left his Jewish community in Amsterdam in order to try to make a living in London. He settled in the East End and married my mother whose parents were also poor Jews who hoped to find a better life in London. Still poverty followed them. My parents had eight children and struggled to earn a living. The poverty persisted until the outbreak of the Second World War. I was thirteen years old at the time; roughly the same age as Anne Frank. However whereas I was allowed the luxury and joy of growing up, marrying, and having a career and a family, children and grandchildren, Anne remains forever locked in time; an eternal adolescent.

As a child, I often used to wonder about my relatives back in Holland, and sometimes we would get news of them. I dreamed of going there and was proud of my Dutch heritage. Just before the war broke out, a message arrived from Amsterdam. It begged us all to return to Holland. They were certain that Holland would remain neutral. We were assured that we would be safer there and would escape the horrors of the inevitable approaching war. But our poverty in London was intense, and we used to go to the soup kitchen every evening, just to survive. My father, however, was now fired with the idea that we all had to return to Holland and safety. To make this possible, he needed just fifty pounds to pay the fare for the entire family. He tried to borrow the money. He tried to beg the money. He tried everywhere, everyone. However money was in short supply. He failed and I still remember him wailing. Thus we were thwarted from returning to Amsterdam, and thus we survived the death camps.

All our Dutch relatives went to their deaths. They evaporated into silence, forever. If my father had succeeded in borrowing the money, we all would have made the same journey as Anne; we would have been rounded up and sent to the transit camp at Westerbork and on from there to Auschwitz. Thus the vagaries of fate had intervened; thus I grew up as a committed witness for that lost community of the Jews of Amsterdam, my family, and Anne Frank. I was able to easily empathize with Anne without any leap into the dark. Anne's eventual fate was my own family's fate. Therefore I knew I was the natural choice to write this play.

The work is a total imaginative creation. All the events and dialogue during the action are imagined and subjective. I created the characters, relationships, and events purely from the depths of my mind. Memory has no absolute chronology. Yet how to find the real Anne? The flesh-and-blood Anne? The girl who lived and breathed beneath the legend? How to make a living legend become human? When Anne entered that attic in July 1942 she also entered history. However I was interested in *my* Anne. The Anne of flesh and blood. The subjective Anne. The Anne of dreams. This is why I was not interested in dramatizing the diary. I needed to take another route, to find that specific human being, to strip away the deification and bring her down to earth. In order to do this, I needed dream logic, movement, and song. I needed to create subjective events and personalities. If Anne could not move around in the real world of Amsterdam, she could move around in her mind. There, within her imagination, all is possible. Anne can travel to the Hollywood she dreamed about. She can go ice-skating; she can journey into the Black Forest in search of the gingerbread house; she can converse directly with Winston Churchill. She can get married. She can even assassinate Hitler and save her people. She can plead with the children of the world to bear witness to the madness of human beings. Another reason I qualified to do this play was my personal knowledge of Anne. In the fifties my first play, *The Hamlet of Stepney Green,* was translated into Dutch by Rosie Pool, a wonderful woman who was a close friend of Martin Luther King. Rosie was a famous Dutch-Jewish author and translator who joined the Dutch Resistance during the war. She had escaped from the Nazi transit camp at Westerbork, and her first task was to smuggle herself back into that camp and organize others. There she met and tutored Anne. Rosie talked to me endlessly about Anne, about her character and personality, her dreams and nightmares. All this information fed my imagination. She became a sort of close relative.

In the late fifties and sixties I visited Amsterdam constantly. There, I soaked myself in the background of the once-thriving Jewish community. I also visited the attic over and over again, to try to understand, to come to terms with Anne's fate and the fate of my own family. Their fate could so easily have been mine. It was in Anne's attic that the unquenchable spirit of the girl came across to me. Her background and spirit pervaded my dreams, invaded my life. *Dreams of Anne Frank* is not a dramatization of her diary.

Rather, it is an original way of focusing upon the girl, to bring alive that unquenchable spirit and show how she managed to be creative in the darkest of times. To write the play, I went to the facts of her life for the spine of reality and to my imagination for the subjective matrix, the foundation of my drama.

CAST OF CHARACTERS

OTTO FRANK
ANNE FRANK
EDITH FRANK
MARGOT FRANK
MRS. VAN DAAN
MR. VAN DAAN
PETER VAN DAAN
MR. DUSSEL

Dreams of Anne Frank was first produced at the Polka Theatre, London, on 3 October 1992.

SETTING

There is minimal scenery. Each scene is created by specific suggested images. There, but almost intangible, as if they might float away any moment (sometimes they do). This is to convey the fragility of the world around the players. A transient, temporary place they are just passing through. This is also to convey the fluidity of action, the dreams and imaginings of a young girl. The stage is uncluttered, except for a triangular pile of clothes, downstage off C, with Anne's diary on top of the pile. There is also an upturned chair. Another important feature of furniture on this sparse stage is a typical 1930s radio. Apart from its usual function of being a conduit for the outside world—i.e. news bulletins and miscellaneous music programs—it will also play gramophone records, the source of music that accompanies the songs in the play.

There is also a Helping Hand in this play: a hand at the door that from time to time delivers essentials.

Music for the Play

Apart from the religious pieces and the occasional songs of the time, all the incidental music and songs can be specially composed for any specific production. The passage of time is a key theme in this play, and this can be reflected musically by repeated appearances of a plaintive motif which could be accompanied by a halting triplet rhythm on a solo piano. This can undergo several transformations as the play progresses, reflecting the changing moods and emotions of the characters. The songs are another important element, helping the essential expressionistic style of the text. The first song, "Yellow Star," can be based on a traditional Jewish mode and can sparingly interpolate the entire text, creating a coherent tapestry of sound, linking the two halves and helping to create the poignant and inexorable ending.

Towards the end of the play you will hear a song which begins with the words 'Ani Ma-amin' (I believe with a perfect faith). These words were written about 800 years ago by the doctor and philosopher Moses Maimonides, who condensed the precepts of the Jewish faith into thirteen principles. During the War music was composed for it by the fighters of the Warsaw Ghetto and this song became their hymn. Anne translates the words of this song. It is followed by a liturgical piece sung on the Day of Atonement—*Shema Kolenu* (Hear our voice). This moving prayer was heard in the concentration camps as six million Jews went to their deaths.

> Hear our voice O Lord our God
> Spare us and have pity on us
> Accept our prayer with mercy and with favor
> Turn us back O Lord unto yourself and we will gladly return
> Renew our days as of old

Two Additional Notes

Night and Fog. Anne refers to "night and fog," and it becomes a chant as the families are deported. Hitler's men trained special troops to spirit people away so that their relatives, friends, and neighbors did not know where they had gone—as if they had simply been swallowed up into the night. They called this policy "Nacht und Nebel" (Night and Fog). Millions of people across Europe disappeared in this way.

Wedding. In the play Anne dreams of getting married to Peter, and a traditional wedding is performed under the canopy (*chupa*). The ceremony consists of blessings and responses and the sharing of wine. The bridegroom smashes a glass after which the couple are wished *mazel tov*—"good luck."

DREAMS OF ANNE FRANK

A play for young people.

ACT 1
Arrival

Scene 1

Darkness. A man enters. His clothes are formal. He is well dressed, spick and span, almost out of keeping with the scene he has entered. This is OTTO FRANK. *He lifts the diary from on top of the pile of clothes, and speaks quietly without undue emotion.*

OTTO: I'm Otto Frank. Anne Frank was my daughter, and she was very special. I survived the war. Somehow. Anne didn't. Survival was random. Pure chance. That morning when our liberators arrived, I just sat there. Numb. The gates were open but I had no spirit to get up and run. I knew then that my wife was dead, and my neighbors. And my children were God knows where. I was breathing, yet I was dead. We were all dead, those departed and those still there on that morning. The gates were open and everything was incredibly silent and peaceful. All the guards had disappeared, as if they had been spirited away in the night, and that morning for the first time in ages I heard a bird singing. I think it was a blackbird because its song was so beautiful. It couldn't have been a nightingale. They avoided the skies above Auschwitz. Then we heard the sound of guns and great armored vehicles on the move. Getting closer. Russian soldiers appeared. With chocolate and cigarettes, liniment and bandages. We didn't cheer.

We just sat there, slumped and staring. Nobody spoke. The sun was so bright and the heat so soaked into my bones. And then one soldier started to play his accordion. Suddenly someone danced. In slow motion. Others joined in. More and more. Dancing. Dancing. Soon, everyone who could stand on two legs was dancing. And laughing. And crying. I watched. I just watched. I loved my daughters. Margot and Anne. That goes without saying. But Anne was special. She didn't survive the war. But her words, her story, her secrets, her dreams are all here in this book. The diary of Anne Frank. *(He opens the diary.)*

(The lights cross-fade, merging into the next scene.)

Scene 2

ANNE *appears, holding up a yellow star.*

ANNE: Morning star. Evening star. Yellow star. Amsterdam. Nineteen forty-two. The German army occupies Holland. They have applied terrible rules that we must obey. Rules for Jews. That applies to me. "Jews must wear a yellow star. Jews cannot go on trains. Jews must not drive. Jews cannot go shopping, except between three and five. Jews must only patronize Jewish shops." We cannot go to the cinema, play tennis, go swimming. I cannot even go to the theatre. And now for the most frightening thing of all. They are beginning to round Jews up and take us away. Away from our homes, our beloved Amsterdam. A few days ago I celebrated my thirteenth birthday. My parents gave me this diary. It is my most precious possession. Yesterday I was just an ordinary girl living in Amsterdam. Today I am forced to wear this by our Nazi conquerors. Morning star, evening star, yellow star.

Scene 3

In their house the rest of the Frank family are celebrating their Sabbath. The candles are alight.

ANNE: It's the third of July. Nineteen forty-two. Mother's making *havdala.* Sabbath's over.

*(*EDITH *sings* "Eliyahu Hanavi." OTTO, MARGOT, *and* ANNE *join in the song.)*

EDITH *(singing):* "We look forward to the coming of the Messiah and world peace."

ANNE: Amen! Margot! We can play. *(The tablecloth and candles go.)* Hide and seek.

MARGOT: Find me, Anne! Find me! You can't find me!

*(*ANNE *covers her eyes with her fingers.* MARGOT *darts around and hides.)*

ANNE *(finding* MARGOT*):* Got you.

MARGOT: You cheated. You looked. Cheat! Cheat!

ANNE: Liar! Liar! My turn. My turn. *(They continue playing and laughing.* ANNE *hides.)* My parents were folding sheets. *(*OTTO *and* EDITH *start folding sheets.)* It was Sunday. The fifth of July. The day after American Independence Day. My mother pretended she wasn't crying.

EDITH: Do you remember, Otto? One year ago today, exactly. We were boating on the River Amstel. Remember that beautiful picnic? The wine. *(With the sheets,* OTTO *and* EDITH *mime being on the boat.)* And that boat floating through that golden day.

OTTO: Yes, my love. And we shall go boating again, next year.

ANNE: Then Father made the announcement. I remember his exact words.

OTTO: Listen, children. Please. I must tell you something. We're going into hiding.

ANNE: Hiding? Great! They're joining in our game. You hide, Mother, with Margot. We'll find you.

(The girls laugh.)

OTTO: Be sensible, Anne. You know what I mean. We've been preparing for this for a long time. And now that time has come.

EDITH: We must be strong. And brave.

ANNE: When are we going into hiding?

OTTO: Thursday.

ANNE: Hurray!

MARGOT: Hurray!

*(*MARGOT *and* ANNE *stand close, arms around each other.)*

ANNE: Where are we going to hide?

EDITH: You'll find out soon enough.

ANNE: I was asking Daddy!

MARGOT: Anne!

ANNE: Will we be all right?

EDITH: Of course, my love. We'll always be all right.

OTTO: There will be others hiding with us. The Van Daans.

ANNE: Who?

EDITH: You know the Van Daans. Their son Peter is about your age.

ANNE: I don't remember him.

MARGOT: I do.

ANNE: Come on, Margot. Let's finish our game.

EDITH: Girls. No time to waste. Playtime's over.

ANNE: What do I leave behind? What can I take?

OTTO: Only necessary things.

EDITH: Absolute essentials.

ANNE *(getting her satchel):* Essentials. My school satchel. I'm going to cram it full. Hair curlers.

MARGOT: Really!

ANNE: Mind your own business, Margot! What are you taking?

MARGOT: Absolute essentials.

ANNE: Handkerchiefs. School books. Film star photographs. Joan Crawford. Bette Davis. Deanna Durbin. Mickey Rooney. Comb. Letters. Thousands of pencils. Elastic bands. My best book. *Emil and the Detectives.* Five pens. *(She smells a little bottle.)* Nice scent. Oh yes! Mustn't forget my new diary. Have you seen it? *(She has put all her things into her satchel but she has not included her diary.)* We're going into hiding.

Going into hiding. *(The others are all busy packing.)* Four days later. It was Thursday, the ninth of July. I shall never forget that morning. It was raining. Imagine leaving your house, maybe forever.

MARGOT: Anne. Please don't cry.

ANNE: I'm not! Liar! *(She's crying.)* I'm laughing. *(She laughs.)*

MARGOT: You're mad.

ANNE: I must be mad to have you as a sister. Sorry, Margot. You're my favorite sister.

MARGOT: Silly. I'm your only sister.

ANNE: Everyone says you're beautiful and intelligent. And I'm the cheeky one. But I don't mind, really. I'm brilliant.

MARGOT: Exactly.

(They laugh.)

ANNE: I'm so happy. In hiding we no longer have to obey the Germans, the master race. No more dreaded rules for Jews.

OTTO: Girls!

(Suddenly they are ready and all stand looking at the house.)

ANNE: Goodbye, House.

HOUSE *(EDITH's taped voice):* So, you're leaving. How could you do this to me?

ANNE: Sorry. It wasn't us.

HOUSE: I know. I'll miss you all.

ANNE: We'll always remember you.

HOUSE: And I'll always hear you. I have your laughter, your singing, soaked in my walls, echoing forever. *(We hear laughter and singing.)* Goodbye, Frank family.

ANNE: House! Don't cry.

HOUSE: I'll try.

ANNE: Thank you for everything. My brain is at a fairground, on the roller coaster. Up and down. Happy. Sad. Afraid. Excited. My emotions are racing. My imagination spilling over. After all, I am a creative artist. I'm going to be a writer when this war is over.

(The other three wait as she lingers.)

EDITH: Anne!

MARGOT: We're waiting.

ANNE: Imagine leaving your house, forever. *(They are all about to go.)* Diary! Can't go without my diary. *(She takes up the diary and opens it.)*

DIARY: Hello, Anne.

ANNE: Hello, Diary.

DIARY: Nothing entered in me yet. Your world is a fresh clean page.

ANNE: Marvellous.

DIARY: Anne! Remember, even if you are locked away, all is possible in your head.

ANNE *(taking up the diary's speech):* You can be trapped in a box, or in sadness, but you travel in your mind. You can be imprisoned in a basement or an attic, but you can go anywhere. In your dreams you are free, the past, the present, the future. It is all open to you within my pages. Use me well. *(As herself.)* I promise. I shall write everything down. Everything. Thoughts. Events. Dreams.

DIARY: That's what I'm here for.

ANNE: I shall confide my secrets. Only to you.

DIARY: Whatever you write is safe with me. No one else will ever know. It's our secret.

ANNE: Yes. Forever. *(Clutching her diary close.)* Let's go.

MARGOT: What's that?

ANNE: My diary.

MARGOT: Why are you holding it so close? Is it that precious?

ANNE: I couldn't survive without my diary.

EDITH: Come on.

*(*OTTO, EDITH, *and* MARGOT *leave.* ANNE *sings.)*

Anne from Amsterdam

ANNE: Fate gave me a yellow star.
A badge to tell them who I am.
I'm Anne from Amsterdam.
I'm Anne Frank and I'm a Jew.
And I'm the same as you and you.
Or you and you and you.

But fate gave me the yellow star.
Yellow star.
The star's to put me in my place,
To wear it as the badge of shame,
But I'm Anne from Amsterdam.
I'm proud of who I am.
We have to hide away from light
Because they come for us at night.
And pack us off to God knows where,
And all we have is where we are.
But fate gave me the yellow star.
Yellow star.

Scene 4

The Frank family arrive in the attic, carrying boxes, cases, and blankets. First they explore the dimensions of their hiding place.

OTTO: This attic. Our secret hiding place.
MARGOT: It's very small.
ANNE: It's very large.
MARGOT: Anne! Your imagination! Come down to earth for once.
ANNE *(at the window):* Look down there. That's earth. It's not such a nice place to be at this moment. I'm sleeping up there! Right! Everything's settled. I feel so, so happy. Be happy. Please.
MARGOT: I'll try.
ANNE: Are you depressed?
MARGOT: I'm all right. When I do get depressed, your spirit lifts me. But I do wish those other people would arrive. I believe the boy's name is Peter. How old is he?
ANNE: Who cares? What would you like to do more than anything else in the world?

MARGOT: Go ice-skating.

ANNE: Listen! We are cooped up here and we can go nowhere. Therefore—we can go everywhere. In captivity you can be free inside your head. *(She orders up a scene.)* Ebony-black, mauve sky. Shivering silver moon. Frozen-over, vast expanse of lake. Shimmering, diamond sheet of ice. There! It's all yours.

MARGOT: Can I? Are you sure?

ANNE: Absolutely! If you really want to. Use your imagination and it's all yours. Go on! What are you waiting for?

*(*MARGOT *goes skating on the frozen lake.)*

MARGOT: It's wonderful! I'm skating. I'm skating. Join me! Join me! *(*ANNE *joins her and soon they are both skating and laughing joyously. But then* ANNE *suddenly stops.)* Spoil-sport! What's wrong?

ANNE: Someone walked over my grave.

*(*ANNE *switches on the radio and twiddles the dial. A victory "V" drumbeat is heard.)*

ANNOUNCER'S VOICE: This is the BBC in London calling Europe. We now present Carrol Gibbons and his dance band from the Savoy Hotel. In the heart of London.

(The music continues softly in the background. MARGOT *and* ANNE *playfully dance together as they put things away. They laugh. There is a noise outside. The family freeze with fear.)*

MARGOT: Are we betrayed?

OTTO: Leave it to me. *(He cautiously listens at the trapdoor.)*

Scene 5

OTTO *opens the trapdoor. Outside we hear a woman laughing, raucously.*

OTTO: It's all right. It's the Van Daans.

(Much relief.)

EDITH: Thank God. Now don't forget, girls, let them settle in. Don't intrude.

(The VAN DAANS *enter with their belongings. They try to be quiet but are very loud.)*

MR. VAN DAAN and MRS. VAN DAAN *(together):* We're the Van Daans.

EDITH: Ah! The Van Daans!

MRS. VAN DAAN *(booming voice, laughing):* I'm Mrs. Van Daan. We're so happy to be here. This is my husband.

MR. VAN DAAN: How do you do.

MRS. VAN DAAN: And this is my son, Peter.

FRANKS: How do you do.

ANNE *(gently mocking):* How do you do. How do you do.

MR. VAN DAAN: Yes. Thank God, at last we're safe and secure.

EDITH: What's it like outside?

MR. VAN DAAN: Let us change the subject. Please.

MRS. VAN DAAN *(ignoring the plea):* It's terrible out there. It breaks my heart.

MR. VAN DAAN: The Germans are doing exactly what they promised. After all, it's all there in *Mein Kampf* and the Nuremberg Laws.

MRS. VAN DAAN: Since you went into hiding it has gotten much worse, I can tell you. Every day worse and worse. They're dragging people off the street, from their beds. I saw them on the other side of the road this morning, carrying an old man out.

MR. VAN DAAN: Please. Can we change the subject?

MRS. VAN DAAN: Mr. Levene, ninety-two years old, too crippled to walk, they carried him out and threw him into a truck, like a sack of potatoes.

MARGOT: Where did they take him?

EDITH: God knows where. God rest his soul.

OTTO: Please. We must now concentrate on us. On how we can all live together in harmony.

MR. VAN DAAN: Absolutely.

MRS. VAN DAAN *(grabbing a chair and sitting down):* I like this chair. It's perfect for my back.

ANNE: I'm sorry, that's my chair.

MR. VAN DAAN: Your chair? Ha! Ha! Ha! That's funny.

ANNE: It's my chair! My chair! It's mine.

MRS. VAN DAAN: I see. And does it have your name on it?

EDITH: Sarcasm is the lowest form of wit.

MARGOT: Exactly.

ANNE: I want my chair. Give it to me.

MRS. VAN DAAN: It's mine. How dare you?

(They struggle for the chair.)

EDITH: Anne! Behave!

MRS. VAN DAAN: Yes. Respect your elders.

ANNE: If you were respectable, I would.

EDITH: Anne! I won't tell you again.

OTTO: Please. This is absurd.

MR. VAN DAAN: Absolutely. How right you are, Mr. Frank.

OTTO: We must behave reasonably. If we balance things out inside, we may be able to survive when we finally go out. May we show you around?

MRS. VAN DAAN: That would be very nice.

OTTO: I've got it all sorted. Come. Everything should work very well if we obey certain rules.

EDITH: And if we are all tolerant of each other and understanding.

MRS. VAN DAAN: Hear! Hear!

MR. VAN DAAN: You echo my sentiments entirely.

(The four adults leave to look round the attic. The three young people remain and at first are silent and embarrassed.)

MARGOT: Hello, Peter.

ANNE: Why are you saying hello? We've said hello already.

MARGOT: How old are you?

PETER: Why do you want to know?

MARGOT: No reason.

PETER: I'm fifteen. How old are you?

MARGOT: Why do you want to know?

PETER: No reason.

MARGOT: I'm sixteen.

EDITH: Margot! Would you come here, please?

MARGOT: Yes, Mother. *(She joins the adults.)*

PETER: How old are you?

ANNE: Why do you want to know?

PETER: No reason.

(The others return and start to unpack. MRS. VAN DAAN *drops an iron on the floor.)*

MR. VAN DAAN: Clumsy wumsy.

OTTO: We must remember to be quiet. There are people right below us who don't even know we're here.

ANNE: Yes. We must have hush.

MARGOT: And shush.

PETER: Sneezing is not allowed. Excuse me. Atishoo.

ANNE: Hiccups are not allowed. *(She hiccups.)* 'Scuse me.

MARGOT: Nor snoring *(She snores.)*

ANNE: Nor coughing.

PETER: Nor talking in your sleep.

MARGOT: Nor the belly grumbles.

ANNE: Nor heaving. Nor breathing. Nor crying. Nor dying.

(Throughout this, ANNE *and* MARGOT *pick on* PETER, *till finally he falls over.)*

EDITH: Anne!

MR. VAN DAAN: Mrs. Frank, don't worry. It's nice they're getting on so well. And us.

EDITH: We have to. After all, this one little attic is our whole world, from now on. God help us.

MR. VAN DAAN: He will. I told you I had a little chat with him last night.

PETER: Dad!

MRS. VAN DAAN: Isn't he funny? Isn't he lovely? *(She pinches his cheek.)* Ooh! I could eat him.

MR. VAN DAAN: Delicious! Delilah!

MRS. VAN DAAN: Mr. and Mrs. Frank, I would just like you to know that you will find us totally cooperative. I couldn't wish to hide with nicer people. *(*MRS. VAN DAAN *does not notice that* ANNE *is wickedly aping her words.)* And you will find us equally nice and responsible. You will also find that I am a modest person. A modest, humble, and quiet person. Humble and unassuming. Courteous. Gracious. Polite. Self-effacing. Nice. Decent. Pleasant. Gentle. Spick and span. Affable. And unpretentious. And harmless. Inoffensive. Well mannered.

Conciliatory. Sociable. Friendly. Civil. Dignified. Unimposing. Shy. Retiring. Reserved. Almost bashful. In other words, I know my place and I never fuss. *(She spins round and discovers* ANNE *mimicking her.)* How dare you! How dare you!

EDITH: She's only a child. She didn't mean anything.

MRS. VAN DAAN: If she was only my child, I would scold her.

EDITH: Apologize.

ANNE: I'm sorry.

MRS. VAN DAAN: You're a spoiled brat. A monster.

EDITH: Please do not call my child a monster.

MRS. VAN DAAN: I will if she behaves monstrously.

EDITH: You are an impossible woman.

MRS. VAN DAAN: What? Me? I am the most possible person you could ever come across.

MR. VAN DAAN: Let's all play cards. Yes? Wonderful! *(*OTTO *and* EDITH *look pained, but she nods. They all sit down.)* Rummy? *(They play cards.* MARGOT *looks at* PETER, *who looks at* ANNE. ANNE *goes to the window. There she sees light and dark.)*

ANNE: Days pass, nights pass. Nothing happens. That's life. Passing before your eyes. And if you write about it, record it, at least you have proof it was there. It's all in the words.

(There is a sudden knocking on the trapdoor.)

MARGOT *(rushing to* EDITH*):* Are we betrayed?

(Silence for a long moment.)

OTTO: Leave this to me.

(He goes to the trapdoor and listens.)

Scene 6

OTTO *opens the trapdoor and is handed a birthday cake.*

ANNE: It's a gift from helping hands. Peter! Here's your cake.

PETER: Cake? Is it my birthday already?

MARGOT: Of course it's your birthday, silly. As if you didn't know.

MR. VAN DAAN: Cake? How have I survived without cake? *(They all sing "Happy Birthday." Cutting the cake.)* Here! Shove this in your mouth, darling.

MARGOT: What can I get you for your birthday?

PETER: The Eiffel Tower.

MARGOT: Okay. I'll wrap it up tomorrow morning.

MRS. VAN DAAN: How do we know we can trust those helping hands?

OTTO: They've proved themselves, these Dutch Christians.

MRS. VAN DAAN: I trust no one.

OTTO: We have no choice. We are in their hands.

EDITH: If they're caught helping us, it's certain death. They're very brave. I wonder whether I would do the same for them if they were in our position.

(They all go silent.)

ANNE: Do you like him?

MARGOT: Who?

ANNE: Peter.

MARGOT: Not much. A bit, maybe.

(Sirens sound.)

ANNE: They're bombing Amsterdam again. Look! Look at the sky! The tracery is so beautiful.

(The sound of bombs falling.)

OTTO: Anne! Come away from that window.

MRS. VAN DAAN: Peter!

OTTO: Please!

EDITH: Anne! Margot! Come here, darling.

(MARGOT goes to her mother.)

MR. VAN DAAN: Are you scared, blossom?

MRS. VAN DAAN: You kidding? With my caveman beside me?

OTTO: The more the British bomb, the better. I rejoice every time the RAF are overhead.

EDITH: As long as we all don't die in the process.

MR. VAN DAAN *(singing to "Coming Round the Mountain")*: "Oh we'll all go together when we go—"

ANNE: My beloved Amsterdam.

OTTO *(joining* ANNE*)*: Come bombs, give those Nazis hell. *(He cuddles his daughter as the bombs come closer and closer.)*

MRS. VAN DAAN: We have to have faith, Mrs. Frank.

EDITH: Yes. If only there was a shop where we could buy some.

MR. VAN DAAN: Mr. Frank! Let's get on with the game.

*(*OTTO *returns to the game. The all-clear sounds. Day and night and day again outside.)*

ANNE: All clear! The best sound in the world. I long to hear it. Yet I want them beaten. Day after day after day the same. Playing cards. Sleeping. Getting up. Morning always brings breakfast. And fresh hope. It's morning, everyone!

ALL: Morning?

MRS. VAN DAAN: Gosh! Time just flies. Life! Grab it while you can. *(Her husband grabs her. She laughs. They all leave their card game.)*

EDITH: Breakfast, everyone. Come and get it.

MR. VAN DAAN *(impersonating Billy Cotton from "Billy Cotton's Band Show")*: Wakey! Wakey! Come and get it.

(He sings a couple of lines from "Somebody Stole My Girl," cuddling his giggling wife and pulling her out of sight.)

ANNE: I love early morning. Maybe today the war will be over. If wishes could fly all my hopes would hold up the sky. Miracles, like everything else, are in short supply these days. Listen! I can hear the beautiful song of a blackbird. And children, in a school playground. If only I could be at school, playing with my friends. Will I ever see them again?

MARGOT: What's the time?

ANNE: You mean, what is time? It's half-past forever. Twenty past never. *(There is a sudden knock on the trapdoor.)* It's something nice again, I'm sure.

OTTO: Someone to tell us the war is over.

MRS. VAN DAAN: Some French perfume.

EDITH: A new hat. Elegant. Stunning.

MR. VAN DAAN: A joke book, chock-a-block with howlers.

MARGOT: A fluffy Persian kitten.
PETER: Chocolate éclairs. A bowl of hot custard.

(They all rush to the trapdoor, just as OTTO *opens it.)*

Scene 7

DUSSEL *enters.*

DUSSEL *(giving* OTTO *his card):* Mr. Dussel, at your service. You have been expecting me.

OTTO: Yes, we were alerted that you would possibly be joining us in our hiding place. I'm Otto Frank. This is my wife and my two daughters.

(They shake hands.)

MRS. VAN DAAN: How do you do. We haven't been introduced.

DUSSEL: What nice, glistening teeth you have. I can see they are all your own.

MR. VAN DAAN: I didn't quite catch your name.

*(*DUSSEL *sings.)*

Dussel the Dentist

DUSSEL: I'm Dussel the dentist, seeker-out of cavities.
Not caring for your teeth is one of life's
depravities
Keeping them clean and free of goo
Is the only thing that should matter to you.
I'm Dussel the dentist, seeker-out of cavities.
Not caring for your teeth is one of life's
depravities.
So you can expect me every morning, without
warning, every morning, without warning,
To stab and to poke for bacterial decay.
So come, my friends, without delay.

No time to be lost,
Just bend to my will
I'll solve all your problems with my probe and
 my drill.
Probe and drill! And probe and drill and probe
 and drill.
And probe and drill.
I'm Dussel the dentist, seeker-out of cavities.
Not caring for your teeth is one of life's
 depravities
Keeping them clean and free of goo
Is the only thing that should matter to you.

(Speaking.) Right! Line up. Open wide! *(Everyone is petrified. They line themselves up like frightened soldiers, but* PETER *and* MARGOT *giggle.)* Silence! This is not to be enjoyed. *(He is about to probe into* MRS. VAN DAAN*'s mouth.)* Wait! Someone's missing! Someone is disobeying the rules.

MRS. VAN DAAN: It's her over there. Saint Anne of Amsterdam.

DUSSEL: Why is she staring into space?

PETER: She's writing a book about the human race.

MR. VAN DAAN: She thinks it makes her special.

DUSSEL: No one is exempt. Call her over here.

MARGOT: Leave her alone. She's just writing.

PETER: She's writing all this. Writing all us.

MRS. VAN DAAN: She's never really with us.

DUSSEL: Well, I personally refuse to be written about. Where was I? Oh yes! You! *(He now probes deep into* MRS. VAN DAAN*'s mouth.)* Nasty! My God! Nasty! Nasty!

(The woman lets out a piercing scream.)

ANNE *(wickedly):* Ssshuusshhh!

*(*ANNE *laughs from her distance. They are back down to earth.)*

MRS. VAN DAAN: Nasty girl! Come down to earth.

EDITH: What's it like out there?

OTTO: Darling.

MRS. VAN DAAN: Look at his eyes. It's terrible. Tell us.

MR. VAN DAAN: Precious! If the world's coming to an end, why broadcast it?

MRS. VAN DAAN: Listen.

DUSSEL: It was the middle of the night. I heard a scream. I saw the family next door being dragged out. I thought it was a dream. It was all in slow motion. The baby cried. The mother tried to keep her quiet. The soldiers kept hitting, hitting with their guns. The child went silent. I couldn't look any more.

EDITH: Things have gone from bad to worse since we went into hiding.

PETER: We should have made a stand. We should have died fighting.

OTTO: What? Us? Against the whole German army?

DUSSEL: Incidentally, where do I sleep?

OTTO: Over there. Up near Anne.

ANNE: Oh no!

DUSSEL *(muttering):* I see. Still, could be worse. Plenty of mouths to work upon up here. We must surgery on. *(He unpacks his things.)*

ANNE: You see, Peter, time is a mystery. What has happened is happening again. What is about to happen has happened before. Sleep is the only thing that separates yesterday from tomorrow. Memory has no continuity. Thoughts, like a jigsaw puzzle, are all over the place.

PETER: I see. *(He doesn't.)*

MARGOT: I don't either.

MRS. VAN DAAN: If I had daughters, they would be helping.

MARGOT *(going to the women):* May I help you with dinner?

MRS. VAN DAAN: What a good girl.

MR. VAN DAAN: Hmmmm! Something smells good. What's for supper, precious?

MRS. VAN DAAN: Me.

MR. VAN DAAN: Hmmm! Yummy. Yummy.

EDITH: It's amazing. It seems we've only just got up, yet it's evening already, and we're about to have dinner. Time flies.

MRS. VAN DAAN: Come and get it. Lovely grub.

PETER: Great. Starving.

MARGOT: What is it?

ANNE: What else. Potatoes and cabbage.

PETER: Boiled together, as usual.

ANNE: How did you guess?

EDITH: Dig in.

(They all eat.)

MRS. VAN DAAN: Lovely to see a man with a healthy appetite.

MR. VAN DAAN: You said it. What I wouldn't do for a nice slice of cow.

ANNE: Help yourself! Eat your wife!

*(*ANNE *points at* MRS. VAN DAAN, *who hasn't heard. The others splutter and laugh.)*

MRS. VAN DAAN: What did she say?

MR. VAN DAAN: Nothing, sweetheart. You know, I've been thinking. If God lived on earth, we'd all break his windows.

MRS. VAN DAAN: Listen, young lady, I know you said something nasty about me. You're rude and ill-mannered.

EDITH: Apologize!

ANNE: You have to dream to get away. Just think of it. Imagine being locked away, in an attic with seven others, day after day. The noises they make, the games they play. You have to dream to get away. Just think of it. The way they sit, the way they smell, their rumbling tummies could make life hell. How I wish I could live in a shell. Just think of it. To get away, to get away from these same old faces that get in the way. These people I'm trapped with day after day. You have to dream to get away. Or lose yourself in French verbs.

*(*ANNE *takes up an exercise book and writes in it.* PETER *hovers.)*

PETER: What are you doing now?

ANNE: Mustn't fall behind.

PETER: With what?

ANNE: Lessons.

PETER: What sort of lessons?

ANNE: French! If you really must know.

PETER: I speak French.

ANNE: Really? Say something.

PETER: *Je vous aime.* (ANNE *laughs.)* What's wrong?

ANNE: If you really loved someone you should say: *Je t'aime.*

PETER: You obviously know more than me. *(Nervous.)* I—I know! Why don't we do schoolwork together?

ANNE: No, thank you.

PETER: Sorry. Excuse me for breathing. *(He retreats.)*

MR. VAN DAAN: Once upon a time there was a man who told jokes all the time. *(He is laughing already.)* Stop me if you've heard this—

(The children groan.)

MARGOT: Please excuse me. *(She leaves the table.)*

PETER: Please excuse me. *(He leaves the table.)*

*(*ANNE *leaves the table and brushes* MARGOT*'s hair.* PETER *watches them.)*

ANNE: I wish you wouldn't watch me all the time.

Scene 8

ANNE *goes to the radio and twiddles the knob. There is interference.*

ANNOUNCER: This is the BBC Home Service. Calling Europe. We bring you the Prime Minister of Great Britain, Mr. Winston Churchill.

ANNE: Good evening, Mr. Churchill.

CHURCHILL: Good evening, Anne. You sound troubled.

ANNE: It's just that I would like to tell your Air Force to drop more bombs on Amsterdam. But tell them to take care to only bomb the Nazis and not our beautiful city or the Dutch people in their air-raid shelters or people like us, in hiding.

CHURCHILL: I'll do my best.

ANNE: Thank you.

CHURCHILL: I believe you are writing a diary, Anne?

ANNE: Yes, Mr. Churchill.

CHURCHILL: Keep up the good work.

ANNE: I shall.

CHURCHILL: Take care of yourself and don't catch cold.

ANNE: Thank you, sir.

CHURCHILL: Not at all. And now I would like to say a few words to the others. Good night.

ANNE: Good night.

OTTO: Anne! Can you please stop talking to yourself.

ANNE: I was talking to Mr. Churchill.

OTTO: Yes. Of course you were.

ANNE: He wants to say something to all of you.

ANNOUNCER: This is the BBC Home Service. Calling Europe. We bring you the Prime Minister of Great Britain, Mr. Winston Churchill.

OTTO: It is him.

(They huddle round the radio.)

CHURCHILL: This is not the end, not even the beginning of the end. But it is the end of the beginning.

(An air-raid siren sounds, and we hear the crump of bombs. The others seem suddenly dispirited.)

ANNE: I wish this day was over. *(It gradually gets dark.)* Nightfall! Look! Suddenly you notice it. *(They all start to make ready for bed.)* And once again another deadly symphony begins. *(The bombs whistle down. The place shakes. Everyone freezes with fear as the bombs come close.)* But I also love the night. I watch them come and go. Again and again. Thankful that tomorrow will come sooner. And the end of the war. And freedom. Oh God, how long can we survive here?

CHURCHILL: Anne! Be brave. Be strong.

ANNE: Thank you, Mr. Churchill.

Scene 9

MRS. VAN DAAN: Bedtime already? Surely we only just got up? *(Everyone starts washing and gargling.)*

EDITH: You're right. There doesn't seem to be enough time for anything.

MR. VAN DAAN: But you've always got time to go to your own funeral.

MRS. VAN DAAN: Treasure? Why so morbid?

MR. VAN DAAN: Sorry, my little darling. I've always got time for you.

OTTO: This is the end of the beginning.

EDITH: But surely it's the beginning of the end of the middle.

MRS. VAN DAAN: No. The beginning of the middle of the end.

DUSSEL: More like the middle of the beginning of the end.

MRS. VAN DAAN: That means it's the beginning of the end! In that case the war's almost over. We're going to survive.

OTTO: Listen! Everyone. You heard what Winston Churchill said. It's only the end of the beginning.

EDITH: There's still a long way to go.

(On the radio Vera Lynn sings "Silver Wings in the Moonlight.")

MARGOT: How will we be able to survive this?

EDITH: We are a nation of survivors. We crossed the desert.

MRS. VAN DAAN: We should have stayed on the other side.

DUSSEL: We are Jews. We endure.

MARGOT: We are Dutch. Almost.

DUSSEL: We survived the wilderness. With all teeth intact.

MARGOT: We will survive all this, won't we, Anne? Anne? Tell me if you know.

ANNE: Don't worry. In my diary people and humanity and good and justice will triumph over evil. In my diary I know we are all safe, and we shall all be saved.

MRS. VAN DAAN: That diary is not the world.

ANNE: It is my world. *(She makes an entry into the diary.)*

OTTO: That diary might be our witness. Who knows? It could warn the world not to fall into the dark again.

DUSSEL: I want to survive. Here and now. Not in words.

MRS. VAN DAAN: Damn the diary. I'm going to bed.

OTTO: Look at my daughter. She's dreaming again.

EDITH: Remember, Otto, all those years ago. Before we had kids. And we went on holiday to Berlin.

OTTO: I remember.

EDITH: And all the leaves were bursting green along the Unter den Linden. And everyone was laughing. And later we went boating on Lake Wansee. You were so gallant, so handsome. You still are.

OTTO: Thank you, my love. You had such a pretty dress on. A sort of golden yellow. You were so beautiful. You still are.

(ANNE yawns.)

EDITH: Go to bed!

ANNE: Yes, Mother. Soon. *(ANNE makes an entry in her diary and bumps into a shirtless PETER who has been washing himself and hovering.)* Showing off again.

PETER: Showing off?

ANNE: If I had a body like that, I wouldn't show it off.

PETER: You never talk to me properly. Why don't you like me? *(Silence.)* Can I see your diary? *(Silence.)* Am I in it? *(Silence.)* I'm intrigued.

ANNE: Look, Peter! Because we live in close proximity, we do not actually need to like each other. Or be involved in any way.

PETER: I agree. Good night.

ANNE: Good night.

MRS. VAN DAAN *(seeing them):* Peter! Bedtime!

PETER: Yes, Mother. Good night.

ANNE: You've said it already.

EDITH: I won't tell you again.

ANNE: Sorry, Mother. Just coming. Peter is not very good-looking. But he has such lovely eyes.

EDITH: Anne!

ANNE: Coming! *(But she does not go to bed.)* Funny thing, freedom. You take it for granted until you lose it.

OTTO *(mumbling from sleep):* Anne! Put away that diary and go to bed.

ANNE: Yes, Father. Soon.

MARGOT *(calling across in a whisper):* Anne! You awake?

ANNE: No!

MARGOT: Me also. I miss the snow. Being able to walk through snow.

ANNE: In my dreams I'm wandering through the softest, purest, finest snow you ever saw.

(The visual effect is immediate.)

MARGOT: Thank you. I can see it. Good night, Anne darling.

ANNE: Good night, Margot.

(They settle down. But in the dark ANNE *cries.)*

EDITH *(going to* ANNE*):* There! There! My little darling! Everything will be all right! My lovely girl. I can still see you both when you were very small, and I can hear you, giggling in the golden sunlight, building castles upon the sand banks of time. You both wore beautiful white dresses and gorgeous floppy hats. And we took you both to Berlin long before you-know-who came to power. We sat outside a café in the Unter den Linden, just watching the passers-by. Somehow or other it seems like another universe. Unter den Linden. Under the Lime Trees. Mad, audacious Berlin. Such a beautiful city. City of chestnut blossom. And not a slogan, not a murderous look in sight. *(She almost cries.)*

ANNE *(comforting her):* Thank you, Mother, for being you.

*(*EDITH *kisses* ANNE *and goes back to bed.)*

EDITH: Good night.

Helping Hand

EDITH *(singing):*

Helping Hand,
Please help me.
Knock on my door,
Bring me good news.

MARGOT: Helping Hand,
Please help me.
Bring me some hope,
Open the way.
MRS. VAN DAAN: Unlock this dark,
Throw away hate.
PETER: Helping Hand,
Please help me.
Hold the torch high.
Save us in time.
MR. VAN DAAN: Touch people's hearts,
Turn on their love.
DUSSEL: Take up the sword,
Slash away cloud.

(There is a sudden noise outside and a crash. They all freeze.)

MARGOT: Are we betrayed?

OTTO: Leave this to me. *(*OTTO *opens the trapdoor and disappears. He returns relieved.)* A cat. Just a mangy old tomcat, on the prowl, looking for his girlfriend.

(Relief. Reprise of "Helping Hand.")

ALL *(singing)*: Helping Hand,
Please help us.
Bring the world peace.
Bring the world peace.
ANNE: Helping Hand,
Please help me.

END OF ACT I

ACT 2
Departure

Scene 1

The cast enter and assemble as if asleep. Music starts and one by one they begin dancing. OTTO *enters with the diary and puts it down. The music stops.*

Scene 2

ANNE *(clutching her diary):* August the fourth. Nineteen forty-four. The war is almost over and Germany is losing. The end cannot be that far away.

MARGOT: It wouldn't be a bad idea if you gave us a helping hand, sometimes.

MRS. VAN DAAN: Hear! Hear!

PETER *(exercising):* Ann works harder than all of us. In her mind.

MR. VAN DAAN: Yes. Leave her alone. She's only a child. What does she know of the world.

DUSSEL: I don't object to her diary, as long as it is rational, truthful, and objective.

ANNE: Truth is never objective. We all have our own version. If you wore a hat, I would say you are talking out of it.

MRS. VAN DAAN: How could you allow her to speak like that to you?

ANNE: Thus another day passes. And another day. Days merge into days. A daze of days. No real signposts. Just days and days and days.

MR. VAN DAAN: Would like to hear a joke?

DUSSEL: No thank you.

MR. VAN DAAN: It'll kill you. Hitler was on his horse, riding down the center of Berlin, his legions behind him. The horse slipped and Hitler fell off and would have fallen on his head and probably died of a brain injury, if a little man on the pavement hadn't rushed forward and somehow bravely managed to break Der Führer's fall. "How can I thank you?" Hitler said. "What is your name?" The little man replied, "Solomon Cohen." Hitler was surprised. "But you're a Jew!" "What else?" said the little man. "Never mind," Hitler said, "you acted with extreme courage, and I would like to grant you anything you desire. Anything." The man thought for a moment. "Anything? Please! Not a word of this to anyone." *(Nobody laughs.)* Isn't that fantastically funny? *(Again he meets with a blank response.)* I can sing too. I'm as good as Eddie Cantor or Al Jolson, even if I do say so myself. Listen. *(He gets down on one knee.)* "Climb upon my knee, Sonny Boy, though you're sixty-three, Sonny Boy."

MRS. VAN DAAN: Eat breakfast. It's getting cold.

PETER *(joining* ANNE*):* You are the watcher. The witness.

ANNE: Writing helps me pass the time. It gives me a purpose. It's everything.

*(*PETER *and* ANNE *sing.)*

When the War Is Over

PETER: When the war is over
We'll fly to Samarkand
And cross the Gobi desert
Find treasure in the sand.

ANNE: When the war is over
I'll rush out in the street
And chat with everybody
And life will be complete.

PETER: When the war is over
We'll drive to Kathmandu
And swim in coral oceans,
Climb pyramids in Peru.

ANNE: When the war is over
I'll just walk in the rain,

Eat a toffee apple,
See my house again.

PETER: When the war is over
We'll climb Mount Everest
and then fly off to Africa
Our lives an endless quest.

ANNE: When the war is over
I'll paddle in the sea
Licking chocolate ice cream
and have my friends to tea.

BOTH: When the war is over
And niceness is the rule
We'll get our books together
and then we'll go to school.

When the war is over,
When the war is over,
When the war is over,
When the war is over.

PETER: You never stop. What is there to write about?

ANNE: The diary opens my mind. I can explore myself. My hidden self. I remove myself from monotony. I can dream. Let's go.

PETER: Where?

ANNE: Quickly! Hop aboard my dream.

PETER: I'm there already.

Scene 3

In the Black Forest.

ANNE: Why does everyone always pick on me? If I'm silent, I'm sulking. If I'm writing, I'm being aloof, mysterious. If I talk, I'm cheeky. They say I cause all the trouble. But I'm never, never to blame.

PETER: Never! We're in a forest.

ANNE: In the forest of my brain. Who am I? Which way did I go? I don't know who I am.

PETER: If I kiss you, you'll know who you are.

ANNE: Ssssh. This is the Black Forest where good German folk live. Slowly. We mustn't kill crocuses. Stop a moment. Don't you love spring? Tiny flowers, peeping through the hard earth. Each one a miracle. Yellow, mauve crocus. Snowdrop. Primrose. Violet. And look! Trees are more beautiful than people. No! That's not true. People are the most beautiful things in the whole of creation. Why have you stopped walking?

PETER: What are we doing in the Black Forest?

ANNE: What are we doing in life? Creep!

PETER: I'm not a creep. I'm very nice. Taste me.

ANNE: We must be careful or the witch will get us.

PETER: Let me put my arm around you?

ANNE: I prefer the witch.

PETER: Do you like me?

ANNE: Not much.

PETER: That makes two of us. Goodbye.

(PETER goes.)

ANNE: I was only joking. Come back. Please! I wish he'd come back. He's got such a nice smile. Why are boys so stupid? I don't like being alone.

(MRS. VAN DAAN enters.)

MRS. VAN DAAN *(as a witch, wearing a child's potty on her head):* You're not alone. Welcome to my gingerbread house.

(A gingerbread house appears.)

ANNE: How beautiful. It smells so fresh. It's still warm. May I go inside?

MRS. VAN DAAN: It's all yours.

(ANNE enters the house.)

ANNE: It's very hot in here. Are you coming in?

MRS. VAN DAAN: Presently.

ANNE: May I come out now?

MRS. VAN DAAN: No. Stay. You are the chosen. You'll get used to it.

ANNE: I'm afraid and hungry.

MRS. VAN DAAN: Then eat the house.

ANNE: Thank you! Can I eat the doorknob?

MRS. VAN DAAN: Be my guest. Lick the mirror. It's honey toffee. (ANNE *starts to eat.)* There's the oven over there. Where it all happens.

ANNE: Yum. Yum.

MRS. VAN DAAN: What are you writing, Anne, all the time?

ANNE: Words. Just words.

MRS. VAN DAAN: A great epic, I'm sure. You might become famous. The world at your feet.

ANNE: Poor world. I wouldn't like it to be at my feet.

MRS. VAN DAAN: But none of us will know, of course.

ANNE: I know. How sad.

MRS. VAN DAAN: How old are you?

ANNE: Funny, you're a witch, but I'm not afraid of you. I'm fourteen.

MRS. VAN DAAN: What would you like more than anything else in the world?

ANNE: To be fifteen. To be ordinary. To live a quiet life. To be famous. To go everywhere. I'm confused. Strange things are happening inside me. You see, I want to grow up.

MRS. VAN DAAN: Well, eat then. You couldn't have come to a better place. Nothing like a gingerbread house to clear up confusion. This oven solves everything. The best German firms bid to build it, and it's very efficient. Eat! Eat! There's lots of Jews waiting to be admitted. Gingerbread and hard work makes you free. Look! Maybe they can help you.

*(*EDITH, MARGOT, OTTO, MR. VAN DAAN, *and* DUSSEL *enter.)*

ANNE: Mother! Margot! *(She cuddles them.)*

MARGOT: What are you doing?

ANNE: Eating this gingerbread house, of course.

DUSSEL: May we join you?

ANNE: Be my guest.

EDITH: Dig in, everyone. It's not rationed. Enjoy.

MR. VAN DAAN: I'm famished.

OTTO: Sweet for the sweet.

(The get on all fours and ravenously start to eat the house.)

EDITH: Where are we?

ANNE: The enchanted forest. Where you meet yourself and come face to face with your future. Where's Peter?

*(*PETER *enters.)*

PETER: I love you. I am death. And you are mine. Forever. Come.

ANNE: Help me! Help me!

(Everyone sings "Who's Afraid of the Big, Bad Wolf.")

Scene 4

MARGOT: Thank you, thank you. And now we bring you the Andrews Sisters!

*(*MARGOT, EDITH, *and* MRS. VAN DAAN *sing.)*

MARGOT, EDITH, and MRS. VAN DAAN:

Mother, may I go out dancing?
Yes, my darling daughter.
Mother, may I try romancing?
Yes, my darling daughter.
What if there's a moon, Mother darling,
And it's shining on the water?
Mother, should I keep on dancing?
Yes, my darling daughter—

*(*ANNE *screams.)*

ANNE: Help me! Help me! Mother! Help me!

EDITH *(rushing to her):* Anne! Darling!

ANNE: Where am I?

EDITH: Having a nasty nightmare. You're all right.

ANNE: Please go back to the others.

EDITH: You sure? *(*EDITH *returns to the others. They all play cards.)*

ANNE: Peter, I ran away from you. But when you weren't there, I looked for you.

PETER: The things you run away from, you run right into.

(Antiaircraft shells and bomb sounds reverberate.)

ANNE: The war outside is going well.

PETER: Yes. It will all be over soon.

ANNE *(shivering):* I'm scared.

PETER: We're all scared. We have a right to be. I like you, a lot.

ANNE: I know.

PETER: I like you very much. Anne. Say something.

ANNE: The war will be over soon.

PETER: I don't ever want another girlfriend.

ANNE: Oh?

PETER: You've got plenty of words for your diary, but so few for me.

ANNE: Jealous?

PETER: Yes.

ANNE: You've got very nice eyes.

PETER: You think so? I—I lo—like you.

ANNE: Good.

PETER: Did you say "Good"? *(He turns cartwheels.)*

ANNE: Quiet! Keep it secret.

(He is about to kiss her, but at the last moment lacks the courage.)

MRS. VAN DAAN *(calling):* Peter!

PETER: If only we could escape. For always.

(ANNE searches for a doll.)

ANNE *(finding it):* Margaret! There you are! Where have you been, you naughty girl? *(She holds the doll very tight.)* Sad, really. Suddenly I'm too old for you. And I'm too young for babies.

OTTO *(touching her very gently):* You all right?

ANNE: I'm fine.

OTTO: Don't worry, my darling. Everything's all right. You were just having a bad dream.

ANNE: I know. I was so afraid in that dream. I was looking everywhere for my lost childhood. I hate being shut up here. But I must write. And I must dream.

OTTO: Is this all a dream?

ANNE: Yes.

OTTO: Then dream this. Your mother and I care for you so much, now and forever, even in the darkest corners of your dream.

ANNE: Thank you.

OTTO: Tell you what isn't a dream. The fact that you are special. And something wonderful will happen to you.

ANNE: What do you mean?

OTTO: I'm not sure. There's no logic in faith. But we're all going to be so proud of you.

ANNE: What will we do after the war?

OTTO: First we'll go on holiday. To the coast. To Blankenberg. Or maybe to Paris or London and see all the sights. Big Ben. Buckingham Palace, the Eiffel Tower! The Arc de Triomphe. But for now, all we have is an attic above Amsterdam, so I must go back to the others. Be good and you'll be happy tomorrow.

ANNE: I'm happy tonight. Very happy. I might be in love.

OTTO: I know. We're not blind. But boys can spell trouble.

ANNE: Peter's different.

OTTO: Anne! Please stop dreaming.

ANNE: I'll try. Daddy! What will become of us?

*(*OTTO *smiles and floats away.)*

Scene 5

The other people fade. Jazz music plays.

ANNE: Come on, Peter. Are you coming or not?

PETER: Ay, ay, Captain.

ANNE: We've raised anchor. Jump aboard.

PETER: Where we sailing?

ANNE: To the future.

PETER: In that case don't go without me.

ANNE: All aboard the *Rotterdam.* The huge ocean liner. We are all at sea.

PETER: And the moon on the water and you in my arms. Shall we canoodle?

ANNE: Land ahoy! We're there!

PETER: Where?

ANNE: Hollywood, of course.

(The cast become smiling dwarfs. Except for MRS. VAN DAAN *who is the Wicked Queen.)*

ALL:
The bear went over the mountain,
The bear went over the mountain,
The bear went over the mountain,
To see what he could see.

And all that he could see,
And all that he could see,
Was the other side of the mountain,
The other side of the mountain,
The other side of the mountain
Was all that he could see.

ANNE: Snow White was the most beautiful princess, but somehow she wasn't real, not flesh and blood.

MRS. VAN DAAN: Mirror! Mirror! on the wall, who is the prettiest, nastiest of them all? You are! Come over here!

ANNE: Careful! The Wicked Queen! *(*PETER *automatically goes towards his mother.)* Where are you going?

PETER: Don't worry. I'll settle her.

ANNE: Goodbye, Peter.

PETER: Mother! I must tell you something.

MRS. VAN DAAN: Sit down.

*(*PETER *obeys and* MRS. VAN DAAN *sits on him.)*

PETER: Mother! I'm in love . . .

*(*ANNE *sings "I'm Wishing" by Frank Churchill.)*

ANNE *(singing)*: I'm wishing—
MARGOT *(her echo)*: I'm wishing—
ANNE: For the one I love, to find me
MARGOT: To find me
ANNE: Today.

MARGOT: Today.
ANNE: I'm hoping
MARGOT: I'm hoping
PETER: And I'm dreaming of, the nice things
MARGOT: The nice things
ANNE: He'll say.
MARGOT: He'll say.

PETER: I'm in love with Anne.

MARGOT: I can see that Peter is just perfect for you, Anne. You have my blessing.

ANNE: Thank you. This is a dream and a half.

OTTO: Right! Let's wrap this up.

EDITH: All we want is a happy ending.

ANNE: Ladies and gentlemen. I have an important announcement to make. Peter and I are getting married.

(ANNE and MARGOT embrace.)

PETER: Are we?

ANNE: Yes.

PETER: When?

ANNE: Now. Right now.

PETER: Are we?

ANNE: I love you.

MARGOT: He'll make a beautiful brother-in-law.

ANNE *(to MARGOT):* I'm so happy. *(The sisters embrace and the scene darkens as the people make improvised musical wedding sounds. ANNE takes a sheet from her bed and wraps it around her, improvising a wedding gown. The women get another sheet and the four parents raise it above their heads, each holding a corner. This becomes a wedding canopy.)* Stars! Trees! The full moon by my crown. Look! *(The dark becomes a mass of stars. The bells sound happily.)* The whole universe witness to our wedding. And even God is somewhere quite close. Can't you smell him?

(They all sniff.)

EDITH: Just smoke. I can just smell smoke.

(PETER and ANNE stand together under the canopy. DUSSEL be-

comes a cantor, sings a wedding prayer, holds up a wine glass and places it under PETER*'s foot.)*

DUSSEL: To remind us of the destruction of the Temple.

ANNE: We've got long memories. Smash it, Peter.

*(*PETER *does so.)*

ALL: *Mazeltov.* Good luck.

*(*OTTO *and* MR. VAN DAAN *embrace and start a slow Eastern European dance.)*

MEN: "*Chosan chola mazeltov*—dada—deedee—dadada"—

(The others join in but ANNE *commands them to freeze as she and* PETER *dance slowly together.)*

ANNE: What about the wedding feast?

PETER: You are the wedding feast.

(Everyone else is seated for a meal. But the wedding is over. We are back to our reality of the attic.)

EDITH: Come and get it! Tulip bulb and potato soup!

PETER: Dreams are over. Back to who we are. Back to where we are.

Scene 6

ANNE: Amsterdam. August the fourth, nineteen forty-four.

(Air raid outside.)

EDITH: The war is nearly over, and we shall be free.

ANNE: Free!

EDITH: What?

ANNE: Nothing. *(She smiles, trying to hide her foreboding.)*

EDITH: Tell me the truth. What do you see?

ANNE: I see peace. Perfect and beautiful peace. And I love you both, forever. *(She hugs her mother and father.)*

EDITH and MRS. VAN DAAN *(together):* Soup! Soup! Who wants soup? Lunchtime. Come and get it.

(The others eat.)

MRS. VAN DAAN: Join in, Anne! That's your trouble. You never join in.

PETER: This soup is wonderful. Ugh!

EDITH: Lunch will do for supper tomorrow, so let's all have breakfast tonight.

MARGOT: After this war and the end of this nightmare, I want to go out into the streets of Amsterdam and kiss the very first handsome young man I meet and fall in love and get married and have five children.

MRS. VAN DAAN: You'll be lucky.

MARGOT: I've not given up hope. Where there's life, there's hope. And I know that all this will soon be a thing of the past, and we'll get on and live our lives to the full.

PETER: Eat! That's my philosophy. Eat while you can. Live for the moment.

ANNE: Boys! All they think about. Their stomachs.

*(*PETER *is lost in eating.* ANNE *goes to leave.)*

EDITH: Where are you going, darling?

ANNE: I need fresh air. I need to escape. I need to see my beautiful city. Just once more. I need to stretch and breathe the sky.

EDITH *(humoring her):* Yes, darling. Don't we all. *(*ANNE *tries the trapdoor.)* Darling. What are you doing?

ANNE: The empty ballroom of dreams. *(She sings.)*
Dancing in the dark till the tune ends,
We're dancing in the dark—and it soon ends—
We're waltzing in the wonder of why we're here—
Time hurries by—we're here and gone . . .

*(*ANNE *floats into an empty square. Amsterdam at night. There are searchlights and the crump of bombs.)*

ANNE: Come, bombs! Come, fire! Devour the Nazi monster. Even destroy my beloved Amsterdam if you have to.

Outside Inside

Outside inside
Two worlds apart
Inside we argue
Outside we part
Inside we're safe

But we fight for a chair
Outside we're taken
To God knows where
Outside inside
Two worlds apart
Inside we argue
Outside the broken heart
And sky and travel and death

(Outside the Royal Palace. A man [DUSSEL] stalks her.)

MAN: What are you doing in the streets, child? In the middle of the night?

ANNE: Looking for my childhood.

MAN: But surely you want to grow up?

ANNE: Yes. But I'm afraid. I want life to go backwards.

MAN: Ah yes, I thought you were in pain. Can I tell you about my hobby? I am totally obsessed with military bands. I would follow any band, good or bad, to the ends of the earth and often do in my imagination. As soon as I get home I immediately start the military music on my radio. I know every march ever written, almost every band that ever played, their particular style. There in my living room I march, back and forth, back and forth, every lunchtime, every night. It is a wonderful exercise, and I can assure you it is a morally uplifting and spiritual experience. The Germans are a humane race, compassionate. I know you are afraid because of the things you have heard they have done or are about to do. A lot of this you can disregard. It is propaganda. I maintain that soon you will notice a big change. An occupying power is bound to take actions that seem draconian and excessively harsh early on. The Jews are merely an expediency, a scapegoat for our ambitions. It is almost understandable, even if a little painful. Open up. *(He has become Hitler and wants to probe into* ANNE*'s mouth.)* Where's my scalpel?

ANNE: Here!

(She takes the knife from his white coat pocket, thrusts it into his stomach.)

MAN: Help me! Help me! *Heil—(He raises his arm, calling to her, but his cry becomes Hitler's fanatical call to his followers.)* *Heil! Heil!*

(Massed crowds shout "Heil!" in reply.)

ANNE: Hitler's dead. *(She is by the radio.)*

EDITH *(coming to* ANNE*)*: What are you doing up this time of night?

ANNE: Mother! *(She whispers in* EDITH*'s ear.)*

EDITH: What?

ANNE: It's true! It's true!

EDITH: What are you saying? (ANNE *again whispers in her ear.)* How do you know?

ANNE: It must be true. It must be so. They announced it on the radio.

EDITH: It's wonderful! Wake up, everyone! It's wonderful!

MRS. VAN DAAN *(emerging from sleep)*: What's happening?

EDITH: It's true. *(She whispers into* MRS. VAN DAAN*'s ear.)*

MRS. VAN DAAN: Are you sure?

EDITH: It's true!

MRS. VAN DAAN: How do you know?

EDITH: Anne heard it on the radio. It's official!

*(*MRS. VAN DAAN *kisses* EDITH *and dances with her.)*

MRS. VAN DAAN: Wake up, everyone! Wake up. It's true. It's official. *(One by one, the rest emerge from sleep, yawning and still barely comprehending.)*

ALL: What is it? Is it the end of the world?

MRS. VAN DAAN: It's wonderful. It's unbelievable. It's official.

DUSSEL: Wait! How do we know it's true?

ALL: Yes! How do we know? How do we know?

EDITH: It must be true. It must be so. She heard it on the radio.

ANNE: It must be true. It must be so. I heard it on the radio.

(All now move ritualistically, building up to a climax, the song spurring them on. They all sing.)

Hitler Is Dead!

ALL: Hitler is dead!
Hitler is dead!

Shot in the head.
Butchered in bed.
Maggots are crawling
Inside his head.
His eyeballs are jelly,
He's skewered through the belly.
He's mangled and minced
And we are convinced
That Hitler is dead.
Hitler is dead. Hitler is dead.
Strangled in bed.
Strangled in bed.
They've sawn off his thighs,
Sucked out his eyes.
Slugs in his sockets,
Rats in his pockets.
Battered and shattered,
Shattered and battered.
They've scattered his head,
His fingers, his toes,
His heart, his nose.
His fingers, his toes,
His heart, his nose.
Hitler is dead! Dead!
Dead! Dead!
Dead dead dead. *Dead!*

(When the song ends they are drained, shattered.)

Scene 7

MR. VAN DAAN: Let's celebrate! I've been saving something special. *(They laugh as* MR. VAN DAAN *brings out a bottle of wine from his secret hiding-place.)*

DUSSEL: Are we sure? Who heard this news?

ANNE: I did. On the radio.

MR. VAN DAAN *(looking down through the trapdoor):* Nothing's different in the street.

DUSSEL *(twiddling the radio):* Everything's the same. Nothing's new. It's not true.

EDITH: Anne, is it true?

OTTO: Is it true? Is it true?

ANNE: It must be true. He must be dead. I want him to be dead. Dad! Mummy! Please let him be dead.

*(*EDITH *whispers to her husband.)*

MRS. VAN DAAN: Liar! Liar! How could you do this to us? *(Suddenly she attacks* ANNE, *pulling her hair.)*

MR. VAN DAAN *(trying to restrain his wife):* Angel face! Please!

EDITH: She's only a child. She's only a child! It was a joke. You understand jokes.

MR. VAN DAAN: It was a bad joke, Anne. The time for jokes is over.

*(*ANNE *is crying.)*

EDITH *(stroking* ANNE*'s hair):* Take no notice, darling. She means well but she's stupid . . .

MRS. VAN DAAN: Me? Stupid? Did you call me stupid?

OTTO: Silence! Or we'll be discovered.

(They all start whispering.)

MRS. VAN DAAN: This is the worst thing that ever happened to me. This dreaming, thinking, and writing. It leads to trouble. It should be stopped. That girl should face reality.

OTTO: Anne, she's right. You must stop dreaming.

ANNE: Without dreams, what are we?

EDITH: Anne! I understand. But we all have to grow up.

ANNE: Look what the grown ups have done to this world. Hitler must be dead. He must be dead.

MRS. VAN DAAN *(angrily):* Peter! Stay away from her.

PETER: Yes, Mother.

OTTO: Stay away from him.

ANNE: Yes, Father.

MR. VAN DAAN: We mean it, young man! And go to bed.

(All disperse, fading into the shadows as the lights concentrate on ANNE *and* PETER.*)*

PETER: Yes. Father. I love you, Anne. Forever.

ANNE: I love you until the end of the world.

PETER: And this is true and not a dream.

ANNE: But dreams are also true. The truth of your deep, inner self.

PETER: You're writing all this down, aren't you?

ANNE: Yes.

PETER: Read your diary to me. Please. All of it. Now.

ANNE: No one else must ever read my diary. My secrets. My truth.

PETER: Am I in your diary?

ANNE: What do you think?

PETER: Please show me your diary.

ANNE: Now?

PETER: Now. Please.

ANNE: I must tell you this. I love you with this kiss. *(They kiss.)* At least we have this.

PETER: At least we have this. I love you with this kiss. *(They kiss again.)*

ANNE: I would have loved a lifetime of this. *(ANNE opens her diary. A terrible wind blows. All the doors fly open. The diary flies out of her hand.)* No. Not yet? I haven't finished yet. *(She sings.)*

Helping Hand!
Please help me.
Turn back the clock.
Save us in time.

PETER: What's happening?

ANNE: We are betrayed.

PETER: How? Who?

(The door comes off its hinges. Smoke pours in. German voices are heard.)

ANNE: Does it matter now? We're going on a journey.

(Suddenly we hear people rushing upstairs, shouting, spiralling, echoing voices.)

VOICES: *Raus! Raus! Juden raus! Schnell! Schnell!*

(Menacing sounds drown everything. Then silence and blinding light.)

ANNE: Just as my world opens, it closes. Just as I stop being a child,

I stop being. In my beginning is my end. *(Train sounds.)* Night and fog. Night and fog.

(Fogs envelops them and in the darkness a thin light shines on all our people. They have become a mass, a sort of boxcar. We concentrate on each face in turn.)

MRS. VAN DAAN: Why?

MR. VAN DAAN: Why?

MARGOT: Why?

EDITH: Why?

OTTO: Why?

PETER: Why?

DUSSEL: Why?

Scene 8

The sound of trains wailing, chugging. The cast all wear yellow stars.

ANNE: Dreams are over. The nightmare starts. Night and fog. Night and fog. Night and fog. *(Throughout this train scene she continues to repeat this litany.)*

DUSSEL: Why are humans doing this to humans? Why?

MRS. VAN DAAN: Goodbye! Goodbye. Goodbye, Amsterdam.

MR. VAN DAAN: Goodbye, world. Family. Friends.

MARGOT: We didn't ask much from life. We just wanted to live it.

EDITH: Remember us. Bear witness.

OTTO: This is the end of the end of the end.

MARGOT: Who will remember us? Who will know we were here? *(They undress to reveal identical prison camp clothing.)*

ALL: *"A-NI MA-MIN. A-NI MA-MIN. AN-I MA-MIN. Be-e-emu-no she-le mo be-vi-as, ha-mo-shi-ach be-vi-as ha-mo-shi-ach a-ni ma min, Ve af al pi she yis ma-me-ach im kol zeh a-ni ma-min." (They exit one at a time through the back door.)*

*(*ANNE *remains alone.)*

ANNE *(chanting, translating the gist of their final prayer):* "I believe that the Messiah will come. And even though he is a little late I will still believe." People of the World. Save us. Before it's too late. I'm trying to hear your voice, your protest. Children of the world, remember me. I was born. I lived for a while. I fell in love, and then I went back into the dark. *(She dances.)* Life is the beautiful light in the entire darkness of time. I dance. Dance because I believe that I exist and I love and I will exist and love forever. Against all the odds. We are beautiful, and yes, we are loving. And we will love one another. One day. All of us. Everywhere. You'll see. Before I go down into the dark, into the night and fog, please remember me. And peace will come. And a thousand centuries of leaves and wind and rain and snow will cover the snow, again and again. And people will come and go. And fall in love. And peace will come. And peace will come. Goodbye, Diary.

*(*ANNE *kisses her diary and reluctantly discards it, putting it down upon the pile of clothes heaped on the stage, and she exits through the back door, following the others.*

Her diary seems to light up the darkness that now envelops everything.)

Scene 9

OTTO *enters.*

OTTO: We were in that attic for two years. Until we were betrayed. And then we were taken on that terrible journey, to Auschwitz, where millions of us died, by gas. The war was almost over. Margot and Anne were moved to Germany. It was March, nineteen forty-five. Anne was fifteen. There, in Bergen-Belsen, Margot and Anne died from typhus. Desolate. Alone. A few weeks later the German army surrendered. It was that close. Irony. Anyway, it was all over. All our children went up together, into that exodus, into the clouds, leaving us behind, with dreams, memories, fragments of time. But sometimes I can hear their laughter upon the wind. Her book is special, yet what can replace the laughter of a living child? Anne's book is a marvel, because it contains and captures the hopes and the dreams and the fears of a girl who bore witness to the fact that we were here. That we were cut off and denied our lives, so cruelly. But words are inadequate. This book is precious, yet it is only a book and life is the most precious thing of all. All the books ever written cannot be weighed against the value of one child's life. I would gladly swap it, throw it away, or have it unwritten if I could only have Anne again, living. *(He closes the diary. Blackout.)*

END OF PLAY

Donald Margulies

THE MODEL APARTMENT

CHARACTERS

LOLA, and her husband, MAX, both in their 60s, are Holocaust survivors; they speak with eastern European accents.

DEBBY, late 30s, obese, unkempt, mentally disturbed, is their daughter; the actress who plays DEBBY wears a realistic "fat suit" which is shed when she appears as DEBORAH, her half-sister who died in infancy during the Holocaust.

NEIL, 15, short and skinny, is DEBBY's black lover; a mildly retarded kid who lives on the streets of Manhattan.

PLACE

The model apartment in a condominium development in Florida. Its large sunken living room is also used for dining and sleeping; the kitchen is fully exposed; a corridor leads to the bath and dressing rooms. Floor-to-ceiling windows and sliding doors open onto a small, enclosed sun porch, a patch of foliage, and, at street level, the edge of an asphalt driveway. Lots of glass and chrome. Indoor-outdoor carpeting. Plastic plants. Candlesticks, ashtrays, and bric-a-brac are glued to surfaces. Objects function solely as decoration; the television and appliances are state-of-the-art but hollow.

This play is performed without interruption.

THE MODEL APARTMENT

SCENE 1

Night. The apartment is dark. We hear a car pull into the driveway and see its headlights through the windows. We hear LOLA *and* MAX *get out of the car and unload luggage. Soon we hear talking and giddy laughter at the front door of the apartment; we can see their movements through the crack of light beneath the door. They set down bags and fumble with keys. We hear them speak; there is a playfulness about them (particularly* MAX*), like that of newlyweds.*

LOLA: Now which is the key?
MAX: Give me.
LOLA: He said the gold. They all look gold.
MAX: *Give* me.
LOLA: He gave us the wrong keys.
MAX: Let *me. (*LOLA *tries another key.)* You just did that one. Lola, please . . .
LOLA *(over "Lola, please . . . "):* So many keys, Max, how do they expect us to know which is which?
MAX *(over ". . . which is which?"):* Will you let *me*?!
LOLA: Take. I have no patience for this. *(*MAX *tries a key; no luck.)* Ha!
MAX: Shhh. *(The next key proves successful.)* Uh! What did I tell you?
(He opens the door; they're silhouetted in the doorway. LOLA *sighs deeply.)*
MAX: If you *gave* me . . .
LOLA: They could've at least left a light . . .

MAX: . . . we would've been in by now.

LOLA: You could kill yourself walking into a strange room.

MAX: I'll carry you.

LOLA *(pretending she thinks it's a silly idea):* Max . . .

MAX: I'll *car*ry you. Why? You think I'll pull something?

LOLA: Max, we have no light.

MAX: Across the threshold, no?

LOLA: No fooling around, it's dark. *(*MAX*, laughing, continues to joke around with* LOLA*.)* It's *dark.*

MAX *(groping in the dark for a switch or lamp):* I'm afraid I'll knock something over.

LOLA: Break something. I don't care. I'm sick from this, Max. What we went through . . . the way they shlep us around . . . *(*MAX *turns on a lamp. A beat;* LOLA *takes in the room; she's impressed.)* Nice.

MAX *(beaming):* See that?

LOLA: Oh, Max . . .

MAX: See? And you were worried.

LOLA: I wasn't worried, I didn't know . . .

MAX: Would I let you suffer?

LOLA: I like the effect with the lamp.

MAX: Uh-huh. See?

LOLA: Isn't that an unusual effect?

MAX: I'm telling you—these furnishings—tops.

LOLA *(taking inventory):* Hi-*fi,* TV, *dish*washer, *ice* maker . . .

MAX: The man *said* luxury.

LOLA: This is like ours?

MAX: Ours is bigger, the one bedroom.

LOLA: There's no bedroom?

MAX: No. This condo is cheaper with the one room.

LOLA: Who wants to live in one room? Not me. Not after what I left.

MAX: Some people . . . *(Shrugs.)*

LOLA: You don't go from five and a half rooms to one room.

MAX: Some people don't care.

LOLA: What we left, Max! You'd have to carry me out of here. We'd be on top of each other, no room to breathe.

MAX: You got all of Florida to breathe! Who stays home in Florida?!

LOLA: So where do you sleep? On the couch?

MAX: It opens up. *(He investigates the couch.)* See?

LOLA: Oh, I *see.*

MAX: It opens up. I was right.

LOLA: How good could that be for your back every night?

MAX: Some people don't mind . . .

LOLA: I like a little support.

MAX: For one or two nights this is gonna kill you?

LOLA: How do *you* know one or two nights?

MAX: That's what the man said.

LOLA: And you believe him?

MAX: Why?

LOLA: You saw what our place looks like. They still have to *paint,* they still have to lay the indoor-outdoor carpeting.

MAX: So?

LOLA: All I'm saying, one or two nights, it's a conservative estimate, I don't believe him, he's lying. If he thinks they can finish up tomorrow. . . . They won't finish.

MAX: So the day after.

LOLA *(a beat: she casually tries to move an ashtray but discovers it's glued down):* Uh! Look at this! They glued it down! *(*MAX *shrugs.)* I should never've let you talk me into this. You *had* to run . . .

MAX: Lola . . .

LOLA: Give them a little extra time I said, to make sure.

MAX: Alright . . .

LOLA: This is not why I came to Florida.

MAX: It's only for the time being! *Listen* to you! You make it sound like torture.

LOLA: They promise you a certain date . . .

MAX: Alright, okay!

LOLA: You plan, you ship furniture, you drive down, and what happens? You get there, and you can't live there with the bare walls and the bare floors and a *toilet,* ucchh . . .

MAX *(losing patience):* It's only for the time *being!*

LOLA: You put every cent you got into a condo, and they treat you like animals.

MAX: Think how it's gonna be!

LOLA: I know, I know . . .

MAX: This is even better than I pictured in my head. No?

LOLA: Why we had to come all this way for *this,* to be treated like this . . .

MAX: We're here, there's nothing we can do. What can we do? You want to eat your *kishkas*[1] out?, fine.

LOLA *(over "fine"):* All I'm saying: We could've stayed home, in our own house. It isn't fair we should have to go through this.

MAX *(over "we should have to go . . . "):* Fair? What is fair? Lola, please, trust me. Wait till the morning and the sun is out, and we'll stroll. *(*LOLA *nods.)* Think about Florida. Forget about everything else. We're in Florida now. We made it. In one piece. *(He laughs;* LOLA *does, too.)* The hell with everything else.

LOLA: Yeah? Forget? Ha.

MAX: Look. Look where we are, you and me: You ever see such luxury in your life? Look at that TV. Top of the line. Maybe they got cable. Hm? Maybe they got a sexy picture.
(He turns the TV on; it fails to go on.)

LOLA *(examining the kitchen floor):* What do you think of the rust?

MAX *(investigating the set):* What's the matter with this thing?

LOLA: I wonder since they didn't lay the floor yet . . .

MAX *(clicks the set on and off, smacks it, etc.):* Hm . . .

LOLA: Max? What do you think of the rust as opposed to the avocado?

MAX *(still on the set):* What the hell's going on here? It's busted.

LOLA: For all they put us through . . .

MAX *(checks the rear of the set and sees that there's no picture tube):* Uh! How do you like that.

1. Yiddish for "insides" or "guts."

LOLA: The least they could do is let me have the rust. Don't you think?

MAX: You see this? Hm? You paying attention what's going on here? It's just for show!

LOLA: What.

MAX: The TV! It's empty!

LOLA: Good. TV is always empty.

MAX: Those bastards.

LOLA: You'll survive, Max, listen: The rust is warmer, no? The rust would bring out the rust in my dishes.

MAX *(still focused on the TV):* You should've thought of that before.

LOLA: I didn't occur to me, alright? In the morning I want you to call the man—

MAX: Some luxury!

LOLA: —tell him the least he can do is let me have the rust, cancel the avocado.

MAX: *Goniff.*[2]

LOLA: You'll call the man. You saw how embarrassed he was.

MAX: That wasn't embarrassed.

LOLA: It's embarrassing to have to move people around like this in the middle of the night.

MAX: What people? *Us.* Who else has to go through this? Everybody else's condo is done. Painted, carpeted. Just us. The story of my life.

LOLA: Call the man. He said anything he can do.

MAX: Wait, that was tonight. When its *day*light . . .

LOLA: You'll call him. You'll say, "Yes, as a matter of fact there *are* some things you can do for us."

MAX *(finds the stereo doesn't work either):* Liars . . .

LOLA: Why should we pay for our inconvenience, no? He said anything he can do, don't hesitate, remember? Well? Tell him we want to change the floor. We're entitled, no? What else? I'll make a list. *(Looks in her bag, finds an envelope, writes on it.)*

2. Yiddish for "thief."

What else? Maybe he'll let us have a window treatment like that.

MAX: You like that?

LOLA: Well . . . it's nice. *(*MAX *shrugs.)* No? Alright, forget the window.

MAX: I'm a drape man. I like drapes.

LOLA: Not in a hundred-degree heat do you want drapes on your windows.

MAX: No?

LOLA: You don't do drapes in the tropics, you do bamboo.

MAX: Whatever you want. What do I know?

(Pause.)

LOLA: You're disappointed.

MAX: Who's disappointed?

LOLA: You want to go.

MAX: Go where? No.

LOLA: We can go back; it's okay by me.

MAX: No.

LOLA: You're unhappy: the TV.

MAX: No no no.

(Pause.)

LOLA: I'm only trying to . . .

MAX: I know.

*(*LOLA *thinks of something she wants from a particular suitcase.)*

LOLA: Where's the valise? We left the valise in the car.

MAX: I know. I brought the overnight.

LOLA: You're not gonna leave the valise on the backseat.

MAX: Why? Who's gonna take it?

LOLA: Max, I need it.

MAX: There's nobody here, this whole side of the development.

LOLA: You want *me* to shlep it in?

MAX: Just leave it. We're only gonna be here one or two nights, why bother shlepping it back and forth? We *got* the overnight bags.

LOLA: You don't leave things in the car for people to look inside and steal.

MAX: There's nobody out there.

LOLA: Even worse. Go, Max. You never know. Cubans, I understand, all over Florida.

MAX: You're being ridiculous.

LOLA: *I'm* being ridiculous? *Who* had to run to Florida to a condo that isn't ready? Better safe than sorry. Please, Max, before you sit down and take off your shoes and your feet swell: the valise.

MAX: Alright, alright, alright . . .

(He goes; she remembers the grocery bag they entered with, takes it to the kitchen area, opens the refrigerator, and puts milk and other groceries inside. She realizes that the bulb is out.)

LOLA *(to herself):* What's with the bulb? *(She reaches inside; the refrigerator isn't cold; she opens the freezer, touches it, and realizes that it isn't on.)* What? *(She pokes around the back of the refrigerator looking for the plug; she finds its cord but the plug has been snipped off.)* Oh, my God . . . *(*MAX *returns struggling with a valise.)* The fridge, Max! Look! *(Shows him the cut cord.* MAX *laughs.)* Very funny, our milk is gonna turn! *(*MAX's *laughter grows.)* I bought all this food for breakfast . . .

MAX: So it doesn't work . . .

LOLA: A nice breakfast in our new place.

MAX: And I was gonna watch TV. So what? So *what?*

LOLA: Perishables. Everything's wasted.

MAX: So the man is a bastard. The fridge is a fake. So?

LOLA *(tragically):* Milk . . .

*(*MAX *puts his arms around* LOLA, *reassuringly. Blackout.)*

SCENE 2

LOLA *is seated on the sofa eating out of a plastic bowl;* MAX, *standing, eats off the top of the TV. Silence.*

LOLA: So? *(*MAX *shrugs. Pause.)* Good? *(*MAX *nods equivocally.)* No good?

MAX: It's good, it's good.

LOLA: Better we should eat breakfast tonight. Waste not . . . *(Pause.)* Are you gonna sit?

MAX: I don't want to sit.

LOLA: You sure?

MAX: I'm sure.

(Pause.)

LOLA: I did something wrong?

MAX: You didn't do anything wrong, I feel like standing. So many hours driving . . .

LOLA: Stand. *(Shrugs. Long pause.)* I wonder what she's doing. *(No response;* MAX *is suddenly depressed. Pause.)* Don't you wonder? *(*MAX *shakes his head no; shrugs; pause.)*

MAX: No. No, I don't wonder.

(Pause.)

LOLA: Uh, *now* I did something wrong. *(Sighs; long pause.)* What did you give her?

MAX: I gave her.

LOLA: How much?

MAX: I don't know, three hundred, five hundred.

LOLA: Which.

MAX: Five hundred I think.

LOLA: No. Yes?

MAX: Four something.

LOLA: That much? *(*MAX *shrugs. Pause.)* I gave her a check.

MAX: Besides what I gave?

LOLA: So?

MAX: I gave her close to five hundred!

LOLA: So I gave her a little more. What is five hundred gonna do. How far is *that* gonna go?

MAX: So what'd you give?

LOLA: A check.

MAX: Yeah, I know, how much?

(Pause.)

LOLA: Twenty-five hundred.

MAX: Twenty-five *hun*dred?!

LOLA: Shhh. I *knew* it . . .

MAX: Why twenty-five hundred?! I gave her *five* hundred.

LOLA: *Four*-something you said.

MAX: You know what she's gonna do with it?! Huh?!

LOLA: Better to give her a nice lump all at once . . . *(*MAX *grumbles.)* She'll leave us alone. Right? Isn't that what you want? If she don't need nothing—anything—if she doesn't need anything . . .

MAX: That's not how we worked it!

LOLA: Max! *(Meaning "quiet.")*

MAX: The more you give, the faster it goes! Don't you know that by now?!

LOLA: But we were going away. For good. It's not the same.

MAX: Oh, God . . . it doesn't stop. It doesn't stop . . .

LOLA *(over "It doesn't stop . . . "):* It's not the same, Max. We left. So I gave her something to tide her over a little. *(*MAX *sighs, grumbles.)* I couldn't give her nothing. She'll leave us alone. *(Long pause.* LOLA *goes to her valise, opens it, takes out a paper bag and a package of plastic cups.* MAX *gestures "What's that?")* I thought a celebration. *(Takes a bottle of wine out of the bag.)*

(Blackout.)

SCENE 3

MAX'S *Walkman is set up on the table, playing opera.* LOLA *is clothed but barefoot;* MAX, *wearing a T-shirt, is also barefoot and his belt is undone. They have been drinking. They move slowly, close together, rhythmically, almost dancing, for a long time.* MAX *hums while gently kissing her face and neck. He unbuttons* LOLA'S *blouse and nestles his head in her breast.*

(Blackout.)

SCENE 4

DEBBY, *grossly obese and unkempt, moves around the room inspecting it; she's like a blimp, the Hindenburg, slowly floating, winding through the apartment, from object to object, while* LOLA *buttons her blouse and* MAX *puts on his shoes.*

DEBBY: Fancy. *(Pause; admires plastic plant.)* Pretty flowers.
MAX: How did you come?
DEBBY: I followed the sun.
MAX: How did you *come.*
DEBBY: I *was* gonna skydive in, but I remembered your heart condition. *(*LOLA *sighs deeply.)* I thought the sight of *me* floating down from the sky might scare you to death so I drove.
MAX: Drove what? What did you drive?
DEBBY: I *have* a car.
MAX: You have a car?
DEBBY: I *have* a car.
MAX: How do you have a car?
LOLA: Max . . .
DEBBY: I have a car because I have a car, Daddy. I was *given* a car.
MAX: Who gave you a car?
DEBBY: Don't look at me like that, Daddy, I don't like you looking at me like that.
MAX: How am I looking?
DEBBY: Stop.
MAX: Alright, I'm not looking . . .
LOLA: There's no food.
DEBBY: I like it here.
LOLA: Did you hear what I said?
DEBBY: Such luxury.
LOLA: There's no food. The fridge is a fake.
DEBBY: Oh, Mommy, this is comfy.
LOLA: I have nothing to offer you.
DEBBY: I like it here. Where do you sleep?
LOLA: Who.

DEBBY: Where do you *sleep.*

LOLA: We sleep here. There is no bedroom. This is it. It's very small.

DEBBY: It's perfect.

LOLA: For the time being. There's no room. This is it. The sofa opens up.

DEBBY *(sings):* "Castro Convertible."[3]

MAX: So you drove in a car.

DEBBY: I followed the sun.

LOLA: I wish I had something to offer you.

DEBBY: I went where the boys are. Isn't this where the boys are? *(*MAX *looks quizzical.)* Connie here?

MAX: Connie?

DEBBY: Connie Francis here?

MAX: I can't talk to you when you're like this.

DEBBY: Like what?

MAX *(to* LOLA*):* This is what I'm paying them for? So she can run away to Florida?

*(*LOLA *shakes her head; she doesn't know.)*

DEBBY *(plops herself into a chair):* Ooo, this is the *life!*

MAX: They're supposed to keep an eye on her. This is how they keep an eye on her? They don't even call to tell us!

LOLA: How they gonna call us, Max? We have no phone . . .

DEBBY: Excuse me . . .

MAX: She wasn't ready for the residence . . .

DEBBY: Excuse me, you got a pool here?

LOLA: A pool? A swimming pool?

DEBBY: There's got to be a pool here. *(*LOLA *shrugs.)* There must be. Oh, come on, there's gotta be. I packed a suit. Two-piece bikini. Hot pink. Two sizes too small, so I'll have to lose weight. What I need, Daddy, I need to sit in the sun, relax a little. Rub on some oil, sleep in a chair, and bake. Last time I was tan, I looked West Indian. Haitian or something. I'm so pale I could

3. This was the advertisement and jingle, famous on television in New York, made for selling a particular brand of a sleeper sofa.

die. I'll roll down my straps, get tan all over. Brown shoulders, brown everything.

MAX: How did you find us?

DEBBY: I told you, I followed the sun.

MAX: We're not where we're supposed to be. How did you find us?

DEBBY: I used my noodle. I *have* a brain.

LOLA *(to* MAX*)*: I'm trying to tell her we have no food.

MAX: No. No food.

LOLA: I have nothing to offer you.

DEBBY: I ate on the road. Howard Johnson's. All the fried clams you can eat I ate. You got to watch out at Howard Johnson's. Ask Connie Francis. It's a front for the Nazis. *(*LOLA *sighs deeply.)* She got raped by a Nazi dressed like a bellboy. I had a close call myself. This Nazi? He was sitting at the counter eating a pistachio sundae. Had a scar on his eye like somebody tried to scratch it out. But very handsome. Like Pat Boone. I memorized his face so I could tell it to the police and they could send sketches to the highway patrol. Very smart, no? *(*MAX *shakes his head in frustration.)* He was gonna sterilize me. I saw shiny tools in his jeep. I got in my car. He followed me. I was gonna double-cross him and pull over and let him screw me in the backseat and kill him with one of his own scalpels just at the point of orgasm and save mankind, but I lost him in traffic. *(*MAX *looks to* LOLA *for corroboration; she shrugs and sighs deeply.)* You gotta watch out at Howard Johnson's. Poor Connie. What she went through! Some comeback, though, hm? Wow, what a triumphant return, hm? Sometimes I wish *I* could go away just so I could come back. Judy Garland. Every *day* for her was a comeback. I would love a comeback. Who would I come back *as*? *(A beat.)* Deb-or-ah. *(*MAX *reacts, looks away.)* No more of this "Debby" shit: "Deborah," tan all the time, ribs showing. Hanging out with surfers. Some of my best friends are surfers. Don't look so *close!*

MAX: Nobody's looking!

DEBBY: My chin, I'm all broken out. I don't know why, over and over, always the same place. Maybe food that drips? Pizza grease maybe? The red stuff that comes out of the cheese? Neil says I drool in my sleep. Maybe my drool runs down my chin, makes me break out always the same place?

MAX: Who?

LOLA *(at the refrigerator):* Completely empty. Just for show.

MAX *(to* LOLA*):* Shhh! *(To* DEBBY.*) Who* says?

DEBBY: Huh?

MAX: Who did you *say*?

(Pause.)

DEBBY: I have a new boyfriend. *(A beat.)* His name is Neil. He loves me.

LOLA: You're seeing a *boy*?

DEBBY: You wouldn't believe how much he loves me, Daddy. Can't keep his hands off me.

LOLA: She's seeing a boy.

DEBBY: I have to tell him to cut it out in public, it embarrasses me. I slap his hands. I blush. I love when people see.

MAX: I'm tired.

DEBBY: The boy can't keep his hands off me, Daddy.

MAX: Good. Lola . . . ?

DEBBY: He squeezes me. Holds me tight. Strokes my hair.

MAX: Lola, I'm tired.

LOLA: What do you want from *me*?

*(*MAX *opens the sofa and makes the bed during the following.)*

DEBBY: He's got big arms, Neil. Muscles you would not believe. Like a strong man. He lifts weights. Lifts me off the ground, I laugh, I shake, carries me 'round like a bag of air. A balloon. Cotton candy. Melts in your mouth not in your hands. He loves my cooking, Mommy.

LOLA: Yes?

DEBBY: He takes me to the movies, Neil. I don't care what. I loovvve the dark. We go to Times Square. Work our way down the block. Movie to movie. Night after night. Triple features sometimes. Kung fu. Neil loves kung fu. He's a black belt world champion himself. And horror. I love horror. I love horror so much. I love to scream. Neil makes believe it bothers him. He puts his hand over my mouth? I make believe I stop. Then he takes it off? I scream again. We do that a lot. He buys me popcorn. Butter. Lets me eat all I want. He doesn't care if I'm chunky. Says he likes a girl he can sink his teeth into. Says he likes a girl with hips he can grab on to.

MAX: I'm tired.

DEBBY: When we fuck? Says it's like fucking all the oceans of the world. *(*LOLA *sighs deeply.* MAX *shakes his head and clicks his tongue in shame.)* This boy is nuts about your Debby, Daddy.

MAX: Very good.

DEBBY: Aren't you happy for me? Hm? Hm, Daddy?

MAX: Very happy.

DEBBY: He would do anything for me. Anything. He wants me to be happy.

MAX: Good.

LOLA: Max . . .

DEBBY: If there's something I want, he gets it for me. I liked this car I saw on the street? Stole it for me just like that. *(Snaps her fingers.)*

*(*LOLA *sighs deeply.)*

MAX: I'm too tired. *(He gets into bed.)*

DEBBY: My face lit up. You should've seen me. I could cry right now just thinking about it. Nobody's ever done anything like that for me before.

MAX: Good night.

DEBBY: What a car. Great mileage.

LOLA: Debby. Dear.

DEBBY *(concerned):* What's the matter, Mommy!

LOLA: What are we going to do with you?

DEBBY: Don't worry, I can take care of myself.

LOLA: I wish I had something to offer you. I have no food.

DEBBY: I know. You said. I ate clams I told you.

LOLA: Where are we going to put you? There's no room.

DEBBY: I'll stay on the floor.

LOLA: No . . .
DEBBY: I'll sleep on the floor, I don't care. I like sleeping on the floor. Like in the camps.
LOLA: Dear, I won't have you sleeping on the floor.
DEBBY *(lying on the floor):* Ooo, comfy.
LOLA: Debby, get up.
DEBBY: Just like in the camps.
LOLA: Debby . . .
DEBBY: Mommy, lie down next to me, you'll see.
LOLA: Get up, you can't sleep on the floor. Max?
DEBBY: Mommy, lie down, I'll hold you. Don't be afraid.
LOLA: Oh, God, Max. Max.
DEBBY: It's not so bad. Mommy?
LOLA: Max, she's on the floor.
MAX: Debby, get off the floor.
DEBBY: I like it.
MAX: Debby, get up off the *floor!*
*(*LOLA *sighs deeply.)*
DEBBY: Don't look at me so funny, Daddy.
MAX: Who's *look*ing at you?
DEBBY: What, I got something hanging out my nose? Look the other way. Look the other *way.* I got enough problems without you looking at me queer.
MAX: Debby, I'm tired. What we went through today.
LOLA: Yes. It's true.
DEBBY *(over "Yes. It's true"):* What you went through! Always what you went through! What about me?! What about what *I* went through?!
LOLA: Shhh . . .
DEBBY *(over "Shhh . . . "):* You think I have it easy?!
LOLA: Nobody said . . .
DEBBY: My own parents! My own mother and father!
MAX *(guiltily; playing dumb):* What.
DEBBY: "What." What do you think? Come on. Skipping out on me! Running out! *Aband*oning me! Ring a bell?!!
LOLA: No. Who.

DEBBY: I went home to see you! For a visit! I rang the door. I rang and rang. I hollered. Fay from next door came out 'cause I was hollering. In her *bath*robe. "Didn't you know, Debby," she says. "Didn't you know? They went to *Flor*ida," she says. "They re*tired*." "Retired?! What do you mean retired? People don't just pick up and re*tire* just like that."

LOLA: Don't you remember, sweetheart?

DEBBY *(over " . . . sweetheart?")*: "My own parents! My own parents don't just pick up and retire." It's a good thing Fay heard me holler. She gave me your address.

MAX *(to LOLA)*: *Who* did?

LOLA *(to MAX)*: Fay from next door. *(MAX shakes his head.)* You don't remember we mentioned it?

DEBBY: *Men*tioned it?!

LOLA: You don't remember we talked about Florida?

DEBBY: I remember we *talk*ed about it . . .

LOLA: You don't remember we told you we were going away?

DEBBY: Not *yet!* You weren't supposed to go *yet!*

LOLA: Yes, darling.

MAX: Yes.

LOLA: Your medication.

DEBBY: *Fuck* my medication!

LOLA: You lose track of time

DEBBY: You're gaslighting me! You're making me crazy!

LOLA: Nobody's making you crazy!

DEBBY: *Next* week! You were supposed to leave *next* week! That's what you said! *Next* week!

(A beat.)

LOLA: So? We decided to get an early start.

DEBBY: By running away in the middle of the night?! Tear ass out of Brooklyn at four in the morning? Fay told me: four in the morning. No notes, no last goodbyes. Just a final *shtup* of *gelt*[4] and on your way. *(LOLA sighs deeply.)* Boy. On the road again you two. Always on the road. Always running away from

4. Yiddish for "pay off."

*some*thing. Load up the car, fill the tank, turn the key. Keep an eye on the rearview mirror, Daddy. You never know when that VW van'll turn on its siren and come and get you. Run, Daddy. Go. Get on the road at four in the morning, before the sun comes up. Make up a name when you check in at Howard Johnson's. You're on the road. You can be anybody on the road. Who knows a Jew from a goy on the road in West Virginia? Don't sweat too much. Don't let your hand shake when you sign in. They're trained to pick up stuff like that. Don't give yourself away. Florida's just across the border. Don't blow your cover. You're almost there. You're almost free! *(Giggles mischievously; a beat; girlishly.)* You can't run away from me, Daddy.

*(*LOLA *opens the kitchen cabinet, revealing a box of corn flakes and milk.)*

LOLA *(lightly with feigned surprise):* Oh! Look what *I* found!

*(*MAX *puffs up his pillow disgustedly and rolls to his side to sleep. Blackout.)*

SCENE 5

MAX *is asleep and* LOLA *is fixing a makeshift bed out of cushions for Debby, who is in the bathroom.*

LOLA *(hums for a while, then talks to* DEBBY*)*: I'm making you a lovely bed. It'll do you fine. We'll figure things out in the morning, after we're rested. You'll eat a little something, you'll sleep. Who can think straight, all those hours on the road, those lights coming at you. Who can *see* straight? The bed I'm putting together for you, is gonna be so cute and so comfortable . . . *(She accidentally brushes into* MAX*'s foot, thinking she's disturbed him.)* Ooo. *(*MAX *snorts, in his sleep, undisturbed; a beat. To* MAX.*)* Sleep, Max. That's right, you sleep. The world is coming to an end. Sleep, darling. *(A beat.)* What a talent you got for escape. How'd you get so lucky? *(A beat.)* How come sleep doesn't trick you? It tricks me. It's no friend to *me.* How did sleep ever get to be your friend? It's so simple with you. You shut your eyes and you're gone. Safe. *(A beat.)* Where, where do you go? What goes on in there? You got some chippie in there with you, Max? That's what I think: Sleep is your mistress. With her you can be safe. She'll tell you all the time how big and strong you are. I don't tell you, right? No, *she* tells you. With her, you can talk. With me . . . no talk. No talk at all. What do *I* get? *(A beat. She looks at him.)* Silence. *(*MAX *snorts again.)* Silence and snoring.

DEBBY *(opens bathroom door a crack)*: Mommy, no toilet paper. *(Shuts the door.)*

LOLA: Oh, my . . . no toil—wait. *(Looks around, thinking.)* Don't do anything *yet* . . . oh, God . . . don't worry. Just sit tight.

DEBBY *(off)*: Mommy, what am I gonna—

LOLA *(over "what am I gonna—")*: Just sit tight, I told you. *(Remembers she has tissues in her handbag and gets them.)* Okay . . . *(Knocks on bathroom door.)* Open up.

DEBBY *(off)*: What.

LOLA: I got.

DEBBY: Don't look.

LOLA: I won't look, open up. I'm your mother.

*(*DEBBY *opens the door a crack, snatches the tissues from* LOLA*'s hand, shuts the door.)*

MAX *(calls softly, in his sleep):* Deborah?

*(*LOLA *turns suddenly to look at* MAX, *her eyes filling with tears. Blackout.)*

SCENE 6

MAX *is alone. The apartment is in darkness except for the occasional lights of cars passing in the night.*

MAX: Deborah? *Dvoyreh? (We become aware of the presence of a figure, a lithe young woman,* DEBORAH, *who drifts elusively around the furniture.* MAX *senses her presence, sits up and listens for a moment before speaking to her as if she were a little girl.)* Darling . . .

(She giggles softly.)

MAX *(playfully):* I hear you! Please . . . *Neshomeh mayneh* . . . I need to see that face. *Loz mikh zen dayn shayn peniml!* [Let me see that pretty face!] *(He waits; she still lurks in the dark.)* Don't tease me! You're always slipping away from me! *Dvoyreh, hartzenyu mayns* . . . [My sweetheart.] *(A beat.* DEBORAH *comes out of the darkness for a moment; then, giggling, she recedes into the shadows again.* MAX *smiles.)* Uh! Okay. *Ot doh biztu. Bizt doh, tokhter mayneh.* There you are! *Oy, mayn lebm! Zis kind.* [My sweet child.] I knew you'd be back. You tease me, you do, but *du koomst alehmol tzurik! Sar'a nakhess bizt du! Bizt mayn nakhess. Mayn teyer kind!* [. . . you always come back! What a pleasure you are! My darling child!] *(*DEBORAH *smiles shyly.) A zah shmeykhl! A zah lieb shmeykhl!* [Such a pretty smile!]

DEBORAH: *Tateh* . . .

MAX: Shhh . . . *zitz mit mir.* Sit. *Mer bet ich nisht.* [Sit with me; that's all I ask.] *(He waits a beat; she sits.)* That's my girl! *Mayn zis meydeleh.* [My sweet little girl.] Let me just look at you. Look what a beauty you turned out! So pretty! So polite! So respectful! *Oy,* what a girl! My angel!

DEBORAH: *Tateh* . . .

MAX: I love how you say "Tateh."

DEBORAH: *Tateh.*

MAX *(gently; he doesn't want her to speak):* Shhh. *(Long pause; they look at one another.* MAX *begins singing a Yiddish lul-*

laby to her in a sweet voice. After a while, DEBORAH *gets up and drifts into the shadows again but he is too enraptured by his nostalgic song to notice. He stops singing only when he realizes that she is gone. A beat. Suddenly frightened.)* Deborah?

(Blackout.)

SCENE 7

LOLA and MAX, as they were at the end of scene five: she, standing, looking at him; he, sleeping. DEBBY, in the bathroom, opens the door a crack and passes through something ripped out of a newspaper. LOLA, perplexed, takes it and looks at it as DEBBY closes the door.

LOLA *(meaning, "What are you doing?"):* What.

DEBBY *(off):* Coupons.

LOLA: Coupons?

DEBBY *(off):* Q-pons. *(The toilet flushes and DEBBY emerges from the bathroom fixing her clothing and carrying a newspaper.)* Cottonelle bathroom tissue. Cottony soft. Thirty cents off. You need toilet paper. Never hurts to have extra, right? No such thing as too much toilet paper. Stock up. You never know. *(Tears more coupons from the paper and hands them to LOLA.)* Here: "Save twenty-five cents on new Sara Lee Bagel Time Bagels." Thirty cents on 7-Up. Hershey's Syrup, "Twenty cents off."

LOLA *(over "Hershey's Syrup . . . "):* What do I need this? No . . . take, take . . . I don't need Hershey's . . . I don't need 7-Up . . .

DEBBY *(during the above; tearing more coupons):* 'Tato Skins! 'Tato Skins! Made from the skin of dead potatoes! Minute Maid, Mommy, you like Minute Maid.

LOLA: Well . . .

DEBBY: Take. No expiration date. That's *good.* That's the best. You got plenty of time. Save it. You never know. Tropicana! Ooo. Twenty-five cents off.

LOLA: I already got Minute Maid.

DEBBY: Take both. Ooo, Bumble Bee, Mommy! Bumble Bee! *(Sings the "Bumble Bee" theme song.)* "Bum-Bum-Bumble Bee, Bumble Bee Tu-u-na . . . "

LOLA *(over DEBBY's singing):* Enough with the coupons. You want food? Yes or no. *(Takes the paper away from DEBBY.)* Yes or no?

DEBBY: Yes. *(*LOLA *sets down the box of cereal and milk in front of* DEBBY. *Pause. As if she's remembered something.)* I didn't *tell* you!

LOLA *(eagerly):* What?

DEBBY: The last time I visited the concentration camp, they turned it into a bungalow colony. *(*LOLA *sighs deeply, gets ready for bed;* DEBBY *eats out of the cereal box and guzzles milk.)* They put chintzy drapes on the barbed wire. Raisin cookies were in the ovens. The food, Mommy! Such portions! I was stuffed! None of that stale bread and soup shit. All the salad bar you can eat! Shrimp! Like at Beefsteak Charlie's. *(*LOLA *sees the mess* DEBBY *is making; utters a disapproving sound.)* Hugh Downs was Colonel Klink, the concentration camp counselor. And the Nazis' uniforms were in storage. In mothballs. They put on Bermuda shorts and V-neck T-shirts. They looked like Jewish fathers with numbers on their arms.

LOLA: Debby . . .

DEBBY: It was tricky picking out the Nazis from the Jewish fathers, but I could pick 'em out right away. It's a good thing I took those courses. You never know what's gonna save your life. I was the lifeguard. I guarded the pool.

LOLA: Debby . . . watch . . .

DEBBY: I yelled at the children running barefoot where the ground was wet. That's a great way to slip and fall and crack your skull open. I know; I've done it.

LOLA: Watch with the milk. Sweetheart . . . look at yourself . . .

DEBBY: I got a Red Cross lifesaving thing stitched to my bathing suit. I had to pass a test. I loved guarding life, in the sun, swimming, saving children. Best job in the whole camp. I wore a whistle 'round my neck and I didn't hesitate to use it.

LOLA *(trying to wipe* DEBBY*'s face with a tissue):* Come, dear . . .

DEBBY: The Nazis thought I had spunk.

LOLA *(wiping* DEBBY*'s chin; sighs):* The Nazis, the Nazis . . .

DEBBY *(overlap):* They decorated me with the most adorable pink swastikas.

LOLA *(gasps at* DEBBY*'s milk-soaked blouse):* Look at you, young lady . . . come on, off . . .

(During the following, LOLA *struggles to get the blouse off* DEBBY.*)*

DEBBY *(overlap):* I wore a sash across my bathing suit. I was Miss America. Bess Myerson was Eva Braun.[5] What a tour de force for Bess! She was positively adorable. We played bingo together, me and Bess. We won prizes. She won the coveted Oscar and I won the most adorable handbag made of Jewish hair. *(*LOLA *has gotten the blouse off and exits with it to the bathroom;* DEBBY *stays put. Silence.* MAX *is snoring;* DEBBY *speaks softly, in a whisper, in time to his snoring.)* Every night there was singing . . . by the campfire. We sang by the flames. Wood crackled. Sparks flew . . . like fireflies. We were in tune . . . all of us. Stars twinkled in time to the crickets. We all breathed together . . . in and out . . . and in and out and in and out . . . that was my favorite time: singing by the flames.

*(*LOLA *returns with a towel.)*

LOLA *(while wrapping the towel around* DEBBY*):* That blouse is absolutely filthy. I'm soaking it. I don't remember that blouse. I didn't get you that blouse.

DEBBY: Mommy, I love dreams, don't you?

LOLA *(pouring cereal and milk into a bowl):* Let's try this again.

DEBBY: This is a dream.

*(*LOLA *settles in next to* DEBBY *and feeds her cereal with a plastic spoon.)* I was trying on a dress at A&S? In one of those rooms?

LOLA: Shhh . . . not while you're eating . . . *(*DEBBY *takes a few spoonfuls in silence.)* Good girl . . .

DEBBY: I took off my pants, and my shirt, and my shoes. And I looked at myself in the mirror only it was *your* face and you told me to get ready for the gas chamber. *(*LOLA *sighs deeply*

5. Bess Myerson was the first and only Jewish Miss America (1945). Eva Braun was Hitler's mistress.

while shaking her head.) So I took off my bra and my panties and I screamed, "The gas shower's starting," and I ran out, and the lady who gives out the numbers when you walk in yelled after me and I ran past stacks of coats and skirts and a black security guard grabbed me and put one of the coats on me, took it right off the rack, something I never in a million years would've picked—glen plaid—and took me to the manager's office. *(Getting sleepy, she rests her head on* LOLA.*)* Everybody was watching.

LOLA *(lulling her):* Shhh . . .

DEBBY *(softly):* Everybody was watching, Mommy. I fell asleep in the manager's office. *(A beat; even more softly.)* Woke up all wrinkled. *(*DEBBY *begins falling asleep while* LOLA *rocks her for a long beat. A sleepy whisper.)* Mommy, I love dreams, don't you?

*(*LOLA *continues to rock* DEBBY *gently to sleep. Blackout.)*

SCENE 8

A bedside lamp illuminates the room. DEBBY *is asleep on cushions on the floor.* LOLA, *distressed, has awakened from a bad dream.*

LOLA *(a small, frightened voice):* I didn't look. I was afraid to look.

MAX *(whispers; weary but sympathetic):* What good is it?

LOLA: If I looked . . . if I looked, they'd've seen me looking.

MAX: Shhh . . . go to sleep . . .

LOLA: They'd've made the connection. They'd've sent me *with* her . . . (MAX *nods, "I know.")* You don't want to call attention to yourself.

MAX: I know. *(Changing the subject.)* Tomorrow . . .

LOLA: They'd've sent me, too.

MAX: Tomorrow you'll put on a hat . . . *(*LOLA *smiles, nods.)* We'll walk around, get to know the place.

*(*LOLA *smiles.* MAX *kisses her good night, turns over to sleep. Pause.)*

LOLA *(a voice haunts her; far away):* "Lo-la . . . Lo*la!* Look at me!"

MAX *(with his back to her):* What good is it?

LOLA: I didn't look. She called me, her voice was torn up from screaming, but I walked, I kept on walking. I didn't look back. *(Lights, and* LOLA*'s voice, begin to fade.)* Like my own mother was a stranger. I didn't look . . . I didn't look . . .

(Fade to black.)

SCENE 9

MAX *and* LOLA *are sleeping.* DEBBY *is asleep on the floor. Glass shatters. Someone, unseen, is heard entering the apartment through the bathroom window.* MAX *is jolted awake. Terribly frightened, he nudges* LOLA.

LOLA: Hm? *(*MAX *gestures for* LOLA *to be quiet.)* What, Max, what? *(*DEBBY *turns, makes stirring sounds.)*

MAX *(whispers):* Listen. Someone.

DEBBY *(singsong):* What'sa matter?

MAX: Shhh . . .

LOLA *(whispers to* DEBBY*):* Somebody's here he says.

DEBBY *(soothingly):* Don't worry, Daddy, it's America.

(A stranger enters the dark room; he's a short, wiry, black teenager who is mildly retarded. He freezes when he sees the three of them. LOLA *gasps. A beat.)*

STRANGER: Debby?

*(*DEBBY *stands; a beat.)*

DEBBY: Neil? *(She steps forward to get a better look.)* I don't believe it . . . oh, my God . . . *(Her hand over her mouth in shock, like a contestant on "The Price is Right,"* DEBBY *bounds toward* NEIL, *bursting into tears of joy and hysteria; we can't understand everything she says through her blathering. Her language is foul, but the mood is conciliatory.)* You little fuck . . .

NEIL: Debby, I'm sorry . . .

DEBBY: You know how worried I was about you? Huh?

NEIL *(embracing her; breaking down, too):* Sorry . . . I'm sorry . . .

DEBBY: Where did you go? Where did you *go?*

NEIL: I came *down* here.

DEBBY: No, no, be*fore.* Where'd you go when you went? *(Teeth gritted, she punches him.)* You fuckin' piece of shit, how could you walk out on me like that?

NEIL: No I din't . . . no I *din*'t.

DEBBY: I wake up and you're gone. What am I supposed to think? Huh? What am I supposed to think?

NEIL *(over ". . . huh? . . . "):* I din't walk out, I had to go.

DEBBY: You lie to me, Neilly, you lie to me all the time . . .

NEIL: I *swear* . . . went back to the shtreet . . .

DEBBY: Oh, God . . .

NEIL: No, I came back to your house . . . you were gone!

DEBBY: I love you too much! It's no good for me how much I love you!

NEIL: I'm sorry . . .

DEBBY: You're not sorry, you're not sorry . . .

NEIL *(bawling and shrieking):* I am! Debby, I *am!* Come down looking for you! To Florida?! I ain't sorry?!

DEBBY *(over "I am!"; kissing him):* I know . . . I know you are, sweetie pie . . . I know you are, lover boy . . . I know . . .

NEIL: Don't run away no more . . .

DEBBY: I won't . . . I won't . . . I go crazy, Neil, I go nuts . . . *(Still crying. Their kisses become more passionate, and they feverishly grope one another. Whispery and girlish.)* Oh, God, Neil . . . I love you too much . . . I can't help it . . . You make me crazy . . . I can't help it . . . Oh, God, Neil . . . *(They fumble with clothing and in an instant they're having intercourse.* LOLA *and* MAX, *still in the darkness in the midst of all this, are appalled but too fascinated to do or say anything;* LOLA *averts her eyes but* MAX *cannot avert his.)* Oh, God, oh, Neil . . . oh, God, oh, Neil . . . don't take it out, don't take it out . . . oh, God, oh, Neil . . . oh, God, oh, Neil . . . *(Lights begin to fade.)* . . . don't take it out, don't take it out . . . oh, God, oh, Neil . . . don't . . . don't . . . good . . . good . . . good . . .

*(*LOLA *shakes her head and clicks her tongue. Fade to black.)*

SCENE 10

The lights are on. DEBBY *stands beaming beside* NEIL, *her arm laced through his.*

DEBBY: Mommy? Daddy? I'd like you to meet Neil. (NEIL *tries to pick up an ashtray, but it's glued to the table; he laughs.)* Neil? (NEIL *laughs while making a show of trying to lift up the ashtray.)* This is my mother and my father.

NEIL *(still working at the ashtray):* Oh, man . . .

MAX: What is he doing?

DEBBY: Neil? Honey, stop.

NEIL: Stuck.

MAX: Tell him to leave it.

DEBBY: Neilly? Stop.

(NEIL *succeeds in tearing the ashtray off the tabletop.)*

MAX: Hey! What the hell you think you're doing?!

DEBBY: Wow. I told you he was strong.

(NEIL *hands* LOLA *the ashtray.)*

MAX: You want to get us all in trouble?

DEBBY: Make a muscle. (LOLA *takes the ashtray from* NEIL; *she smiles, nods her thanks.* MAX *snatches the ashtray from* LOLA.*)* Make a muscle. He's a muscleman, I'm telling you. *(Stroking* NEIL*'s arm.)* Make a muscle.

(NEIL *yanks his arm away from her.)*

MAX *(trying to replace the ashtray):* He broke it. Look at that, he broke it.

LOLA: Shhh . . .

DEBBY *(over "Shhh"; cradles* NEIL*'s head; like a little girl talking about her dolly):* Isn't he sweet? He's my baby.

(NEIL *enjoys the tenderness, but embarrassed, he pulls away from* DEBBY *to explore the room.)*

MAX *(still fiddling with the ashtray):* They'll make us pay. Supposed to leave it the way we found it and look what he does.

NEIL: Man, this place . . .

DEBBY *(to* NEIL*):* Sit, honey.

NEIL: Rich.

MAX: *Now* what is he doing?

DEBBY: What. *(*MAX *gestures toward* NEIL *with incredulity.)* You never liked my friends. *(To* NEIL.*)* Honey, sit.

*(*NEIL *does, and seems to relish sitting in a comfortable chair; he pulls off his sneakers.)*

MAX: Who said to make himself at home?

LOLA *(to* NEIL*)*: I have no food. *(Shrugs apologetically.)*

*(*MAX *glares at* LOLA. NEIL *remembers something; reaches for a paper bag in his jacket pocket, gives it to* LOLA. LOLA *looks at him quizzically.)*

DEBBY: Isn't that nice? Neil brought a present. *(Makes a spiteful face at* MAX.*)*

LOLA: I don't want a present . . .

*(*NEIL *gestures for her to take it.)*

DEBBY: Mommy you gotta.

MAX *(to* LOLA*)*: You don't want anything from him.

*(*LOLA *hesitates, then reaches for the bag.)*

NEIL *(sees the tattooed numbers on* LOLA*'s forearm and pulls up his sleeve)*: Hey. I got one, too. *(Reveals a tattoo on his arm.)*

DEBBY: Isn't that cute?

LOLA *(smiles uncomfortably as she self-consciously covers her arm and pulls a plastic-wrapped package from the bag)*: Bagels?

NEIL: Sara Lee.

DEBBY: Sara Lee Bagel Time Bagels?! Oh, Neil, you shouldn't have . . .

*(*DEBBY *hugs and kisses him all over his face.* NEIL, *embarrassed, wriggles out of her hold.* DEBBY, *giggling, continues to make kissing sounds and gestures toward* NEIL.

NEIL *(angrily pulls away from her)*: Stop!

DEBBY *(wounded, repentant)*: I'm sorry. I'm sorry, honey . . .

MAX *(to* DEBBY*)*: What does he want?

DEBBY: Daddy, be nice.

MAX: What's he doing here?

LOLA: Max . . .

DEBBY: He loves me. He came after me.

MAX *(to* NEIL): This isn't a hotel, I'm very sorry.

LOLA *(softly; to* DEBBY*):* He came from New York?

DEBBY: *Ask* him. (LOLA *shrugs, at a loss.) Talk* to him. I want you should get to know him.

(NEIL *laughs as he snaps a glued candlestick off the dining room table.)*

MAX: *Uy! Now* what?!

(MAX *yanks the candlestick away from* NEIL *and tries to replace it.* NEIL *looks at* MAX *for a beat, then snaps off the other candlestick.) Uy Gut . . .*

DEBBY: What are you so scared of?

MAX: They'll make us pay!

DEBBY: So what?

(NEIL *hands* MAX *the second candlestick and giggles.)*

MAX: He can't *do* what he pleases. We don't live here, we're guests here! They'll bill us!

LOLA *(over "They'll bill us!"):* Shhh . . .

DEBBY: Oh, Daddy . . .

MAX: We promised the man: leave it the way we found it.

LOLA *(smiles compassionately):* It was an accident.

DEBBY: Yeah.

MAX *(over "Yeah"):* What are you *talk*ing "an accident"?! You saw: He—

LOLA: Oh . . . *(Gestures, "Don't make such a big deal.")*

MAX *(to* NEIL*):* How would you like it if somebody came into *your* home?

(NEIL *looks at* MAX *with genuine innocence.)*

LOLA: He doesn't understand.

MAX: Huh?

LOLA: He wanted to pick it up.

NEIL *(shrugs):* Wanted to pick it up.

LOLA: Yes. *(To* MAX.*)* See?

MAX: They didn't *want* you to move it, that's why they glued it down.

NEIL: Why?

MAX: Why? How do *I* know why? This is their place, this is how they want it. Who are we to judge?

DEBBY *(opens the bag of bagels, begins eating):* Such a coward. My own father, I don't believe it.

MAX *(to* DEBBY; *over "I don't believe it"):* You shut up.

LOLA: He doesn't understand, Max.

MAX *(to* NEIL*):* These are the rules. You go by the rule. You don't like them?: too bad.

DEBBY: Don't Make Waves: the story of his life.

LOLA: He doesn't understand.

MAX *(over "He doesn't understand"):* You come here, out of nowhere, you rip the place apart . . .

LOLA: He's not ripping the place apart, Max, he's only . . .

DEBBY *(over "Max, he's only . . . "):* Such a scaredy cat. I swear. Everybody's a Nazi to you.

MAX: Don't start with your Nazis!

DEBBY: Hotsy totsy, a newborn Nazi. What did Hitler say when Eva Braun had a baby?

NEIL: What?

DEBBY: "Hotsy totsy, a newborn Nazi." *(Laughs hysterically.)*

LOLA *(through the laughter):* Neil? *(A beat.)* Neil? You came from New York?

DEBBY: Neil? Talk to Mommy, she wants to talk to you.

NEIL: Yeah? *(Meaning "What is it?")*

LOLA *(a beat):* You came from New York?

NEIL: Uh-huh.

LOLA *(nods: "That's nice"; a beat):* How's the weather?

NEIL: Cold. *(Shrugs.)* Freezing.

LOLA: Is that so? *(Clicks her tongue.)* We got here just in time, Max, they're freezing in New York.

MAX *(whispers to* LOLA*):* What is the matter with you?

LOLA: What.

MAX: Making conver*sation* with him?

DEBBY *(girlishly):* What are you whispering?

LOLA *(overlap; whispers to* MAX*):* What *should* I do? I'm trying to make the best of it . . .

NEIL: The cops come load everybody up off the shtreet.

(The three look at NEIL*; a beat.)*

MAX: Huh?

NEIL: It's freezing they make you. Y'understand? Debby lets me stay her place.

*(*MAX *looks at* DEBBY*, who shrugs.)*

MAX: You pick strangers up off the *street?!*—

DEBBY: I *knew* you were gonna say that . . .

MAX: —let them stay in your *home?* Debby Debby Debby, you *sleep* with this boy?

DEBBY: Oh, Daddy . . .

MAX *(Over "Oh, Daddy . . ."):* Who knows where he's been? Don't you hear what's going on with people like this?

DEBBY: What, you never slept in the dirt?

LOLA *(to* NEIL*):* You have family?

*(*NEIL *looks to* DEBBY *for support.)*

DEBBY: Well?

NEIL *(after a beat):* My grandma.

LOLA: Your grandma?

NEIL: My grandma she died.

LOLA: Oh.

NEIL: She look after me.

LOLA: Yes.

NEIL: Cook and stuff.

LOLA: Yes.

NEIL: Like a mother.

LOLA: Aw . . . Max, *d'hairst?* [You hear?]

*(*MAX *gestures to leave him out of it.)*

NEIL: Burned up.

LOLA *(gasps):* A fire?

NEIL *(nods):* Uh-huh.

LOLA: What a shame. . . . A fire, Max.

MAX *(his compassion awakened in spite of himself):* Yeah, yeah.

NEIL: Got too much smoke when the building caught fire's what they say.

LOLA: Ah yes.

NEIL: Took her out, tried to y'know make her breathe?

LOLA: Yes?

NEIL: Took her shirt off, tried to make her breathe right there on the shtreet, everybody watching, but no, got too much smoke. *(*LOLA *sighs.)* Yeah. She look after me. So . . . then I go to the shtreet. Y'understand?

LOLA: Yes. *(Sighs.)* All alone in the world.

NEIL: Eighth Avenue.

DEBBY: That's where I found him, all dirty . . .

NEIL: Debby she come up, talk to me. Ax me stuff. Took me to Olympic for hot cocoa. She was nice. *(Shrugs; a beat.)* Took me to *her* house. *(Shrugs.)* Wash my clothes. Give me a bath. Soap. *(Shrugs.)* Fucked in the bathtub.
*(*MAX *shakes his head in disbelief.)*

LOLA *(calming* MAX*):* Alright, alright . . .

NEIL *(overlap):* Man, there was water going fast. Floor. Man. Never fucked a woman so fat. Like the ocean. She was nice to me. *(Shrugs.)* Let me sleep in her bed. Sheets and stuff. *(Shrugs; a beat.)* She was nice. *(Shrugs.)* I guess she's like my girlfriend.

DEBBY: Aw, he is sooo sweet . . . *(Kisses* NEIL*'s head.)*

LOLA *(to* NEIL*):* Your mother? Where is she?

NEIL: Jail? Dead? Brooklyn? *(Shrugs.)*

LOLA: Brooklyn? You're from Brooklyn? Where in Brooklyn?

NEIL: Beverley Road?

LOLA: Isn't that something?! Beverley Road! *We* used to live on Beverley Road! You hear this, Max?: Beverley Road.

MAX: Very nice.

LOLA *(to* NEIL*):* What number?

NEIL: 619? *(Shrugs.)*

LOLA: 619? We were 630! How do you like that? We were neighbors! Small world. You hear this, Max?: practically next-door neighbors! Across the street from each other. I don't remember you. Isn't that funny? We lived there eleven years. Must've just missed each other. The neighborhood . . . changed . . . *you* know. Beverley Road, I can't get over it. What a coincidence. Of all the streets in the world . . . yes, Beverley Road, that's where we lived, our first apartment. Yes. Right after the war.

MAX: I'm looking at my watch and I don't believe it. *(Gets into bed.)*

LOLA: Neil will get a kick out of this.

DEBBY *(knows where this is headed; groans):* No he won't.

LOLA: Neil?

MAX: Lola, what are you starting?

LOLA: Neil, you'll get a kick out of this.

DEBBY *(stomps around the room):* Mommmmyyy . . .

MAX: Debby, shhh! Lola . . .

LOLA: Neil?

NEIL: Yeah?

LOLA: During the war?

DEBBY *(to* NEIL; *she lays his head on her lap):* A bedtime story. One of Mommy's bedtime stories.

LOLA *(brightly launches into her story, which she's told dozens of times before):* There was this girl I knew there, in Belsen.

DEBBY *(starting a limerick):* There was a young girl from Belsen . . .

LOLA: A young girl, younger than me. *(*DEBBY *hums the second line of the limerick.)* With the blackest eyes. Like shiny marbles. Eyes you just *had* to look into, you couldn't look away, that's the kind of eyes this girl had. Anna her name was.

DEBBY: Anne Frank, Anna Frank.

LOLA *(over "Anna Frank"):* Anna Frank from Amsterdam. Yes. The same.

MAX: Lola, *must* you?!

LOLA: And we were friends there, the two of us.

DEBBY: Like sisters.

LOLA *(simultaneously):* Like sisters—

MAX: Lola, enough. Look at the time!

LOLA: —like she was my baby sister, that's how we were. I was all of eighteen, remember, and already buried *(Sighs.)* my mother *and* my father, and my sisters and I thought my brother was dead, too, only it turned out that he survived the war but went crazy after, I lost him *that* way.

DEBBY *(over "I lost him that way"):* Mommy, just tell it. God . . .

LOLA: And Max, I didn't meet Max till after. And he, he just came out of hiding, in the woods—

MAX: Lola!

LOLA: —and when he came out—

MAX *(trying to stop her):* Hey hey hey.

LOLA: —when he came out, he found out his bride and a little baby girl, a little girl named Deborah—

MAX: Wait wait wait . . . what are you doing?!

LOLA: —a little girl named Deborah he was crazy about—

MAX: What are you *do*ing?

LOLA: —and when he came out, they were dead—

MAX: This is mine to tell!

LOLA: —they died, while he was hiding, in the woods.

MAX: Shut up with that! Who *asked* you?! That's *my* life! When I want to discuss *my*—

LOLA *(to* MAX*):* What am I saying? I'm saying fact.

MAX: Yes, and when I want to discuss—

LOLA: When do you ever discuss? You never!

MAX: I'm talked out! No more!

LOLA: So *I* should shut up? Because *you*—

MAX: Yes! What does the boy care?

LOLA *(over "care?"):* It's interesting! *(To* NEIL.*)* Isn't this interesting?

NEIL: Uh-huh.

LOLA: See? You never let me talk.

DEBBY: I wish we had popcorn.

MAX: What good is it, Lola? What good is it, over and over—

LOLA: Go to sleep! Sleep! Like you always do! *(*MAX *covers his head with a pillow.)* Good! Perfect! Sleep! *(A beat; tries to remember where she left off.)* So . . . there was this girl I knew there, in Belsen.[6]

DEBBY *(over "in Belsen"):* No, no, you did that already.

LOLA: Oh.

6. The concentration camp, Bergen-Belsen, where Anne Frank died.

DEBBY: Later, much later. "Alone in the world."

LOLA: Yes? *(Shrugs; resumes.)* So, I was alone. All alone in the world—

NEIL: Like me.

LOLA: Yes. Like you. —I was alone. All alone in the world, and this girl, she was my friend. In the camp. Two people couldn't be closer. We helped each other get through each day and each night. Every morning we woke up was a triumph. We filled the time with talk, me and my little friend Anna. We told each other stories about what *was* and what *will* be.

DEBBY: What stories she told!

LOLA: What stories she told! You know the expression "like an artist"? She painted pictures with words.

DEBBY: Pictures with words.

LOLA: You had a perfect picture in your head of everything she described. You knew what all the faces looked like, every member of her family, her cat, the boy she wanted to marry, Peter. "Anna, you tell such wonderful stories," I told her.

DEBBY: "You should be a writer."

LOLA *(simultaneously):* "You should be a writer." And she told me,

DEBBY: "I *am* a writer."

LOLA *(simultaneously):* "I *am* a writer. As a matter of fact, I've written a whole book." "What kind of book," I asked, "does such a young girl write?" And she told me, "A book of ideas and observations, ideas about life. A kind of a diary," she said. "And where *is* this diary of yours," I asked my young friend. And she smiled. "You'll see, one day you'll see." And I didn't think anything of it except her black eyes twinkled in such a way I can see them right now. And then I said to her, "Well, why don't you keep a book *here,* here in the camp?" And she said,

DEBBY: "Lola, what a good idea, I can't thank you enough."

LOLA *(simultaneously):* "Lola, what a good idea, I can't thank you enough." So, thanks to me, all the time we were at Belsen, she secretly kept a book. A diary, another diary. Where she found the paper to write on I'll never know. Whatever she could get her hands on. Little scraps, rags. She wrote things down all the time. Whenever you saw her, she was jotting something down. All day long. She'd be too weak to eat, but there was Anna, writing. In plain sight, writing. Finally I had to say something. "Anna, what's with all the writing? The guards are gonna find out and murder you." And do you know what she said to me?

(Pause.)

DEBBY *(prompting* LOLA*):* "I don't care *what . . .* "

LOLA: "I don't care *what* happens to me," she said. "I many not survive the war but I must write down everything, everything I see and everything I feel. All I care about is people should see what I write and know the truth and remember. I want people to remember." She kept on writing, right till the end. Sometimes she was too starved to keep her head up, but I held it up for her so she could write. When she got too sick—typhus she had—too sick to hold even a matchstick to write with, *I* wrote for her, I took dictation from Anna Frank. *(A beat.)* As you would imagine, I was a big character in this book. I was the hero—

DEBBY *(correcting her):* Heroine.

LOLA: The heroine. Well, it was *her* book, true, but I was there, on every single page. "Lola did *this,*" or "Lola said *this* today." "Lola gives me the strength to go on." "Lola has such courage." Can you imagine? *Me,* Lola, I gave Anna Frank the will to live may she rest in peace.

(A beat.)

DEBBY: When she died in my arms.

LOLA: When she died in my arms, and I'll never forget it as long as I live, she made me promise: "Hide my book, Lola." Her voice was weak, I had to bend my ear close. "Don't let them take it," she said. "Make sure people read what I wrote, people should know. Promise me, Lola, promise me." I promised. And little Anna Frank smiled and closed her eyes and she was gone, right in my arms. *(Becoming choked up.)* I did the best I could. I tried to save it. It was my story. I promised Anna. I kept it hidden. Every day I lived in fear. I trusted no one. If only the Nazis didn't find it and piss all over it . . .

DEBBY: That's new.

LOLA: If only that book lasted through the war . . . I'm telling you, I was the heroine, it was my story. She wrote about *me!* I could've given people hope. But my story, *Lola*'s story, told by Anne Frank, went up in flames with her at Belsen. The Belsen diary. The *other* diary. The diary nobody knows about. The diary *I* told her to keep.

DEBBY: She's so fulla shit.

LOLA *(to* NEIL*):* Believe me, I was there.

DEBBY: And I was at Woodstock.

LOLA: There was another diary. I know; I was in it. On every page.

DEBBY *(over "On every page"):* Who's gonna say no? Huh? Who's around to say no?

LOLA: On every single page: my name. "Lola this and Lola that . . ."

DEBBY: Mommy, you don't know what's what anymore. You *think* you knew Anne Frank.

LOLA: I DID! I DID! But who knew this little girl, the young friend I gave my crumbs to, my little sister, who *I* inspired, who knew what she would become? This girl with black eyes writing, writing all the time. Who knew what she would mean to the world? Just a girl, but a magical girl. Her name was Anna. Anna Frank from Amsterdam. Yes. The same. *(A beat.)* Years go by. Our boat comes into New York in fog so thick, I never got to see the Statue of Liberty. Then. One day, in Brooklyn, in my kitchen, on Beverley Road, I see in *Life* magazine a story about a diary found in Amsterdam, and a picture, a picture of a girl with eyes like black marbles and I say, Anna! You said to me, "One day you'll see!" Anna, my little friend! *(A beat.)* And that, Neil, is the story of me and Anne Frank.

(Long pause.)

NEIL: Who?

(Blackout.)

SCENE 11

MAX, *alone in the dark room.*

MAX *(dreaming; urgently, agitated):* Deborah? Where did you go now? Please . . . *Tokhter mayneh* . . . come back. I can't see you.—*Dvoyrehleh? (He waits anxiously for a moment, approaches where he thinks he sees her.) Koom, ich muz redn mit dir.* [Talk to me.] Listen . . . help me . . . all my life, I'm homesick . . . . This hole in *mayn hartz* . . . it doesn't stop . . . *(*DEBORAH *appears, winds through the shadows;* MAX *tries to follow her.)* Hello, darling . . . forgive me . . . I never sat shiva[7] for you. This ache . . . it doesn't go away . . . it gets worse with time. Not better, worse. Tell me, sweetheart . . . tell me: When does it end?

DEBORAH: *Es nemt keynmol nisht keim soff.* [It never ends.]

MAX: No, don't say that! *(*DEBORAH *shakes her head no as she recedes into the shadows.)* It must end! It must! *(Looking around for her.)* Deborah?
(Blackout.)

7. The traditional seven-day period of mourning in a Jewish home.

SCENE 12

MAX *awakens with a start at the sound of* DEBBY *and* NEIL *laughing in the bathroom. Water is running;* DEBBY *is giving* NEIL *a bath.* MAX *reorients himself and sees that he and* LOLA *are alone. Suddenly, he gets out of bed and urgently gathers his things.*

LOLA: What. *(Meaning, "What are you doing?")*

MAX: Come, we're going.

LOLA: What?

MAX: We're getting out of her.

LOLA: Max . . .

MAX: We can escape.

LOLA: What are you talking "escape"?

MAX: We have to do something, Lola, this'll never end.

LOLA *(scared, she watches him pack for a beat):* Where? Where would we go?

MAX: A motel, we find a motel for the night.

LOLA: Why? When we're here?

MAX: Are you listening to me or what?

LOLA *(over "or what?"):* Max, no, you don't mean it. Just leave her here?

MAX: She'll survive. She always does. She'll survive.

LOLA *(over "She'll survive"):* Not again, Max. We tried that before. We left her in Brooklyn. It didn't work, she followed us all this way. She needs us.

MAX: She doesn't need us. She needs to *torture* us.

LOLA: So what if they sleep on the floor, it's the middle of the night.

MAX: No.

LOLA: It's comfortable here.

*(*DEBBY *and* NEIL *are heard laughing wildly in the bathroom.)*

MAX: "Comfortable." Ha. Get your things, we're going right now.

LOLA: I don't like traveling in the dark for no reason.

MAX: What "no reason"?! Listen what's going on here! This is a nut house!

LOLA: *I don't want to travel in the dark! (A beat.)* I don't want to leave all this.

MAX: What? What are you leaving?

LOLA: I like it here. Everything we could want, Max. It's nice.

MAX: *Lis*ten to you! Stay! Stay like your mother stayed! *(*LOLA *winces.)* She didn't want to leave her beautiful home and her, her *furniture,* so she stayed! She could've gotten out—

LOLA: Sha! *(Meaning "shut up.")*

(Pause.)

MAX: Lola, Lola . . . they won't find us. I promise. We'll get in the car and go.

LOLA: I don't want to run, Max, please. No more running.

MAX *(stuffing her things into suitcases):* We'll find a motel. A TV that works. A hard mattress. A *mattress.* A decent night's sleep—

(Suddenly the bathroom door opens, and DEBBY, *in a bright mood, her face a mask of red lipstick, bursts in singing;* NEIL *follows, laughing.* MAX *shakes his head in frustration.)*

DEBBY: " . . . I feel pretty and shitty and gay! And I pity—"

LOLA *(to* DEBBY, *as she goes to her):* What did you do?

MAX *(to* LOLA*):* Just leave her.

DEBBY: "—any girl who isn't me today!"

LOLA: My lipstick . . .

NEIL: I helped.

LOLA: You certainly did. *(Moistens a tissue with her saliva and cleans* DEBBY*'s face.)*

DEBBY: "—See the pretty girl in that mirror there?—"

NEIL *(laughing):* She's funny.

LOLA: Very funny.

MAX *(overlap; to* LOLA*):* Leave her! Just leave her!

LOLA *(overlap; to* DEBBY*):* I can't turn my back on you for two minutes . . .

DEBBY: "—What mirror, where?—"

LOLA *(sighs while wiping her face):* Debby Debby Debby . . .

DEBBY: "—Who can that attractive girl be-e?—"

MAX *(to* DEBBY*):* All right, listen.

DEBBY: "Such a pretty face, such a pretty face—"
MAX *(overlap; to* LOLA*):* You see?
DEBBY: "—such a pretty face, such a pretty face, such a pretty MEEE!!"
MAX: *LISTEN!*
DEBBY: WHAT!
MAX: Enough. This has to stop.
DEBBY: We're having a pajama party. Don't be a poop.
MAX: *Listen* to me . . .
DEBBY: Party poop. Such a party poop.
MAX: Your mother and I had a talk.
DEBBY: A talk? What kind of talk? *(To* LOLA.*)* Mommy?
LOLA *(shrugs):* Your father . . .
DEBBY: You never let me have fun. Such a killjoy. Such a poop.
MAX: This isn't gonna work. You shouldn't've come.
DEBBY: Why? I'm *here.*
MAX: It's no good. You follow us, why do you follow us?
DEBBY *(trying to embrace him):* 'Cause I wuv you, Daddy.
MAX *(taking her arms off him):* We're getting out of here.
DEBBY: We are?
MAX: Not you. Your mother and me, we're gonna go.
DEBBY: *Now?* Mommy . . . what do you mean "go"?
NEIL *(to* DEBBY*):* Where they going?
LOLA *(to* DEBBY*):* Your father . . . I don't know . . . a motel . . .
DEBBY: It's like three o'clock in the morning . . .
MAX: We can't all stay here together.
DEBBY: But we *are* . . . we *are* all together.
NEIL *(to* DEBBY*):* They're going away?
LOLA: We *are* managing, Max.
NEIL: Debby?
MAX: This is managing?
DEBBY *(overlap):* What do you want? You want us to be quiet?, we'll be quiet. Neil, shut up. *(Punches* NEIL*'s arm.)*
NEIL: Ow . . .
DEBBY: No noise, I said . . . *(To* MAX.*)* Here . . . You want room? We'll make room . . . *(Pushes furniture.)*

LOLA: Debby . . .

DEBBY: I'm making room . . . Neil . . . ?

(NEIL also moves furniture.)

MAX: Stop it! Leave the place the way we found it!

DEBBY *(continues disrupting the room):* I'm making room . . . I'm making room . . .

MAX *(overlap):* Hey . . . hey . . . *(To LOLA.)* They'll tear the place apart. *(To DEBBY.)* Look—stop that!—look . . . *(Takes money from his wallet.)* Here, the two of you find a motel.

DEBBY: Motel?!

MAX: Better you should go.

DEBBY: I don't *wanna* go . . .

LOLA: Max . . .

DEBBY: . . . I wanna stay with *you* . . .

MAX *(handing NEIL money):* Here . . .

DEBBY: Don't, Neil . . .

NEIL *(taking the money from MAX):* If you want to give me money, give me money.

MAX: More? *(Gives him more from his wallet.)* Take more.

NEIL: You want to give me money?, I'll *take* your money . . . *(DEBBY slaps his hand. To DEBBY.)* If he wants . . .

DEBBY *(snatches money from NEIL):* You don't want his money.

MAX: That's it. That's all. My pockets are empty. No more.

LOLA *(over the above, to MAX):* Where they gonna go, what they gonna do?

MAX: There are motels we passed, right off the highway.

DEBBY: I'm unforgettable. You can't forget me. I'm unforgettable. Nat King Cole sang that song about me. I'm Mona Lisa.

(MAX shakes his head; he's had it.)

NEIL: Mister. Please? Just a place to sleep.

DEBBY *(sings):* "Unforgettable, that's what I am . . . " *(Etc.)*

MAX *(over DEBBY's singing):* Come on, get your stuff . . .

LOLA: Max . . .

NEIL: Got no place to go. Please, mister.

MAX *(over "Please, mister"):* The both of you. Whatever you've got . . .

LOLA: You can't just—

NEIL: I'll be quiet.

MAX: I walked out of the woods. For what? For *this?*

DEBBY *(sings):* "Call me unforgettable . . . call me . . . unreliable . . . "

MAX *(to* NEIL*):* The last Jew in Europe. Sure. What kind of last Jew? What do I got to show for it? Hm? A condo in Florida? A daughter? Some daughter.

DEBBY *(to* MAX*):* You don't like me, huh?

*(*MAX *looks as if that's the biggest understatement yet.)*

LOLA: Don't talk like that. . . . Of course he likes you. He loves you. We both love you.

DEBBY *(stalking* MAX *around the room):* What, I'm not svelte enough? Not pretty enough? Not smart enough?

LOLA: You're very smart . . .

DEBBY: I won a scholarship award in fourth grade. Just me and Carol Ann Wiener. She was my best friend. What do you want me to do, Daddy? Rip off my rolls? Tear off my skin?

MAX: Lola, I will not—

DEBBY: Starve myself to death? Would that make you happy? Huh? How could I possibly be as pretty as Deborah? Skin and bones. Stick my finger down my throat. Vomit rots your teeth. Mengele[8] was my dentist. He was Mister Wizard. He put my teeth in Coca-Cola. They burned like acid. Mengele taught you brain surgery.

MAX: What Hitler didn't do to me, *you* are doing . . . !

*(*DEBBY *gasps in mock horror.)*

LOLA: Max!

MAX: It's true! What *he* didn't do . . .

DEBBY: You made me, Daddy-O. You and Mengele and Frankenstein.

MAX: Uh! *Franken*stein now!

DEBBY: All the brain surgery you did on me! Night after night! Anne Frank was in the next bed. You rewired my brain! Took out my memory! That's why my head always aches!

8. Dr. Josef Mengele: the notorious murderer/torturer at Auschwitz.

LOLA: What should we have done? Not told you anything . . . ?

DEBBY: Mommy?

LOLA: Yes, dear, what?

DEBBY: They're all inside me. All of them. Anne Frank. The Six Million. Bubbie and Zaydie[9] and Hitler and Deborah. When my stomach talks, it's *them* talking. Telling me they're hungry. I eat for them so they won't be hungry. Sometimes I don't know what I'm saying 'cause it's *them* talking . . .

LOLA *(over "talking . . . "; to* MAX*)*: See? She doesn't know . . .

DEBBY *(over "she doesn't know . . . ")*: Deborah talks to me. She tells me to do things. It all started with her, you know. You thought it was me. It's her fault. She was the life of the party, but the party died before I got here. I can sing! I can pass out pigs in the blanket! I can be a lampshade! I'M ALIVE! I CAN'T HELP IT I WASN'T EXTERMINATED!

MAX *(singsong)*: I'm not listening . . .

NEIL: Don't be sick, Debby . . . please . . .

DEBBY: I was in the woods with you, Daddy. Covered with leaves. I remember things I never saw. I was gonna save you. Hiding from the Nazis . . . night after night . . . waiting for the Nazis to come. And you always had that picture . . . that picture you carried in your shoe all through the war. This little doll. This little broken doll. This little Deborah made you cry and cry. I NEVER HAD A CHANCE! YOU EVEN GAVE ME HER NAME! HOW COULD YOU GIVE ME HER NAME?!

MAX: *Dos nemt nisht kim soff!* [This never ends!]

LOLA: *Zee ken sich nisht helfen.* [She can't help it.]

MAX: *Vos sie vil rayst zee dir orois!* [What she wants, she rips out of you!]

DEBBY: SPEAK ENGLISH! I hate when you do that! You're in America now! We speak English! This isn't the UN! This isn't Judgment at Nuremberg with Maximilian Schell!! Speak English! I'm sick of all the whispering in Yiddish and German! I could never understand what the doctors were saying, but I knew they were talking about me, sticking things in me, cut-

9. Yiddish for "grandmother" and "grandfather."

ting me open and stuffing all these dead people inside me. Millions and millions of dead people inside me. It's so crowded and noisy in here, I can't hear myself *think* anymore! This is not my heart. My heart never sounded like *this.* Where is *me?* What happened to *me?* How was I supposed to *sleep* with Nazi doctors screwing around with me all night? AND YOU LET THEM! *(She attacks* MAX.*)*

MAX: NO!

DEBBY: YOU LET THEM DO WHAT THEY WANTED!

MAX: STOP IT!!

DEBBY *(overlap):* I should've been dreaming sweet dreams like other little girls—YOU LET THEM IN THE HOUSE! YOU LET THEM IN MY ROOM!

*(*DEBBY *begins strangling* MAX.*)*

MAX *(struggling to free himself of* DEBBY; *screaming):* Help me! She's killing me!

*(*DEBBY *is out of control;* LOLA *and* NEIL *try to get her away from* MAX. *Blackout.)*

SCENE 13

DEBBY *is tied up and gagged.* MAX *strokes her hair and speaks gently, reasonably.* LOLA *waits at the window;* NEIL *is crying.*

MAX: Debby. *(Shrugs.)* I pour everything I got into you. Nothing works. Special schools, special doctors. Hospitals. "Residences." In-patient, out-patient. My head spins from you. *(A small chuckle.)* You're amazing! I never knew a person like you. You don't give up. You come after us no matter what. You're amazing! We don't sleep at night, worried what you might do. We live our *lives* worried what you might do. We gotta face the facts: You gotta help yourself. I can't make you get well. Your *mother* can't make you get well. You gotta get well your*self. (A beat.)* It's time we go our separate ways I think. *(*DEBBY *struggles to speak in protest under her gag.* MAX *soothingly touches her hair.)* Shh shh shh. You think I en*joy* this? The way we have to live? Yelling and carrying on? No good. How many good years we got left, your mother and me? Think about it. *(Shrugs: "What am I supposed to do?")* I'm a simple man, nothing special. I walked out of the woods. For what? So I could come to America? Sell sportswear in Flatbush? For this I walked out of the woods? Where are the children? Where are the grandchildren? *(A beat.)* Look, darling . . . all I want . . . I want to clip on my clip-on sunglasses, put up my feet, sit in the Florida sun, read my *Wall Street Journal,* see how my stocks are doing. *(A beat.)* Sweetheart . . . *(Pause.)* Debby . . . *(A very deep sigh.)* Why can't we just shake hands, wish each other luck. Hm? Is that so terrible? Shake hands, *zy'gesunt.*[10] *(*DEBBY *just looks at him.)* Am I so bad? I'm such a bad person? Such a bad father? *(An ambulance siren is heard approaching. A beat;* MAX *shrugs.)* All I want is a little peace. Is that so terrible?
(Blackout.)

10. Yiddish for "be well."

SCENE 14

LOLA *stands by the open front door.* MAX *faces away from her. The ambulance's red light spins off the walls of the apartment. Silence.*

LOLA: You won't ride with her? *(Silence.)* You don't have to. I will. You can follow in the car. *(Silence.)* I can't turn my back. Maybe you can, I can't turn my back.

MAX *(a realization):* Uh! You're glad she came.

LOLA: What?

MAX: You're glad she came.

LOLA: I'm glad she's safe now, yes. I was worried.

MAX *(over "yes. I was worried"):* You're glad she *came.* You need her.

LOLA: She *is* my child.

MAX: You *need* her. You need her *mishagas.*[11]

LOLA: You don't understand a mother.

MAX: Oh, no?

LOLA: No, you don't.

MAX: She is hopeless, Lola. Let her go. Stay with me.
(Pause.)

LOLA: I'm responsible. Who's responsible if not me?

MAX: A trick of fate. I'm not responsible.

LOLA: Max, I'm responsible and you're responsible, too.

MAX: Madmen are born the same way as sane men. A trick. Why am I alive today: It's all a trick.

LOLA: She's our daughter, Max. You don't turn your back on your own child.

MAX: "Child." You make her sound like an infant. An infant needs taking care of. An infant you keep clean and fed. This is no child. She can *crush* me, Lola! She can kill me and she will! If this keeps up . . . *(A beat. Softly.)* Let her go.
*(*LOLA *shakes her head no. Pause.)*

11. Yiddish for "craziness."

MAX: Then why did we come?

(Pause.)

LOLA: You wanted it.

MAX *(nods, hurt; pause):* And you?

LOLA *(with uncertainty):* I wanted it, too. For you.

MAX: Ah.

LOLA *(with more conviction):* You wanted it and I wanted it, too.

(Pause.)

MAX: We talked about coming down here . . .

LOLA: Yes.

MAX: For years and years: Florida. Was it gonna be something! Florida.

LOLA: Yes.

MAX: We'll buy our place in the sun and we'll enjoy.

LOLA: Yes.

MAX: Once and for all: you and me, just us. Florida.

(Long pause.)

LOLA: I can't deny her, Max. She exists. What am I supposed to do? Shut my eyes and ears?

MAX: Yes.

LOLA: You don't mean it.

MAX: *I shut my eyes and ears.*

LOLA: And what do you see?

MAX: What I *wish* to see.

LOLA: And what you do *not* wish to see?

(Long pause; they look at one another. Sadly; her eyes filling.)

My darling Max . . .

(Blackout.)

THE LAST SCENE

Lights up, very brightly. The next morning. MAX, *wearing a cabana suit, is asleep on a chaise lounge on the sun deck. The* Wall Street Journal *has fallen to the ground. We hear the tape of an opera he's listening to on his Walkman.* DEBORAH *enters. Silence.*

DEBORAH: I miss you at *Pesach,*[12] *Tateh.* Everyone is there but you. We always talk about you. We do. We haven't forgotten. We wonder how you survived. Everyone is very old now, but healthy. Smashed bones are mended, muscles are restored. Hair has grown in nicely. Thick, shiny hair. And we've all put back the weight we lost, some of us *too* much. Everyone is dressed in their best, their fanciest clothes reserved for holy days. You should see. We look like ourselves again. A very handsome family. I'm still the youngest, so I get to ask the *feir kashas.*[13] I let the boy cousins compete for the *afikoman.*[14] I won't play with them. They're wild. They tease me and run around the living room. They're restless, I know. I am, too. But I like to stay with the men. Zaydie Duvid and Zaydie Schmuel conduct the seder together and argue about everything. The seder goes on into the night. I'm hungry, so hungry, but I can hardly keep my eyes open. The boys shriek and tug on my hair. Mameh and Bubbie Sura and Bubbie Bessie and Aunt Chaya and Aunt Rifke and Aunt Freyda—all the women—they all worry about the food, keeping the food fresh and warm. There is so much food! The kitchen is noisy with women. The dining room is cloudy with smoke and opinions. It's like it used to be when we were all together. No, it's noisier, there are more of us together now than there were before, so many of us. *(Lights begin to fade slowly.)* It's *Pesach* all the time, *Tateh.* I can't remember when it wasn't *Pesach.* I

12. The Jewish holiday of Passover.

13. The "four questions" asked by the youngest child at the passover meal (seder).

14. The special piece of unleavened bread (matzah) hidden during the seder to be found by the children and "bought back" with a prize.

miss you all the time. The men are always arguing. And a feast is always awaiting us in the kitchen. And I'm always hungry, always hungry. And the boys are always running wild. And the arguing in the dining room goes on and on, into the night. And I can't keep my eyes open, I've sipped too much wine, and I don't want to go to sleep hungry, but my eyes are closing, they're closing, and I don't want to fall asleep and miss the feast, I don't want to miss the feast . . .

(Fade to black.)

George Steiner

THE PORTAGE TO SAN CRISTOBAL OF A. H.

adapted for the stage by Christopher Hampton

Hartford Stage, *The Portage to San Cristobal of A. H.* (1982).
Photograph by Lanny Nagler.

CHARACTERS

SIMEON
GIDEON BENASSERAF
JOHN ASHER
ELIE BARACH
ISAAC AMSEL
EMMANUEL LIEBER
GUARD
OLD MAN
A. H.
PROFESSOR SIR EVELYN RYDER
BENNETT
HOVING
COLONEL SHEPILOV
NIKOLAI MAXIMOVITCH GRUZDEV
RODRIGUEZ KULKEN
INDIAN WOMAN
MARVIN CROWNBACKER
TEKU
DR. GERVINUS RÖTHLING
ANNA ELISABETH RÖTHLING
ROLF HANFMANN
INDIAN
BLAISE JOSQUIN
V
AVERY LOCKYER

The play is set in May 1979 in a remote area of Brazil, and in Oxford, Moscow, Cologne, Paris, and Washington.

The non-Brazilian scenes should be cross-cast as follows:
First actor: RYDER, GRUZDEV, RÖTHLING, LOCKYER
Second actor: BENNETT, SHEPILOV, JOSQUIN
Third actor: HOVING, HANFMANN
Actress: ANNA, V

The interval is optional.

THE PORTAGE TO SAN CRISTOBAL OF A. H.

SCENE 1

Just before dawn; a clearing in the depths of the Amazonian jungle.

As dawn breaks, quickly, and the light modulates from darkness to the dim ecclesiastical shade of day, a wall of sound erupts, a jungle cacophony which will form a background to all the Brazilian scenes. At the same time, we become aware of the motionless shapes of five men, lying on the ground, facing upstage, their clothing, roughly speaking, paramilitary, their bodies tense with concentration. Most of them have rifles or submachine guns tucked into their shoulders, aiming offstage.

They are:

SIMEON, *the leader, a tough, grizzled man in his fifties;*
GIDEON BENASSERAF, *big, bearded, still, despite his recent illness, a figure of reassuring solidity;*
JOHN ASHER, *grey-haired, calm, enigmatic, a little apart from the others;*
ELIE BARACH, *the rabbi, slight, dark, unarmed, wearing a skullcap.*
ISAAC AMSEL, *clumsy, impetuous, much the youngest of them.*

As soon as this image registers, another: an old man, to one side and isolated by a spotlight, in profile, wearing earphones and leaning into a radio transmitter. At the same time the crackles and whistles of a radio frequency begin to invade and overlay the jungle sounds.

EMMANUEL LIEBER *is pale and shrivelled, his eyes bright behind thick glasses. His voice is low and urgent; it sighs across the air-waves as he sits, silently staring at the transmitter.*

LIEBER'S VOICE: Ayalon calling. Do you read me? Come in, Nimrod. Are you receiving me? Over.

(The sounds of the radio fade. No movement. LIEBER *waits. Then he flicks a switch, leans forward and begins speaking into the transmitter.)*

LIEBER: Ayalon to Nimrod. Listen. You must not let him speak. Gag him if necessary, or stop your ears. If he is allowed speech, he will trick you and escape. His tongue is like no other. As it is written in the learned Nathaniel of Mainz: There shall come upon the earth in the time of night a man surpassing eloquent. When God made the Word, He made possible also its contrary. Silence is not the contrary of the Word, but its guardian. No, He created on the night-side of language a speech for hell. Whose words mean hatred and vomit of life. Few men can learn that speech or speak it for long. It burns their mouths. But there shall come a man whose mouth shall be as a furnace and whose tongue as a sword laying waste. He will know the grammar of hell and teach it to others. He will know the sounds of madness and loathing and make them seem music. Are you receiving me? Over. *(Pause. He flicks the switch, waits, flicks it again.)* Let him speak to you, and you will think of him as a man. If he asks for water, fill the cup. If you let him ask twice, he would no longer be a stranger. Give him fresh linen before he needs it. A man's smell can break the heart. You will be so close now. You will think him a man and no longer believe what he did. That he almost drove us from the face of the earth. That his words tore up our lives by the root. Can you hear me? Ayalon calling. This is an order. Gag him. Words are warmer than fresh bread; share them with him and your hate will grow to a burden. Do not look too much at him. He wears a human mask. Let him sit apart and move at the end of a long rope. Do not stare at his nakedness. Lest it be like yours.

(Light snaps out on LIEBER. *Pause. Suddenly, with minute movements, the men on the stage tense and prepare themselves. Two men appear: one, a* GUARD, *armed with an old rifle, dark, young, probably Brazilian; the other, an* OLD MAN, *one-armed, wearing grey fatigues. The* OLD MAN *begins scratching vaguely at the ground; the* GUARD *sits, relaxing, his rifle across his knees. He puts a cigarette to his lips, strikes a match.* ISAAC AMSEL *half rises and fires a burst from his submachine gun.* SIMEON *cries out, simultaneously.)*

SIMEON: No! *(The* OLD MAN *collapses and the* GUARD *topples over backwards, the match still between his fingers. Then* AMSEL *is up on his feet and charging across the clearing.)* Wait!

*(*AMSEL *goes crashing to the ground, caught by a trip wire. But he's up again and thunders offstage. The others rise cautiously and hurry to take up a position facing offstage, whence comes the sound of* AMSEL *smashing his way through an unseen door.* GIDEON *picks up the* GUARD*'s rifle and drags the bodies to one side. Silence. They wait, facing offstage in a semi-circle. Suddenly, hurled onstage so that he sprawls full-length on the ground, an ancient man appears. Of medium height, scrawny but pot-bellied, sparse white hair, unshaven, burning eyes, unhealthy, yellowish skin, a ninety-year-old cadaverous hermit: but, for all that, unmistakably,* ADOLF HITLER. *The men stare at him, mesmerized.* AMSEL *appears, reaches down, gathers* HITLER*'s collar and drags him to his feet.)*

AMSEL: You. *(*HITLER *doesn't answer. He looks at* AMSEL, *chewing his lip.)* You. Is it really? Look at you. It is you. Isn't it? We have you. We have you. Everyone will know. The whole world. But not yet. You're ours. You know that, don't you? The living God. Delivered you into our hands. *(*HITLER *ceases to attend. His eye flicks indifferently over the corpses of the* GUARD *and the* OLD MAN. *The others watch him, paralyzed.)* Silent now? Whose voice could. They say your voice could. Burn cities. They say that when you spoke. Leaves turning to ash and men weeping. They say that women, just to hear your voice, that women. Would tear their clothes off, just to hear your voice. *(*HITLER*'s eye returns to* AMSEL. *He looks at him with insolent calm.* AMSEL *loses his temper, seizes him by the collar again, shouting.)* Why don't you speak? They'll make you speak. They'll tear it out of you. We have you now. Thirty years hunting. Kaplan dead. And Weiss. And Amsel, my father. You'll talk. We'll have the skin off you. *(He pushes* HITLER *away so abruptly that the old man falls.* SIMEON *steps forward involuntarily, then checks his movement. He's bathed in sweat, his expression desperately agitated.* HITLER *picks himself off the ground, stays crouching, looking up at them, finally speaks softly.)*

HITLER: *Ich?*[1]

(His eyes flash. SIMEON *suddenly snaps out of his trance.)*

SIMEON: *AUFSTEHEN! LOS!*[2]

1. German for "I."
2. German for "Get up! Move!"

SCENE 2

Professor Sir Evelyn Ryder's rooms in Oxford. Autumn evening. RYDER *stands at the window, looking out. Sprawled in two armchairs, lit by the glow of the fire, are* BENNETT, *sixtyish, carefully but not expensively dressed, large feet; and* HOVING, *sharper, in his early thirties. Silence. After a time,* RYDER *turns abruptly to the others.*

RYDER: More sherry?

(He picks up the decanter, without waiting for a reply, moves towards them.)

BENNETT: Why not?

HOVING: Thank you, sir.

*(*RYDER *begins speaking as he pours the palest sherry into their glasses and his own.)*

RYDER: You remember Amsel, Bennett?

BENNETT: Poland?

RYDER: Yes, he got in and out twice during the war. His obsession was trying to get bomber command to do something about the railway lines. Kept on and on at me to go and tell the old man about the ovens. Wouldn't have done the least bit of good.

BENNETT: The old man didn't want to know about any of that. Not his kind of war.

RYDER: Anyway, Amsel got out and joined Lieber after the war.

BENNETT: And he's still with them.

RYDER: No, no, this is the thing. End of the fifties he disappeared somewhere in Paraguay. Most mysterious. I mean, he was so frightfully good at his job. Alpha material.

HOVING: But Lieber carried on operating?

BENNETT: Oh, yes. They never believed us. Or the Russians.

RYDER: They've always insisted that Hitler escaped a few days before the bunker was surrounded. There *was* a passenger on that plane, you know. Needn't necessarily have been Bormann.[3]

3. Martin Bormann: head of the Nazi Party and Hitler's closest aide by the war's end. His death was never officially recorded and rumors said he escaped to South America; he was declared officially dead in 1973.

BENNETT: No proof he was even in Berlin at the time.

RYDER: And there never was a trace of the plane. Just the testimony that it got away through the smoke and turned south. *(Silence.* RYDER *paces up and down for a moment.)* I'm certain there's nothing in it. Almost certain. He was an actor. That was his secret, you know, mad keen on theatre. Supreme judge of an audience. He'd never have missed the curtain like that. Too great an artist. In his own insane way. I've been through the evidence again and again. Of course, the Russians made off with the chauffeur and the doctor. And did them to death, far as we know. But the identification was . . . pretty certain. And there's the dentures, the teeth.

BENNETT: All we've got on that is the woman who said she helped make the plate. And Smithson thought she was a bit dubious.

RYDER: I know, but I'm inclined to believe her. We can account for every hour in those last days. What he ate, whom he saw, when he went to the lavatory, if you really want to know. If he'd got away, someone would have talked.

HOVING: Suppose . . . suppose there was a double.

RYDER: Oh, there was.

HOVING: Really?

RYDER: Oh, yes. Bennett will correct me if I'm wrong, but we identified a double on two occasions, I believe: once in Prague, and once at a field hospital at the Eastern Front in '44. But my point is, you see, he'd hardly send on a double at the climax of the show, would he?

BENNETT: But mightn't he have been thinking in terms of a comeback?

RYDER: What, you mean Barbarossa?[4] The storm king in the mountain lair. And out to vengeance when his people called. No, it was too late for all that. He knew that. He just wanted to bring everything down with him. He was a romantic mountebank. *(He breaks off, sighs.)* Now are we sure about the signal?

HOVING: We're almost sure we've got the cipher right, sir. It's fairly

4. Barbarossa was the legendary medieval emperor said to have escaped death and to have hidden until a time propitious for his return. Hitler named his planned invasion of Russia "Operation Barbarossa."

straightforward. Pretty elementary set of permutations. And we've put a man in there, at Orosso, the nearest airstrip. Name of Kulken. He's monitoring the whole operation. The signals are very weak now. Far as we can tell there's never been a party up beyond the Chevaqua Falls.

(RYDER *pours himself another glass of sherry, replaces the stopper in the decanter thoughtfully.)*

RYDER: It's just possible. Just. Million to one. I don't think that plane could possibly have got out. Those last days the sky was like a furnace. Anyway, I can't believe he was aboard. No. It's just not on. *(He downs his sherry as the chimes begin for hall.* BENNETT *and* HOVING *rise.* RYDER *crosses to the door and takes his gown. He's halfway into it, when a thought strikes him.)* Unless . . . no. Perhaps the one they've caught is the double. What about that? Rather a piquant notion, don't you think? *(He chuckles, opening the door. The others smile and move over towards the door, which* RYDER *is holding open for them.)* Now, give me the message again. What was it?

BENNETT: Well, the first word was indecipherable. Monosyllable, but we couldn't quite. . . .

RYDER: Oh, surely. I'd have said it was obvious.

HOVING: What, sir?

RYDER: Must be. Found.

(He closes the door behind them. Blackout. In the darkness the crackle and whine of static. Then SIMEON*'s voice, the first word indeed indistinct, but the rest of the message ringing out clear.)*

SIMEON'S VOICE: Found. Praise be to Him. Thou art remembered, O Jerusalem.[5]

(In response to this, LIEBER*'s voice, triumphant.)*

LIEBER'S VOICE: Message received. Glory to God. In the highest. And forever. Now there is light again, at Gilead and in Hebron, and to the ends of the earth. I tell you there is light as never before. And tonight the stars will dance over Arad. And the world stand still to draw breath and the dew be like the cymbals in the grass. Because he is ours.

5. An allusion to Psalm 137.

SCENE 3

The clearing. The noise of the rain forest.

Downstage left, HITLER *sits cross-legged, his wrists bound, staring out in front of him, expressionless.* AMSEL, *self-conscious, towers above him, cradling his submachine gun, on guard.*

Downstage right, SIMEON *is poring over the innards of his radio.* GIDEON *stands anxiously nearby.* ASHER *moves over to join them.*

ASHER: Did you get through, Capitano?

SIMEON: I hope so. Except look at this wiring. Rotten with mold.

ASHER: So would they have picked up the signal?

SIMEON: I think so. Enough to let them know.

GIDEON: They must have done. If we're to get him out alive. Lieber will have heard us. He'll have the plane ready in San Cristobal.

SIMEON: Can you imagine Lieber? Now he knows?

ASHER: All we have to do is get him there alive.

GIDEON: We'll get him there. If we have to carry him. Every stinking mile. That's what we said in our oath. With our lives if need be. If he has to ride on our backs.

ASHER: He might have to. I can't see him walking. He's so old. Born 1889. That's what it says on Lieber's warrant. You think he can walk through the swamp at ninety?

(ELIE *has moved over to join them by now.)*

ELIE: And over the moraine?

ASHER: How strong do you think he is? Did you see what they've been eating? Mice and raw beans and muck scraped off the trees.

GIDEON: Ninety. They made men and women of ninety walk barefoot over the cobbles. And if someone fell behind, they threw water over their feet. So they froze to the stones. And stood there till they died. *(He looks rapidly across at* HITLER, *then back to the others.)* At Chelmno[6] there was a rabbi, a man of wonders. A hundred years old. They tore his tongue out and

6. One of the Nazi extermination camps, located in western Poland.

made him hold it before him and walk. A mile. More than a mile. Till he came to the fire pit. Then they said: Sing. Sing, you man of wonders. *(Silence. Then* GIDEON *adds, decisively.)* All right then, we will carry him. We'll tie one of the hammocks between two poles and make a litter. Spread a poncho on top to keep his carcass dry. Take turns carrying him. Like the ark.

ASHER: And dance before it? You're not serious, Gideon. How can we carry a man through the swamp when it's all we can do to keep our heads above water? Especially you, since the fever. And Elie's right. The rockfall. We've lost nearly all our ropes. You can't get a hammock through that hell. He won't be that light. Bloody paunch on him. No. They'll have to drop us supplies. Blankets, ropes, benzedrine, iodine, crampons, a new transmitter, new sleeping bags, batteries, all that. We need cocoa and fishing lines. I say we wait here. It's all very well for Lieber. He looks at his map: red arrow in, blue arrow out. We'll never, never make San Cristobal, Capo. Look at the rabbi's boots. I can see his corns bleeding. We'd be mad. And *he'd* die on us inside a week. Why shouldn't they send us helicopters, medics, the lot? It's no more than we deserve. They can't expect us to drown in that muck.

SIMEON: Even if I could get the transmitter to work . . .

ELIE: They're not going to come. Lieber can't get access to all that stuff, you know that. They all think he's sick in the head, no one's going to believe him for a minute. At the Ministry, they told him he'd spent too much time out in the sun.

SIMEON: It's not that. He could get help. He could get a helicopter in. Don't you see, if the news was released, we could have an airport built right here. Bigger than Lod.[7] With a Hilton. And a television studio. But we'd lose *him.* They'd whisk him off to New York or Moscow or Nuremberg. And that would be that. We'd have waded up to our eyes through all that filth, just for their benefit. Like that story of the old man and the

7. Location of Israel's international airport.

big fish and by the time he gets it back to the dock, the sharks have stripped it to the bone. We have to move fast and keep quiet and be secret. Until we have him home. Then go to the four corners of the city and blow your trumpets. But not now. Anyone finds out we have him now, they wouldn't leave us his shadow.

GIDEON: Can't we go out another way?

SIMEON: Not at first. That's why he came here. The mud bank in the dead center of the swamp. There's no way out except back through the black water.

ASHER: Bleeding Jesus, I'd rather rot here.

(SIMEON *has calmly unfolded his map.)*

SIMEON: There's no other way. Look for yourself. We have to head for Jiaro so we can dig up our stores.

ASHER: Supper for termites.

SIMEON: After Jiaro there might be an easier way. North of the falls, look. Supposed to be an old Indian road here, stone slabs leading to the blue stone quarries. Here, just above Orosso.

GIDEON: There's a landing strip at Orosso, isn't there?

SIMEON: Yes, but Lieber said not to use it. It's got to be north. Across the Colombian border to San Cristobal.

ELIE: That means the mountains.

ASHER: Carrying the old pig on our backs. You're mad.

(SIMEON *nods, smiling. He folds up his map.)*

SIMEON: Right. Who's going to build the litter?

SCENE 4

A featureless office in the Historical Section of the KGB in Moscow. COLONEL SHEPILOV *stands behind his desk, with his back to it, looking out of the window. Facing his desk is an empty chair, at present brilliantly lit by a shaft of sunlight.*

A knock at the door. SHEPILOV *grunts and* NIKOLAI MAXIMOVITCH GRUZDEV *steps cautiously into the room. He hesitates on the threshold, then advances uncertainly, a few steps, before coming to a halt again. He's about sixty-five, faintly shabby with a straggly grey beard, his clothes an obvious contrast to* SHEPILOV*'s new but unpleasant brown suit.* SHEPILOV, *meanwhile, has rounded the desk, hand outstretched, his greeting formal rather than effusive.*

SHEPILOV: Nikolai Maximovitch. I'm sorry it was necessary to rouse you so early in the morning. It's a rather important matter.
(GRUZDEV *shakes his hand warily.)*

GRUZDEV: Of course. *(He looks at* SHEPILOV *in the ensuing pause, frowning slightly.)* Haven't we met before, Comrade Colonel?

SHEPILOV: I don't believe so. Please sit down. *(He indicates the chair.* GRUZDEV *sits and* SHEPILOV *moves back behind his desk.)* Just one or two details. We're only bookworms here in the Historical Section. All this paper. Every now and then we like to close a file.

GRUZDEV: May I smoke, Comrade Colonel?

SHEPILOV: Certainly you may. *(*GRUZDEV *lights a cigarette, and* SHEPILOV *pushes an ashtray across the desk towards him.)* Sometimes we find there's an . . . untidiness and we have to go back over small things. *(He sits down and the sun blazes into* GRUZDEV*'s eyes. He flinches.)*

GRUZDEV: Yes, I'm sure.

SHEPILOV: It's very good of you to give us the benefit of your advice, Nikolai Maximovitch. Make yourself comfortable. The sun's very bright this morning. I hope it's not inconveniencing you.

GRUZDEV: No, no.

(Silence. SHEPILOV *rifles through some papers.* GRUZDEV *takes a handkerchief from his breast pocket and dabs at the corners of his mouth.)*

SHEPILOV: Now what we're interested in is the testimony you gave. At first, I mean. Before the later interrogations.

GRUZDEV: That's thirty years ago, Comrade Colonel. My memory . . .

SHEPILOV: Quite. But the file is here. And what we want to know, purely as historians you understand, is what made you so certain.

GRUZDEV: I was wrong. That must be in your file. Absolutely mistaken. I made a full statement admitting all my errors.

SHEPILOV: You see, even after SS Adjutant Rattenhuber assured you in front of witnesses, that he had helped to burn the bodies, even after your long interview with Heinz Linge, Hitler's valet, here it is scribbled in the margin in your handwriting: I continue to believe the body shown me by Captain Fyodor Pavlovitch Vassiliki on May the 11th last was not that of Adolf Hitler. Now, I confess I'm puzzled. What made you so certain?

GRUZDEV: But all my denials were erroneous. I even made a mistake about Rattenhuber's rank.

SHEPILOV: Yes, I know, subsequently you withdrew all these statements and concurred unreservedly in the findings of the official tribunal: to wit, that the bodies of Hitler and the woman Braun had been identified beyond any possible doubt by Captain Vassiliki and dental mechanic Fritz Echtmann. You also admitted that propaganda originating from western intelligence had been the cause of your original obstinacy.

GRUZDEV: Comrade Colonel. Is all this necessary?

SHEPILOV: No. We're well aware that certain, quite illegal persuasions were used to make you change your mind. No one wants to rake all that up. What concerns us is your original opinion. *Before* you were questioned by Major Berkoff and his staff. What was it made you so certain Hitler was alive?

GRUZDEV: You know, Stalin himself believed Hitler had survived. He said at the Potsdam Conference, Hitler was being sheltered by Fascism in Spain or Latin America. When Major Berkoff told me Stalin had changed his mind, all my doubts were resolved.

SHEPILOV: We're really not interested in what Stalin believed. It's you, Doctor.

GRUZDEV: Strange, I really can't remember why I was so stubborn. I remember the dentist.

SHEPILOV: Käte Heusemann.

GRUZDEV: Heusemann, yes. She said I was mad. She said I didn't know the first thing about dental fittings. But if a man shoots himself in the mouth. . . . If the angle of trajectory was what the X-rays showed, the bridge on the upper jaw and the window crown on the incisor would certainly have been broken. *(For the first time, a certain confidence and enthusiasm animate his voice.)* The fittings shown to me were intact, except for some crude scratches on the metal clip. Those scratches stuck in my mind. They were white at the edges, as if they'd been made very recently, by a nail file, say, in haste. Then there was the right arm. We know from Dr. Morrell's files precisely where Hitler's arm was injured in the July 21st explosion and how the bones set. The right arm on the body submitted to my department for autopsy was badly charred. The wrist and elbow joint were like ash. All the same, my reconstruction accorded perfectly with the pathology recorded by Morrell. The cracks in the metacarpus, the sutures, the chipping of the bone immediately below the shoulder, all there, perfect. And that made me uneasy. You see, things that mend naturally or that retain a partial dislocation, they're more blurred. I thought it was possible we were meant to observe the lesions and be deceived. Forensic medicine is well acquainted with these devices. I remember one of my first cases in Kharkov, disfigured corpse with a tattoo, which Trenin was able to prove had been applied after death . . . *(He breaks off, suddenly aware that* SHEPILOV *is staring coldly at him.)* What else can I say? The dental fittings and certain aspects of the brachial anatomy. That's why I was misled. *(Silence.* GRUZDEV *slumps back in his chair, screwing up his eyes against the light.)*

SHEPILOV: But were you? Perhaps you were right. What do you think about it today?

GRUZDEV: Today? What is it you gentlemen want me to think? I'm an old man, Comrade Colonel.

SHEPILOV: You had a hypothesis, did you not, to account for the scratches on the dentures and the fractures in the third phalange?

GRUZDEV: Yes.

SHEPILOV: Well?

GRUZDEV: A double. It was a double. They broke his arm, shot him in the mouth and inserted the dentures.

SHEPILOV: And do you still regard that as a viable hypothesis?

GRUZDEV: I don't know. They pulled my fingernails out to make me say he was dead. So I'll say whatever you want me to say. *(He passes a hand in front of his eyes.)* Do you think I could have a glass of water? *(*SHEPILOV *rises without a word and moves across and out of the room.* GRUZDEV *shakes his head.)* Hitler is alive. *(He closes his eyes. The sound of grunts, cries, and repeated blows.* GRUZDEV *gropes again for his handkerchief, mops at his face. He opens his eyes to find* SHEPILOV *standing above him, holding a paper cup of water. Silence.* GRUZDEV *takes the cup, shuddering.)* The cold, Colonel Shepilov. The cold remains.

SHEPILOV: I was there too.

(He's standing there, his hand half-extended, as if afraid GRUZDEV *is going to make off with the cup.* GRUZDEV *sips, hands the cup back to* SHEPILOV.*)*

GRUZDEV: We have met. I remember now.

SHEPILOV: Well. That will be all, Nikolai Maximovitch. For now.

SCENE 5

The swamp. SIMEON *leads on, the radio strapped to his back. Then the others struggle on, each carrying on his shoulder a pole of the makeshift litter:* GIDEON *and* ASHER *in front,* AMSEL *and* ELIE *behind.*

They stagger painfully across the stage until, suddenly AMSEL, *who is downstage, cries out and recoils from something. The others, unbalanced, stumble precariously. A hand flashes out through the blankets which form the curtains of the litter, and then* HITLER *falls from the upstage side of the litter.* ASHER *drops his pole and grabs for him, gets him by the hair and hauls him up, bedraggled, shaking his head, slightly stunned.* ASHER *lets him go and utters a short bark of laughter. The others join in except for* AMSEL.

AMSEL: I'm sorry. It was a snake.

(Then he briefly laughs too, a touch hysterically.)

SIMEON: All right. We'll take a break. On that mud bank over there. *(They wade across to it. The sound of the swamp is less densely cacophonous than that of the jungle, but nevertheless forms a solid hum behind the scene.* SIMEON *swings the radio off his back.* ASHER *gathers up the sodden litter and struggles across to the mud bank, helped by* GIDEON. HITLER *stays where he is for the moment, watching them.)* Elie, prepare some food. I'm going to see what I can raise on this thing. *(He attends to the radio: presently from it, the stutter and whine off static. After a time,* LIEBER*'s voice cuts through it.)*

LIEBER'S VOICE: Ayalon calling. Come in Nimrod.

*(*SIMEON *frowns and strains, listening, as if catching some faint echo of this. Then he begins tuning. Spotlight on* LIEBER. *While he speaks, the following actions on stage:*

HITLER *takes off his trousers and wrings them out meticulously.*

ELIE *opens tins, prepares a meal of cold meats and noodles.*

SIMEON *and* GIDEON *work on the radio, opening it, delicately cleaning and oiling the innards.*
ASHER *lies back on his pack, his eyes closed, relaxing.*
AMSEL *covertly watches* HITLER.
HITLER *puts on his trousers.*
ELIE *distributes the food, then pours water into tin cups and distributes them.*
They eat.)

LIEBER: I want you to remember
Tell me you remember
The garden in Salonika where Mordechai Zathsmar, the cantor's youngest son, ate excrement
The Hoofstraat in Arnheim where they took Leah Burstein and made her watch while her father
The two lime trees where the road to Montrouge turns south on which they hung the meat hooks and
The pantry on the third floor, Nowy Swiat eleven, where Jakov Kaplan, author of *The History of Algebraic Thought in Eastern Europe 1280–1655* had to dance on the body of
The Mauerallee in Hanover, where three louts drifting home from an SS recruitment spree came across Rahel Nadelmann, tied her legs and with a truncheon
The latrine in the police station in Wörgel which Doktor Ruth Levin and her niece had to clean with their hair.
Elias Kornfeld, Sarah Ellbogen, Robert Heimann, in front of the biology class, Newald Gymnasium, Lower Saxony, stripped to the waist, mouths wide open so that Professor Horst Küntzer could demonstrate to his pupils the obvious racial
Lilian Gourevitch, given two work passes for her three children in Tver Street and ordered to choose which of the children was to go on the next transport
Lilian Gourevitch, given two work passes, yellow, serial numbers BJ 7732781 and 2, for her three children in Tver Street and ordered to choose
Lilian Gourevitch

Dorfmann, George Benjamin Dorfmann, collector of prints of the late seventeenth century, doctor, viola player, lying, no, kneeling, no, squatting in the punishment cell at Buchenwald, six foot by four and a half, the concrete cracked with ice, watching the pus break from his torn nails, whispering the catalog numbers of the Hobbemas in the Albertina, until the guard took a whip and

Ann Casanova, 21, rue du Chapon, Liège, called to the door, asking the two men to wait outside so that her mother would not know and then seeing the old woman fall on to the bonnet of the starting car, from the fourth floor window

Hannah, the silken-haired retriever, dying of hunger in the locked apartment after the Küllmanns had been taken, sinking her teeth into the master's houseshoes, custom-made to the measure of his handsome foot by Samuel Rossbach, who also

Hagadio, who in the shoe factory at Treblinka was caught splitting leather, sabotage, and made to crawl alive into the quicklime, while at the edge Reuben Cohen, aged eleven, had to proclaim, 'So shall all saboteurs and subverters of the united front'

Hagadio

Hagadio

until the neighbors, Ebert and Ilse Schmidt, today Ebert Schmidt, City Engineer, broke down the door, found the dog almost dead, dropped it in the garbage pit and rifled Küllmann's closets, his wife's dressing table, his children's attic with its rocking horse, jack-in-the-box, and chemistry set, while on the railway siding near Dornbach

Hagadio

the child, thrown from the train by its parents, with money sewn into its jacket and a note begging for water and help, was found by two men coming home from seeding and laid on the tracks a hundred yards from the north switch, gagged, feet tied, till the next train, which it heard a long way off in the still of the summer evening, the two men watching and eating and voiding their bowels

Hagadio

the Küllmanns knowing the smell of gas was the smell of gas but thinking their child safe, which, as the thundering air blew nearer, spoke into its gag, twice, the name of the silken-haired bitch Hannah and then could not close its eyes against the rushing shadow

(Long pause. The light now has narrowed to isolate LIEBER *and* HITLER, *who sits, some way apart from the others, blankly shovelling food into his mouth.)*

He did it.

(Spotlight on LIEBER *snaps off. Another pause, during which the onstage lights fade up to normal.* SIMEON, *the receiver to his ear, suddenly straightens up.)*

SIMEON: Wait a minute. That was something. *(He peers at the receiver, delicately tuning.)* It's Lieber's wavelength. *(He makes further adjustments.)* There we are. Listen.

(Crackling faintly through the ether, a woman's voice: a sentimental Brazilian pop song. SIMEON *reaches for the dial, sighing angrily, but* ASHER *catches his wrist.)*

ASHER: Leave it for a moment.

*(*SIMEON *leaves it. The five gather round the set. They listen to the song, rapt. After a time,* HITLER *puts down his mess tin, rises silently and moves over to the group. His fly-buttons are undone. He's standing alongside them; none of them has noticed him. The woman's voice emotes thinly to a tango rhythm.* HITLER *smiles.)*

HITLER: *Musik.*

(The others turn to look at him, shocked. Blackout.)

SCENE 6

The woman's voice swells in the darkness, to be overlaid eventually, as the lights come up, by the sound of a light aircraft coming in to land nearby.

A hut in Orosso. Siesta time. An INDIAN WOMAN *is asleep on the crumpled double bed, facing upstage, visible through the mosquito net, the downstage side of which is folded up on itself. She wears a grubby white nightdress. A little way off, sitting facing a formidable bank of radio equipment, his face on the desk, asleep, is* RODRIGUEZ KULKEN. *He's still holding the headphones in one hand. He's wearing stained striped pajamas; he's overweight and unshaven.*

The aircraft lands and taxis in. When the engines are cut, the woman's voice reestablishes itself against the sounds of the encroaching jungle.

KULKEN *jerks awake suddenly. He picks up his headphones, listens for a second. His face wrinkles with disgust. He reaches out and snaps off the radio.*

KULKEN: Shit. *(He gets up and shambles across the room, glancing at the* WOMAN, *opens a battered meat safe, reaches in, brings out a bottle of beer, opens it on a bottle opener fixed to the side of the safe and returns to his chair. He sits there for a moment, then takes a swig of beer.)* Shit.

(He picks up the headphones, switches on the radio, puts on the headphones, and catches the end of the song. He reaches for the tuner and begins searching the airwaves slowly and carefully. After a time, LIEBER*'s voice breaks in.)*

LIEBER'S VOICE: . . . who spat at us and threw stones through our windows. The ones who wouldn't give visas. They all helped. The Poles who killed all but thirty-nine of the six hundred who escaped from Treblinka saying Jews belong in Treblinka. It couldn't have been done without the indifferent and the helpers and those who said in England or France or America that it was all exaggerated, the Jews whining again and peddling horrors. Not without D initialing a memo to B-W at Printing House Square, which said: No more atrocity stories. Probably overplayed. Not without the State Department offering seventy-five visas above the quota when they could have saved a hundred thousand children. Not without . . .

(KULKEN *leans forward and switches the radio off, sighing heavily.)*

KULKEN: Merde.

(He removes the headphones, takes a swig of beer, and spends a moment or two ruminatively picking his nose and inspecting the results. Then he looks over at the WOMAN. *He watches her for a moment, then puts the bottle down and crosses to the bed. He looks down at her, his eyes narrow. Then he kneels on the bed and unceremoniously pulls up her nightdress. She grunts, scarcely stirring. He reaches out, the beginnings of a caress, when the screen door suddenly crashes open.* KULKEN *whips around, taken entirely by surprise.*

Standing in the doorway, still wearing his flying helmet, his pilot's goggles pushed up on top of his head, is the towering figure of MARVIN CROWNBACKER. *He beams at the couple, who are both fumbling with their clothes,* KULKEN *in confusion, the* WOMAN *much more relaxed.)*

CROWNBACKER: Hi. Mr. Kulken? This is Orosso, am I right?

KULKEN: *Scheisse.*

SCENE 7

Night. The roar of the jungle. The lap of water nearby. Darkness broken by the red, smouldering tip of a cigarillo. Gradually a dimly visible area defines itself out of the surrounding blackness.

GIDEON BENASSERAF *crouches, his submachine gun across his knees, smoking. Near him is a stake driven into the ground. There's a rope tied round it which goes snaking away into the darkness.*

GIDEON *looks up sharply as* ISAAC AMSEL *appears beside him. He frowns up at* AMSEL *discouragingly, but* AMSEL *seems not to notice.*

AMSEL: I can't sleep. Not with him out there. *(He sits down beside* GIDEON, *indicates his gun.)* Is it loaded?

GIDEON: No. Why should it be?

AMSEL: Well, he might try to escape.

GIDEON: Where to?

AMSEL: I would if I was him. I'd bite through the rope if I had to.

GIDEON: What for? He couldn't get anywhere on his own. Did you see the ants back there?

AMSEL: No.

GIDEON: Like a cloud of red pepper blowing along the ground.

AMSEL: Better the ants than what we're going to do with him.

GIDEON: Oh? What are we gong to do with him?

AMSEL: Well, that's up to Lieber, isn't it? And the others. They'll try him in the Supreme Court. And hang him. After breakfast. That's not what I would do. *(Pause.* GIDEON *draws on his cigarillo.)* I wouldn't do it that way at all. I'd do it so he knew what was being done. I'd hang him on a pulley over a vat of acid. People could draw lots to turn the handle and dip him in. One turn if you've lost a wife, two for each child. I'd squeeze his balls in a vice. I'd skin his legs to make lampshades.

GIDEON: You're not talking about him. You're emptying the garbage in your own mind.

AMSEL: What about you, Gideon, what would you do?

GIDEON: I haven't thought about it. I'd let him go.

AMSEL: What?

GIDEON: I'd let him go wherever he wanted to inside Israel. With just the clothes on his back. Every time he wanted something, food or water or shelter, he'd have to ask for it and say who he was. Everyone would know, but I'd make him say it. I'd make him say: I am Adolf Hitler; please can I have some water? I am Adolf Hitler; will you give me shelter in your house?

AMSEL: Well, if that's all you want, why not just turn him loose in the jungle?

GIDEON: Why not? Except I'd like him to die a fat old tourist in the land of Israel.

AMSEL: If you feel that way, why are you here?

GIDEON: We're all here for our own little reasons.

AMSEL: I'm here because my father died looking for him.

GIDEON: Also because you've seen too many movies.

AMSEL: You didn't want me to come at all, did you?

GIDEON: No, I didn't, no.

AMSEL: Why not?

GIDEON: You're too young. I know you think you understand what we feel but you're . . . too young.

AMSEL: I want vengeance, just the same as you.

GIDEON: Vengeance? There can be no vengeance. Why should history apologize to the Jews? Don't stare at me, Amsel, as if you knew what I was trying to say. You don't. You think the dead will sit up just because we've got Hitler? They won't. You can dip him in boiling oil six million times. What's that going to mean to a man who's seen his six-year-old daughter so terrified she dirtied herself before they killed her? You think that can be made good? *(He breaks off. Pause.)* What's the difference? There's only two kinds of Jews. The dead and those who are a bit crazy. *(Pause.)*

That's why I don't want any of us to touch him. If we hang him, we'll be pretending what he did can be made good. History will draw a line and forget even faster. That's exactly what they want. They want us to do the job for them. Let the

Jews hang him. We nailed up Christ, now they want us to finish Hitler. So they can be acquitted. That's why I say, the first town we come to, we should leave him in an armchair at the hotel and scatter. Let them get on with it. He's *theirs. (Pause.* GIDEON *breathes out, slowly, calms himself.)* You don't want to listen to this. Check the paraffin and go to sleep.

AMSEL: Will you take me with you afterwards? To Paris?

GIDEON: Paris?

AMSEL: I want to be a film director. I want to make a film about how we marched into the jungle and found Hitler. Wide screen. No one's ever really known how to use wide screen properly. Antonioni just faked it, he's a stills photographer. Kurosawa maybe . . .

(He breaks off, seeing GIDEON*'s not altogether friendly smile.)*

GIDEON: What makes you think I want to go to Paris?

AMSEL: During the fever, I heard you say it to John. I heard you say it was the only place where you might be able to forgive.

GIDEON: No. Not forgive. Never forgive. *(Slowly, the rope goes taut. The two men stare at it, transfixed. Time passes. They're unable to take their eyes off the rope. They watch, motionless. Finally, it goes slack again.)* At the end of that rope there's a man who . . . *(Long pause.* GIDEON *seems to reconsider a moment before going on.)* . . . gassed my wife and sons and . . . *(Another pause, shorter.)* . . . burned my daughter Rebecca alive. If I thought I could go back to literary life in the cafés of Paris, then I must have been delirious.

AMSEL: Then where will you go?

GIDEON: Afterwards? I'll go look for Adolf Hitler.

SCENE 8

KULKEN*'s hut, as at the end of scene six:* KULKEN *and the* INDIAN WOMAN *still on the bed,* CROWNBACKER *in the doorway.* KULKEN *struggles to his feet; the* WOMAN *scrambles off the bed and retreats to a corner of the room;* CROWNBACKER *moves over to inspect* KULKEN*'s radio, whistling appreciatively.*

CROWNBACKER: Nice.

KULKEN: What . . . ?

CROWNBACKER: A 207 range finder. Mounted on a dk circuit.
(KULKEN *plucks nervously at his pajama bottoms.)*

KULKEN: Who the hell are you?

CROWNBACKER: Marvin Crownbacker. Pleased to meet you, Mr. Kulken. *(He moves across to* KULKEN, *reaching into his top pocket, to* KULKEN*'s alarm, and produces a wallet, which he flips open.)* Here's my ID.

KULKEN: That's no good to me. Only queers and Belgians travel under their own names.

CROWNBACKER: Well, you can call me Charlie.

KULKEN: Why?

CROWNBACKER: Everybody always does. *(He slaps at his cheek.)* Jesus, what a dump. *(He smiles pleasantly at the* INDIAN WOMAN.*)* No offence, lady. *(He slaps again, this time at his forearm.)* Goddamn bugs. Got any DDT?
(He unstraps his helmet and takes it off.)

KULKEN: Will you get out of my house!
(CROWNBACKER *pulls a steel three-legged stool out from under the table and sits for a moment facing the radio. He flips a switch, listens to the hum for a moment, then switches off and turns back to* KULKEN.*)*

CROWNBACKER: See, I'm a radio ham myself. *(He indicates the equipment.)* Nothing like this, but . . . I picked up on your circuit with Montevideo. Then I caught one or two whispers from those guys in the rain forest. *(He breaks off.)* I could use some coffee.

(KULKEN *hesitates, then turns and barks harshly at the* INDIAN WOMAN.)

KULKEN: Café. *(He returns his attention to* CROWNBACKER.*)* Where do you operate out of?

CROWNBACKER: Brasilia. I'm just a freelance. *(He smiles at* KULKEN *shamelessly.)* I lucked out. I was just drifting through the airwaves and I found you. Then when I heard the others, I knew that if we played it right, you and me, we were on to two, three million bucks. So I hired that goddamn old Cessna and here I am.

KULKEN: You're crazy.

CROWNBACKER: Listen, you know and I know those boys are out of juice. Their radio is kaput. So, when they come sashaying out of the jungle, how are they going to tell the world? *(He points at the radio.)* That's how. Then we got maybe two days before every goddamn journalist from here to Ulan Bator checks in to Orosso airport. Because this is bigger than Jonestown.[8] This is the biggest fucking story of the century. *(The* INDIAN WOMAN *arrives with a tray: coffee and a plate of seedcakes.* CROWNBACKER *spoons in sugar, takes a mouthful of cake.)* I know. I know the equipment is yours. That's why I'm offering you a bigger cut. Fifty-six forty-four, how does that sound to you?

KULKEN: Ludicrous.

CROWNBACKER: I got all the contracts. They take care of all the subsidiary rights, everything. Newspaper and magazine serialization, anthology digest quotation and abridgment, dramatic, film, radio, television, microphotographic reproduction and picturization, reproduction by gramophone records and other mechanical means by sight, sound, or a combination thereof, translation into any foreign language from Bantu to Yiddish. We even have the goddamn T-shirt and cereal packaging rights. Millions.

8. Location in Guyana, South America, where more than nine hundred followers of Jim Jones, an American evangelist, committed suicide on 18 November 1978.

KULKEN: Cojones. A million dollars for an interview with Martin Bormann?

(CROWNBACKER puts down his cake, rises and leans angrily over towards KULKEN.)

CROWNBACKER: Martin Bormann? Don't fuck with me. Who gives a shit about Martin Bormann? Who they have is Hitler. Adolf Hitler. *(KULKEN pales and throws out a hand to steady himself. CROWNBACKER turns to the INDIAN WOMAN.)* Glass of water. *(She stares at him, uncomprehending. He shouts at her.)* Agua, you stupid bitch. *(She hurries to fetch some water. KULKEN meanwhile has recovered somewhat.)* You okay?

KULKEN: You're wrong. Hitler?

(The WOMAN arrives with the water. KULKEN waves her away impatiently.)

CROWNBACKER: They didn't tell you, huh? Whitehall.

KULKEN: I don't know what you mean, Whitehall.

CROWNBACKER: Listen, that limey faggot you talk to in Montevideo ain't a butterfly collector.

KULKEN: This has all been most interesting, but I mustn't keep you. Buenos días.

CROWNBACKER: I'm not going, Mr. Kulken. You know that and I know that.

KULKEN: My Indians could strip your plane down to the last bolt.

CROWNBACKER: Yeah? Then how would I leave? I'm not going up in that goddamn sewing machine again. I couldn't even if I wanted to. The rains are between here and San Cristobal. Even coming in this morning was like flying through clam chowder. So let's relax till it comes time to say howdy-doody to the Führer. Mm? Partner?

(He smiles at KULKEN, who's staring back at him with undisguised hatred.)

SCENE 9

Twilight. The team, emerging from the swamp, the mud drying on their trousers. AMSEL *leads, clutching his machete. Next come* SIMEON *and* ELIE, *who are supporting* GIDEON, *now in the grip of a malarial spasm, shuddering with fever, running with sweat, racked by the occasional profound hiccup.* HITLER *follows shuffling behind them, watched by* ASHER *who brings up the rear.*

They advance, slowly. Suddenly AMSEL *flinches violently, lets out a guttural cry of horror, and begins swiping at the air with his machete.*

AMSEL: Bats!

(At the same time ELIE *jerks abruptly away from* GIDEON, *unbalancing him and causing him to crash to the ground.* HITLER *ducks and* ASHER *puts a hand up in front of his face. For a moment all of them, except for* GIDEON *who lies prone and* HITLER *who stands calmly in the middle, writhe and stamp as if in some demented dance.* AMSEL *plucks something like an old black glove off his knee and throws it to the ground, crying out again.* ELIE *kneels and grapples invisibly with something on* GIDEON*'s body.* AMSEL *raises his machete in the air.)*

SIMEON: No! You'll have somebody's head off.

(He crushes the black object with the butt of his rifle. ELIE *is stamping on another.* ASHER *is now slapping furiously at himself.* AMSEL *gives another groaning shudder of disgust. Then, as abruptly as before, they are all calm again looking up at the dying light.* HITLER *giggles. He touches the crushed creature delicately with his toe.)*

HITLER: *Die Vampire.*

(He looks up and makes a curious warbling sound: the all-clear. Then another brief smile flits across his face.)

SIMEON: We'll pitch camp here. Elie, help me with Gideon.

(As they begin to prepare camp, lights fade up on LIEBER *sit-*

ting at his radio, headphones on. He speaks into the transmitter.)

LIEBER: Can you hear me?

Do you remember that photograph in the archive in Humboldtstrasse? August 1914, Munich. The crowd listening to the declaration of war. The faces round the plinth. Among them, partially obscured but unmistakable, his. The eyes shining. In two years almost every man in the photograph was dead. If a shell had found him out, a bullet, a grenade splinter, we would have grown old in our houses. There would be children to know our graves.

It was he. None of the others could have done it. Not the fat bully, not the adder. He took garbage and made it into wolves. With his nose for the bestial and the boredom in men's bones. He made real the old dream of murder. Everyman's itch to clear his throat of us. Because we lasted too long, because we foisted Christ on them, because we smell other.

(Light snaps out on LIEBER.*)*

SIMEON: Gideon. Mensch. Have you taken? *(*GIDEON *makes a noise of assent between chattering teeth.)* You must have some more.

GIDEON: I . . . *(*ELIE *taps some powder into his palm.* SIMEON *half sits* GIDEON *up, and* ELIE *holds his hand to* GIDEON*'s mouth, then quickly holds the water bottle to his lips.* GIDEON *chokes and shivers.)* I've had worse.

(He slumps back. SIMEON *gets up, looking down at him, concerned.)*

SIMEON: Stay with him, Elie.

(The light is dwindling fast. AMSEL *returns with the water. He lights the Primus and a hurricane lamp, then puts the water on to boil. Meanwhile,* SIMEON *is distributing what appear to be dog biscuits.* ELIE *covers* GIDEON*'s body with a blanket, but no sooner has he done so, than* GIDEON *jerks up, shaking the blanket off.)*

GIDEON: Elie, Elie.

ELIE: Yes.

GIDEON: Where are we?

ELIE: Out of the swamp now.

GIDEON: We shouldn't be. It's too soon. That means we're too far east.

ELIE: Simeon knows. He decided we had to get out of the swamp. Not only for you. For all of us.

GIDEON: The wind. South wind, can you feel it?

ELIE: Cover yourself. *(He pulls the blanket over* GIDEON *again.)* We'll have you well again. Soon as we get to Jiaro.

GIDEON: I'm tired. Why go to Jiaro?

ELIE: For cold beer. And soap. *(He indicates the soles of* GIDEON*'s boots, now almost worn away.)* And new boots. Then we can get on. To San Cristobal.

GIDEON: Elie?

ELIE: Yes.

GIDEON: Have you ever seen Lieber?

ELIE: Of course I have. When you saw him. That day on the ship. Of course I've seen Lieber.

GIDEON: What did he look like?

ELIE: What did he look like? Don't you remember? Dark glasses. A hat. Old belted raincoat.

GIDEON: His face.

ELIE: Well. Ordinary. Perfectly ordinary. It was dark in the cabin. I didn't especially notice.

(Pause. It's dark now. As GIDEON *speaks light fades up on* LIEBER*'s face. He moves up and down one side of the stage, lost in thought, his expression anguished.)*

GIDEON: Elie. About Lieber. He's the one who really needs Hitler. They need each other. Without Lieber there would be no Hitler. Listen, I don't say there would never have been Hitler. But not now. Not sleeping next to us. Why haven't we seen Lieber's face? Supposing they were. Supposing.

*(*LIEBER *has sat now at his radio, strapped on the headphones, switched on. Now he speaks into the transmitter.)*

LIEBER: At Maidanek ten thousand a day, unimaginable because innumerable, in one corner of Treblinka seven hundred thousand bodies.

I will count them now.

Aaron, Aaronowitch, Aaronson, Abilech, Abraham, I will count seven hundred thousand names and you must listen, I will say Kaddish[9] till the end of time and still not reach the millionth name, at Belzec three hundred thousand.

Friedberg, Friedman, Friedmann, Friedstein

Names gone in fire and gas, ash on the wind at Chelmno, the long black wind at Chelmno, Israel Meyer, Ida Meyer

Four children in the pit at Sobibor

Four hundred and eleven thousand three hundred and eighty-one in section three at Belsen

The one being Belin the tanner whose face they sprinkled with acid and who was dragged through the streets of Kershon behind a dung cart but sang

The one being Georges Walter who when they called him from supper in the rue Marot spoke to his family of an administrative error and refused to pack more than one shirt and still asked why why through his smashed teeth when the shower door closed and the whisper began in the ceiling

The one being all because unnumbered hence unrememberable

Because buried alive at Grodno

Because hung by the feet at Bialystok like Nathansohn, nine hours fourteen minutes under the whip (timed by Wachtmeister Ottmar Prantl, now hotelier in Steyerbrück), the blood, Prantl reporting, splashing out of his hair and mouth like new wine

Two million at, unspeakable because beyond imagining, outside Cracow of the gracious towers, the signpost on the airport road pointing to it still, Auschwitz in sight of the low hills

9. Jewish prayer for the dead.

Because we can imagine the cry of one, the hunger of two, the burning of ten, but past a hundred there is no clear imagining

He understood that

Take a million and belief will not follow not the mind contain, and if each and every one of us were to rise before morning and speak out ten names that day, ten from the ninety-six thousand graven on the wall in Prague, ten from the thirty-one thousand in the crypt in Rome, ten from those at Matthausen, Drancy Birkenau Buchenwald Theresienstadt Babi-Yar, ten out of six million, we should never finish the task, not if we spoke the night through, not till the close of time, nor bring back a single breath

Not that of Isaac Löwy, Berlin, Isaac Löwy, Danzig (with the birthmark on his left shoulder), Isaac Löwy, Zagreb, Isaac Löwy, Vilna, the baker who cried of yeast when the door closed, Isaac Löwy, Toulouse, almost safe, the visa almost granted.

He has made ash of prayer

AND UNTIL EACH NAME is recalled and spoken again, EACH, the names of the nameless in the orphan's house at Szeged, the name of the mute in the sewer at Katowice, the names of the unborn in the women ripped at Matthausen, the name of the girl with the yellow star seen hammering on the door of the shelter in Hamburg of whom there is no record but a brown stain burnt into the pavement, until each name is remembered and spoken to the LAST SYLLABLE, man will have no peace on earth, no liberation from hatred, not until every name, for when spoken, each after the other, with not a single letter omitted, the syllables will make up the hidden name of GOD.

(From now to the end of the speech, LIEBER*'s voice becomes first amplified, then dwindles and vanishes into the engulfing hiss of static. At the same time, the light fades on* LIEBER *himself, who sits motionless, staring ahead of him.)*

LIEBER'S VOICE: Ayalon calling. Come in Nimrod.
I shall wait for you at the edge of the forest.
In San Cristobal.
Over to you, Simeon. Over.
Can you hear me?
This is Lieber calling.
this is Lieber
this is
(The sounds of the jungle reassert themselves. Darkness. Dim light on GIDEON *and* ELIE *watching over him. A strip of light from the hurricane lamp falls across* HITLER*'s face.* GIDEON *groans fitfully and throws his blanket off.* ELIE *leans over him, replacing it.)*

ELIE: Don't Gideon, you're shivering.
*(*GIDEON *sits up on one elbow: a moment of remission and he's suddenly still. He looks across for a moment at* HITLER.*)*

GIDEON: You know what, Elie? We've talked too much for five thousand years. That's why he turned on us. That's how he could tear our guts out. Because he knew how to make words louder than life. He and us. He and Lieber. Such need of each other. *(He sinks bank, begins shivering again, violently.)* Elie? Where are you?

ELIE: I'm here. I'm right here.

GIDEON: There were those who said . . .
(He breaks off.)

ELIE: What?

GIDEON: . . . he's one of us.

ELIE: It's a lie.

GIDEON: There's a tombstone in Bucharest. Under a Star of David, the name Hitler. Adolf Hitler. The week after he became Chancellor the archives in Linz were sacked. Every file burnt. His father's village was destroyed.

ELIE: Journalists' gossip.

GIDEON: Look. Look at his mouth. *(*HITLER*'s lips are moving. They watch for a moment in silence, then* HITLER *flings an arm over* *his face.)* Even in his sleep. An actor's mouth. A Jew's mouth. *(He flings his blanket off again.* ELIE *replaces it.)*

ELIE: You're shaking, Gideon. Stay covered.

GIDEON: That's why he had to kill us all. He couldn't rest as long as one of us was left alive on earth. To recognize him.

ELIE: It's just the fever, Gideon.

GIDEON: How else could he have understood us so perfectly? How else could he know we would walk so calmly into the fire?

ELIE: You must try and sleep. We have to get on tomorrow, before the rains come.

GIDEON: To be the final Adam. That's what he wanted. What's the use of being a Jew, one of the chosen people, if there are millions of others? But to be the only one left. To be the last Jew. *(Pause.)* I shan't make it to San Cristobal. I don't want to. *(Long pause.)*

ELIE: The other Messiah. The Second One, foretold by Malchiel. There shall spring from the seed of Abraham, from the tree of Jesse, absolute good and absolute evil. Only one of our number could have accomplished what he brought to pass. And his lips *are* moving. Even in sleep he says the incessant prayer, the other Kaddish, whose one hundred and nine syllables bring death. Hitler the Jew.

(He's close to tears. He turns away from GIDEON, *burying his face in his arms.* GIDEON *leans across to him.)*

GIDEON: Don't, Elie. It's fantasies. Don't listen to me. *(Pause.)* When we get back, we'll go to the seaside. Sit on a beach all day in the breeze. Say marvelous things like, "what time is it?" or, "chocolate or vanilla?" *(Pause.)* I just thought once we had him everything would be different. *(Pause.)* This taste. *(Pause.)* Elie? *(Pause.)* I need some water. *(Pause.)* Elie?

*(*ELIE*'s asleep.* GIDEON *sighs, pushes the blanket back. He lies there for a moment, then makes an enormous effort and struggles to his feet. He's overtaken by a shivering fit of almost epileptic proportions. He manages to control himself and moves downstage. Then the trembling takes charge of him*

again: he jerks and shudders in an involuntary dance. A crash of thunder and the solid roar of tropical rain. GIDEON *dances, helpless. A flash of lightning illuminates the scene, most especially an Indian,* TEKU,[10] *virtually naked, who stands staring at* GIDEON, *transfixed.*

GIDEON *continues to dance. Another flash of lightning.* GIDEON *collapses.* TEKU *looks up at the sky and drops to one knee beside* GIDEON*'s body.)*

INTERVAL

10. Expression used at the conclusion of discussing a Talmudic passage acknowledging that no agreement was reached or no interpretation predominated; a "draw."

SCENE 10

HITLER *sits in the entrance to the lean-to, sheltering from the perpendicular rain. He is carefully inspecting one of his feet, tending a blister, delicately removing parasites from a sore, concentrating on his task. The rope, now round his waist, is secured to one of the stanchions of the lean-to.*

Way upstage, ignored by him, SIMEON, ASHER, *and* AMSEL *stand around* GIDEON*'s makeshift grave.* ELIE *intones the final verses of the Hebrew service for the dead, his voice rising sonorously above the crashing rain.* AMSEL*'s body is shaken with sobs.*

When the service is over, ELIE *remains where he is, head bowed.* SIMEON *and* ASHER *break away somewhat sheepishly and begin to move off,* SIMEON *to take shelter,* ASHER *with no apparent aim in mind.* AMSEL *stands alone for a moment, controling himself, then turns downstage, his face contorted with rage.*

As AMSEL *strides past him reaching for the knife in his belt,* ASHER *reacts like lightning: before* AMSEL *reaches* HITLER, ASHER *catches up with him and puts an arm round him.* HITLER *looks up, his eye wary. Nothing is said, but the three men are all quite aware of what has happened.* HITLER *subjects* AMSEL *to a withering glare, then, as* ASHER *leads* AMSEL *away, murmuring softly to himself, returns his attention to his foot.*

SCENE 11

n the darkness, swelling, the passage from the last movement of Mahler's Second Symphony immediately preceding the entry of the chorus: the dialogue between the Last Trump and the Bird of Death.

Lights up on the study of Doktor Gervinus Röthling's house in Cologne. RÖTHLING *and his daughter,* ANNA ELISABETH, *a sensitive-looking girl in her late twenties, sit after dinner listening to the record player rapt in concentration. The LP side comes to an end, and* RÖTHLING, *sixtyish, refined, jumps up and crosses to the record player. His movements despite a slight limp are lithe. He stops the turntable, turns the record over, glances at his watch, and turns away from the record player without restarting it. He considers his daughter a moment.*

RÖTHLING: What would you do . . . *(He breaks off, ponders for a while on how to phrase the question.)* What would you do, Anna, if Adolf Hitler were to walk into this room?

ANNA: I should get up. *(*RÖTHLING *smiles quizzically.)* Yes, I should certainly get up from my chair.

RÖTHLING: Why?

ANNA: I don't know. Not to be polite. Shock, perhaps? No, I don't think so, not exactly. *(Pause.)* You remember that time we were going up the Schwarzhorn with Mother, on the mountain railway, and someone said they heard an avalanche? Well, everybody stood up then, do you remember? Perhaps it would be something like that.

RÖTHLING: And you'd curtsy, I shouldn't wonder.

ANNA: Certainly not, Papa. Really! *(*RÖTHLING *smiles, takes a pack of cigarettes from his jacket pocket, extracts one, taps it on the side of the pack, lights it, inhales, and sits down.)* No, I don't know what I'd do. Shout at him, spit in his face, stick a knife in his arm. None of that sounds right.

RÖTHLING: No, well, you young people have no idea of what it was really like, and why should you?

ANNA: Of course we have an idea what it was like.

RÖTHLING: Only from reading. And some of you think that entitles you to take up our national burden. It doesn't. Anyone can say Auschwitz, and if he says it loud enough, people have to lower their eyes and listen. But that's just melodrama. If you weren't alive at the time, how do you know what you'd have done? And none of you seem to have any memories of your own. We all have a fantastic store: and I don't just mean good memories, I don't just mean the comradeship, there's a word you can hardly use nowadays without smirking, I don't just mean falling in love with your mother. I mean a gorge near Mycenae jammed with dead horses, or the corpse of an old man floating down the Grand Canal, or those two partisans I saw strung up beside the road as we moved down out of Norway, eyes gone but so white and graceful. We lived so many lifetimes in that short span, in some ways, you see, it did last a thousand years.

ANNA: First you blame us for remembering, then you blame us for not remembering.

RÖTHLING: You're quite right, it's not your fault. I sometimes think the reason your generation's so dim and cautious is that we used up all the risks. We drank so deep of history, there's very little left in the bottle.

ANNA: Have they sent you the file again, is that what's caused this bout of nostalgia for the Reich? *(*RÖTHLING *nods, smiling suavely in acknowledgment of her barb.)* Why?

RÖTHLING: Someone in Bonn has panicked.

ANNA: Must be another false alarm, isn't it? He can't possibly still be alive.

RÖTHLING: I don't know why you say that. May I remind you, when you were a child, we were governed by a Chancellor almost as old as he would be now. And governed in exemplary fashion. I don't say that makes it likely.

ANNA: Wasn't there some talk of a double?

RÖTHLING: No, no, he was entirely unmistakable. I saw him myself once in a military hospital on the Eastern Front. Apart from anything else, that skin . . . *(He breaks off. Pause.)*

I've asked Rolf to come over to discuss one or two things. I shan't keep him long. I'll send him in to see you when we've finished.

ANNA: I don't know why it amuses you to imagine Rolf and I will get married. Just because he's your assistant.

RÖTHLING: It wasn't my suggestion. And as a matter of fact it doesn't amuse me to imagine you marrying anybody.

(Silence.)

ANNA: I wonder if Herr Hitler's still a bachelor.

RÖTHLING: The last one they found, in that house for senior citizens in upstate New York, was married. And circumcised.

ANNA: Isn't it tiresome to have to go through it all again?

RÖTHLING: Not entirely. For one thing it vindicates the point I made originally, in Munich, when they pronounced him dead, you know, *re* the estate of Paula Hitler. You remember, I objected most strenuously. I begged them to invoke the doctrine of *ratio mortalis.*

ANNA: What's that?

RÖTHLING: The reasonably expected span of mortal life. They wouldn't listen. It's going to be a little difficult, now, insisting on the extradition of someone who's legally dead, wouldn't you think?

(He smiles complacently. A light tap on the door and ROLF HANFMANN *enters, a tall, bespectacled young man carrying a briefcase, earnest and deferential in manner. He crosses to* RÖTHLING *arm outstretched and shakes hands with him, bowing as he does so.)*

HANFMANN: Herr Doktor. *(He puts his briefcase down, then crosses to* ANNA *and pecks her a touch awkwardly on the cheek.)* All right?

ANNA: Yes.

HANFMANN: How's the library?

ANNA: My new children's section is almost ready to open.

HANFMANN: And Fräulein Schalktritt?

ANNA: We're still on speaking terms, just about.

RÖTHLING: Run along now, dear, I shan't keep Rolf for long.

ANNA: Very well, Papa.

(She leaves promptly, apparently almost relieved to go. HANFMANN *sits adjacent to his briefcase, which he leans forward and opens.)*

RÖTHLING: Cognac?

HANFMANN: Thank you, no.

RÖTHLING: Have you drafted the abrogation of the Munich ruling?

HANFMANN: Here, sir. *(He hands a folder to* RÖTHLING.*)* And I've also made a start on drawing up a list of the possible effects of his Austrian nationality.

RÖTHLING: Good. Any comments?

HANFMANN: Not about that, sir, it's complicated but relatively straightforward; no, there's something else I . . .

RÖTHLING: Yes?

HANFMANN: I've been thinking about the conduct of the trial itself.

RÖTHLING: Go on.

HANFMANN: Since the case is quite unprecedented, I've been wondering whether our legal system is sufficiently flexible to deal with it. Isn't this an opportunity to frame some new legislation, to consider, for example, the institution of some new kind of court?

RÖTHLING: No, no, that's the kind of reasoning that led to that disorderly escapade with Eichmann. There are no two ways about it, you see. Either the codex applies to Herr Hitler just the same as it does to anyone else, or you find yourself in danger of supporting his claim that he was above the law. You know my reservations about the Nürnberg trials. *Post facto* law, badly argued. But they did honor a crucial principle: everyone is subject to the law from a hit-and-run driver to Attila the Hun.

HANFMANN: Yes, but surely Attila's crimes were not simply the crimes of one man. That's the point I'd like to see taken into account. What Hitler did required the active support of millions.

(RÖTHLING*'s reply is perceptibly chilly.)*

RÖTHLING: That is an entirely irrelevant consideration. Particularly as we have a perfectly adequate law which has been in existence for hundreds of years. I refer to the concept of the *corpus mysticum* of the ruler, whereby the state is deemed to reside in the actual body of the monarch.

(Silence, during which HANFMANN *decides not to risk developing his point.)*

HANFMANN: Anyway, these rumors can't possibly be true, can they, sir?

RÖTHLING: No, quite. *(Pause.)* I believe you'll find Anna in the drawing room. Unless there's anything else. I have one or two things to attend to, if you'll excuse me.

HANFMANN: Of course.

(They rise. HANFMANN *picks up his briefcase.* RÖTHLING *escorts him to the door, puts an arm loosely round his shoulders.)*

RÖTHLING: This whole Hitler business, you know, it's all greatly exaggerated. It's a kind of upside-down sentimentality, worrying about the whys and wherefores. People who do think they're making profound statements on behalf of the dead. They aren't. They're just puffing up their own little lives. You wouldn't know, you weren't even born. But I can't help wondering if it really was as important as all that.

(They shake hands at the door and HANFMANN *leaves.* RÖTHLING *crosses to the drinks cabinet and pours himself a large snifter of brandy. He puts the glass down on the table beside his chair and moves over to the record player. He starts the turntable, returns to his chair, sits down, lifts the glass, drinks, and smiles to himself, waiting. The Resurrection Ode booms out:* "Aufersteh'n, ja, aufersteh'n wirst du . . ."*)*

SCENE 12

The Mahler continues in the darkness, gradually drowned by the sounds of the jungle and the rain.

Night. The same location as scene 10. The dim shapes of HITLER, ASHER, *and* AMSEL *asleep.* SIMEON *is on watch, or at any rate standing, huddled under a rain cape lost in thought. He starts as* ELIE *materializes out of the darkness at his elbow.*

ELIE: Sleep. You need to. I'll watch.

SIMEON: We're going on tomorrow, rain or no rain.

ELIE: I don't think we can move in this.

SIMEON: No choice. We've had to loop around the swamp, and we're still not back on course. It's going to take us at least a week to reach Jiaro, and who knows what state the supplies there will be in?

ELIE: All the same, we're all very low . . .

SIMEON: Except for him. No fever, sleeps like a baby, even walking better.

ELIE: Yes.

SIMEON: All day, you know, since we stopped carrying him, I listen for his footsteps behind me. At first I couldn't distinguish them from yours and the others, but now I can tell: they're lighter. And surer. He never stumbles. *(Silence.)* We may have to do it ourselves, after all. *(Silence.)* Talk to me about something else.

(ELIE *reflects for a moment.)*

ELIE: You know there's a theory that when God dictated the Torah to Rabbi Jehudah Ben Levi, the Rabbi made a mistake, just one tiny error, which opened a breach through which evil seeped down to envelop the earth. It may only be a letter, a *yod* or a *gimel,* a figure or an accent, or a single word. But which word?

SIMEON: Well?

ELIE: Isaac of Saragossa decided the mistake was in Genesis 22, verse 1: God might command an old man to sacrifice his child, but He would never *tempt* him to do so. And in 1709,

Nathaniel Ben Nathaniel of Danzig conjectured that Rabbi Jehudah must have misheard Exodus 15, verse 20. He argued that though it was right to dance in front of Pharaoh's drowning host, it must surely have been wrong to *strike timbrels.*

SIMEON: And what's your suggestion?

ELIE: My master, Shelomo Bartov, who soon afterwards was burnt at Grodno, told us the word which unleashed all our ills. He said it was the word *and* in Leviticus 10, verse 5. He spoke with such sadness.

SIMEON: But why? Why that word?

ELIE: I asked him. He was angry. He called me a dunce. Why that word, he said. For the reason deeper than reason that it could be any other.

SCENE 13

Late afternoon. The bedroom of V*'s apartment in Paris: elegant but messy, cluttered with bric-à-brac.* BLAISE JOSQUIN, *in his fifties, formal in manner, is knotting his impeccable tie, crouching slightly to take advantage of the dressing table mirror.* V, *thirtyish, is still in bed, watching him, her expression a trace sullen.* JOSQUIN *finishes with his tie, takes a comb from the pocket of his jacket, which is arranged neatly over the back of a chair, and begins the unnecessary task of combing his hair. He breaks off to gesture with some distaste at the dressing table which is awash with pots, tubes and bottles, many of them left open.*

JOSQUIN: I don't know how you can bear to live like this.

V: It's not at all difficult.

*(*JOSQUIN *finishes combing his hair and replaces the comb. He turns to* V.*)*

JOSQUIN: I hope that was all right. I'm afraid just at the moment my mind tends to be elsewhere.

V: Up the Amazon.

JOSQUIN: You might say so.

V: I don't mind. Actually, your body works better when it's here on its own.

JOSQUIN: Yes, I'm feeling better.

V: Good.

JOSQUIN: More indifferent. Better. Only I can't stand having any dealings with Berdier. All those gold chains and loafers and electronic lighters. But he's a gorilla. It always makes me nervous when they bring him in. *(*JOSQUIN *sits on the stool in front of the dressing table and looks across at* V *for a moment.)* My son, Edmond, gave me a fright at breakfast this morning: he suddenly asked me if I'd ever seen Hitler. For a moment I thought there must have been a leak, but it turned out he'd seen some television film last night. So I told him, yes, I had seen him once, at Montoire.

V: I know.

JOSQUIN: He was on his way back from Spain, from what *I* think was the real turning point of the war.

V: You told me.

JOSQUIN: Yes, but I've never been able to fathom why Franco should have refused to give them access to Gibraltar. He was supposed to be their ally; they put him there. How could he have been so cunning?

V: At least *he*'s not still alive.

JOSQUIN: What I remember most about Hitler was the terrible tedium streaming off him like cold air out of a vacuum. As if he was just unspeakably bored with his fame and the vast machinery he'd set in motion and the futility of it all. *(He grunts, lapsing into reverie for a moment.* V *gets up and starts dressing.)* I don't know what to do about Edmond's acne. He glows like a lighthouse. I never had anything like that. I must get my wife to take him to a specialist.

V: Do we have to talk about your children?

JOSQUIN: Sorry.

(Silence.)

V: Are you going to Brazil?

JOSQUIN: Looks like it.

V: You want to tell me about it?

JOSQUIN: We had a very useful meeting today. I mean, we're all agreed on what we don't want. We don't want the Jews to get him, because they'll take him to Israel which at the time of the crimes had no *de facto* existence; we don't want the Brazilians to get him, of course, because nobody understands their extradition laws, least of all the Brazilians themselves; and we don't want the Americans to get him, well, because we don't want the Americans to get him. This is a four-power matter. Which is fine, except that it means dealing with the Russians, who pretend they couldn't care less, while in fact obstructing every initiative we take.

V: But are you agreed on what you do want?

JOSQUIN: Well, naturally, we've agreed there's only one appropriate venue for the trial. The European Court at Strasbourg. But there is an alternative that's been proposed, and that's that there shouldn't be a trial at all.

v: No trial?

JOSQUIN: Well, the argument is that it would just open a lot of old wounds and turn over a lot of stones best left unturned, you know, Vichy, the French camps. Also, what kind of a mad old scarecrow must he be by now? A trial would hardly be a very edifying spectacle. Although it would be interesting to hear that voice again.

v: If there's no trial . . . I mean, what else can you do with him?

JOSQUIN: Well, that's where Berdier comes in. The special section. A discreetly organized accident. "We mustn't let those crazy Jews out of the woods" was the way Berdier put it. Save everyone a lot of trouble and expense. I argued against it of course. Said I thought it would be political folly. But I have to say the Chef de Cabinet seemed intrigued by the idea. *(*v *has finished dressing by now. She moves to stand behind* JOSQUIN, *rests her hands for a moment on his shoulders. Then she ruffles his hair.)* Don't do that! *(He gets up and moves over to the dressing table.)* I wish you wouldn't. Really.

(He crouches in front of the mirror, combing his hair, annoyed. v *stands watching him, her expression coolly unsympathetic.)*

SCENE 14

Dawn. A clearing. The rain has eased off but is still a presence. Upstage, the smouldering embers of a fire. AMSEL *is sitting by the fire alone, knees drawn up to his chin. He's crying.*

ELIE *is clearing up, packing, preparing to leave. He looks hollow-eyed and exhausted.*

HITLER *is downstage left, squatting patiently, tethered to a stake by the long rope, watching* AMSEL.

SIMEON *and* ASHER *are downstage right, conversing in low voices.*

SIMEON: What was it like? In Hertfordshire?

ASHER: What?

SIMEON: At Bishop Romney's Grammar School, wasn't it?

ASHER: How do you know?

SIMEON: Lieber made me learn all the dossiers by heart before he burnt them.

ASHER: Oh. Well, it was all right. I used to like being in the school play, except I never got the parts I wanted. I played Macduff. Whose family is wiped out by the, what is it, fell kite? Hell-kite? Something like that. The boy who played Lady Macduff had a falsetto could peel the skin off an apple. Mm. *(Pause.)* What you really mean is, what the hell am I doing here?

SIMEON: Well, I know, technically, I mean, according to the Talmud, you aren't Jewish.

ASHER: Yes, but I spent a lot of time with my father. His flat in Ladbroke Grove . . .

SIMEON: Yes.

ASHER: It's just I took a notion to it. I couldn't think of anything that interested me more.

SIMEON: And you've kept the thread. Not like the rest of us. We're more or less off our heads. But you're still tied to the outside world. Like that man in the story in the labyrinth. You've kept the thread unbroken. *(He breaks off. A strangled sob from* AMSEL. ELIE *goes across to him and puts his arm around him, murmuring words of comfort.* HITLER *watches them intently.)* He'll be all right. When Gideon died, it was like losing his father all over again. *(He looks across at* HITLER.*)* And he seems to get stronger every day. Our friend. *(He turns back to* ASHER.*)* What I'm saying. Elie and I are finished. Like in that play. *(He smiles.)* Not all the perfumes of Arabia. But you. You get him out. Him and the boy.

ASHER: All right.

(Both of them spin round as TEKU *suddenly appears in the clearing. He's carrying a small bunch of wild flowers. He ignores* SIMEON *and* ASHER *completely and moves right across the stage to* HITLER. *He hands the flowers to him, ceremoniously.* HITLER *takes them.* TEKU *bows to* HITLER, *his expression respectful.* HITLER *nods graciously.)*

HITLER: *Blumen.*

SCENE 15

The crackle of the radio; garbled voices in various languages; finally, one voice, imposing itself.

Lights up on KULKEN*'s hut.* KULKEN *sits in front of his transmitter, headphones on, bewildered expression.* CROWNBACKER *stands beside him listening to an extension headphone, one earpiece of which he holds casually up to his ear.*

KULKEN: What language is that?

CROWNBACKER: Russian, you dumb asshole. *(*KULKEN *listens a moment, perturbed.)* Now do you believe me?

KULKEN: I'm beginning to.

*(*CROWNBACKER *glances at his watch.)*

CROWNBACKER: Come on, turn it around.

*(*KULKEN *reaches forward and turns a dial. The Russian voice disappears to be replaced by flashes of other sound as* KULKEN *adjusts the tuning. Soon he arrives and stops at a reedy English voice.)*

VOICE: . . . kyrie, hello, Siegfried, this is Valkyrie. Are you receiving me? Come in, please. Do you read me, Siegfried? Over.

KULKEN: Hello, Valkyrie, this is Siegfried. Reading you loud and clear. Over.

VOICE: Some rather urgent instructions for you: now the rain has broken, we want you to clear and drain the airfield.

KULKEN: What with, a bucket?

VOICE: We shall be sending in four senior personnel, so would you please organize appropriate quarters for them? Confirm. Over.

KULKEN: This isn't Acapulco, you know. *(*CROWNBACKER *shakes his head. Then he mimes acquiescence, smiling and nodding.)* Roger. Will do. Over.

VOICE: We don't want you to think we're in any way dissatisfied with the job you've done. On the contrary, Head Office have asked me to pass on their congratulations and let it be known you'll be receiving a bonus . . .

KULKEN: Bastards.

VOICE: There's a light aircraft on the strip, what information do you have about this? Over.

*(*CROWNBACKER *shakes his head, finger on his lips.)*

KULKEN: None. Over.

VOICE: Someone must have turned up in Orosso since your arrival? Who? Over.

*(*CROWNBACKER *sticks out his tongue and draws a finger across his throat.)*

KULKEN: Must return to monitoring Russian signal. Will report again 1800 hours. Over and out.

(He spins the dial and flicks the switch, throws down his headphones and gets up, sighing exasperatedly. CROWNBACKER *puts down his headphones.)*

CROWNBACKER: I think you must hate him even worse than you hate me.

KULKEN *(muttering):* Touch and go.

CROWNBACKER: Listen, who gave you this chance?

KULKEN: The CIA, I imagine.

CROWNBACKER: What?

KULKEN: Don't waste time denying it. If you're a radio ham, I'm Colonel Fawcett. What I want to know is have you been told to limit yourself to two-bit deals with the media, or are you just naturally petty-minded?

CROWNBACKER: I don't know what you're talking about.

KULKEN: What's going to happen to him after he's done his interview with the *New York Times?*

CROWNBACKER: I guess they'll take him back to the States. Who cares?

KULKEN: That's exactly what I'm saying.

CROWNBACKER: I agreed to let your Indians kill the goddamn Jews, didn't I? And we could have marketed their stories as well.

KULKEN: Stories! It's governments we should be dealing with, not bloody editors. You assume we'll just let him go back to America, but why shouldn't we see if the Russians would pay more? Why shouldn't we auction him? The British and French would make a joint offer, then start quarreling. The two Germanies would bid against each other. And what about Israel? See what I mean? Bit more bloody exciting than negotiating the serialization rights with the *Daily Express.*

(CROWNBACKER *broods for a moment.)*

CROWNBACKER: I like to keep things simple.

KULKEN: That's what makes us different, Mr. Crownbacker. *(Pause.* KULKEN*'s voice takes on a more businesslike edge.)* Right. Let me just find out what's happening. I tell you, now the rain's stopped, we don't have much time. *(He crosses to the doorway where the* INDIAN WOMAN *waits with a young* INDIAN *dressed in the cast-off rags of civilization. He dismisses the* WOMAN *and begins speaking to the* INDIAN *in a low voice.* CROWNBACKER *slaps wearily at his arm The* WOMAN *comes into the hut and crosses the room. As she passes* CROWNBACKER, *he suddenly flings out an arm and puts it up inside her dress. She stands there passively for a moment, her expression stoical. Then* CROWNBACKER *withdraws his arm and she continues on her way.* KULKEN *comes back into the hut, thoughtful. The* INDIAN *has vanished.)* They've stopped. Haven't moved for two days. The old one, he says, and four white men.

CROWNBACKER: Four?

KULKEN: There's an Indian with them too. A forest Indian. Apparently he's carving some kind of a chair.

CROWNBACKER: A chair?

KULKEN: That's right. So. I've told them to go in, kill them all, and fetch us out old Schickelgruber.

CROWNBACKER: Is Hitler still okay?

KULKEN: He says the old one looks fine. On the other hand. *(Pause.)* Can you hear anything? *(They listen. Maybe, very faintly, a distant, splintering crash.)* He told me he could hear it.

CROWNBACKER: Well, what is it?

KULKEN: Tree fall.

SCENE 16

The light finds TEKU *who is putting the finishing touches to a ceremonial stool, its flat surface shaped to suggest a condor in flight, its legs carved with an abstract motif representing the anteater sigil. He oils it lovingly, caressing the smooth wood. The landscape is more open now between the jungle and the Cordillera and the encampment looks less transitory. The rain has stopped, and there's a hint of coolness in the air from the nearby mountains, although the roar of the jungle is louder than ever.* HITLER *sits downstage, impassive as ever; he's no longer tethered to the stake, but his wrists are tied together.* AMSEL *stands not far off watching him.* SIMEON, *who looks ill and exhausted, is sitting on an empty crate, which is covered by a grey blanket.* ASHER *and* ELIE *move downstage, deep in conversation.*

ASHER: Why me?

ELIE: You know what the wisdom books say of your tribe, the tribe of Asher? A stubborn folk. Who else is there? Simeon must judge. He's the leader of the party. He knows in his own mind why the trial must take place.

ASHER: Why must it?

ELIE: Supplies are low. We still have the mountains to cross. Who knows what chaos waits on the other side? Simeon has prepared, he knows the words which have to be spoken. In any case, he and I, we're dying.

ASHER: No.

ELIE: So Simeon must judge. I must read the Law, blessed be its Name. And the boy. Gideon's death has made him even more self-important. He and the Indian must be the witnesses. And you must defend.

ASHER: I . . .

ELIE: You know about fairness. You know how a man is innocent until proven guilty, in the real world. *(He smiles.)* The real world.

ASHER: But I'm no lawyer.

ELIE: True. We have only ash in hand to kindle a great fire. He of Asher whose name is also in Manasseh.

ASHER: This is just posturing. It's really not far now. Lieber is probably already in Orosso.

ELIE: No. Those waiting for us across the mountains are not ours. Teku is a sign. *(He points to* TEKU, *who is still working.)* To see the trial of a man who sought to banish God, blessed be His name, from creation, a witness out of Eden. *(*ASHER *looks around, smiling bitterly.)*

ASHER: Eden?

ELIE: I know. But still the nearest place to it left on earth. There have been, haven't there, instances?

ASHER: Yes. *(Pause.)* All right.

*(*TEKU *rises, admires his handiwork for a moment, then picks up the stool and moves to put it down center stage.* HITLER *looks up, frowning, sensing something is afoot.* ELIE *crosses to* SIMEON. *They confer for a moment in murmurs. Then* SIMEON *rises.)*

SIMEON: Amsel.

*(*AMSEL *rests his submachine gun against the lean-to and moves swiftly over towards* HITLER *drawing a short, broad knife. He takes* HITLER *by the elbow and stands him up, none too gently.* HITLER*'s eyes blaze. For a moment they stand looking at each other, the old man and the boy with a knife. Then* AMSEL *cuts the rope which binds* HITLER*'s wrists.* ASHER *crosses to join them.* SIMEON *sits down.* ELIE *sits on the ground beside him.* TEKU *moves right downstage and squats, looking back at the stool.* AMSEL *sheathes his knife, moves back to the lean-to, sits down on the ground and reaches over for his gun, which he rests across his knees.* HITLER *glares at* ASHER *for a moment, then looks away and begins gently chafing his right wrist. Tableau.)*

SCENE 17

Tremendous confusion of noise and flashing of bulbs. Television lights blaze up on AVERY LOCKYER, *the Secretary of State, who stands on a rostrum behind a lectern with the presidential seal. He's impeccable in his alpaca suit and raw silk tie, his tan enhanced by a liberal application of makeup. He blinks complacently in the light, smiles skillfully and raises a hand.*

LOCKYER: Ladies and gentlemen, please. One at a time. Please. *(He pauses for a moment, then points.)* Yes?
(A voice rises above the hubbub.)

VOICE: Riffler, *St. Louis Post Dispatch.* Mr. Secretary, is this story true?

LOCKYER: Well, Mr. Riffler, I wish we were in a situation to be able to finalize an answer on that. There does, however, seem to be a reasonable expectation that the man found by what I want to emphasize is a strictly unofficial pursuit party is, yes, the Head of State of the so-called Third Reich.

VOICE: Escomb, *Time* magazine. Sir, do we have anyone on the spot right now?

LOCKYER: I'm sure you'll understand, Bill, that it's against the interests of our government to go into details on that right at this moment. But I can say that on both global and local levels our position is one of extreme readiness.

VOICE: Mr. Secretary, you . . . sorry, Cord Dwyer, *Milwaukee Tribune.* Are you in contact with other governments on this?

LOCKYER: Of course, if Mr. Hitler is positively identified, this will be a matter for international response. All the sovereign states party to the Berlin agreements are involved. So is Brazil, on whose territory the putative Reichschancellor was found. The German Democratic Republic and the German Federal Republic are naturally both extremely interested, as is the Republic of Austria in which the subject was born and from time to time domiciled. I have instructed our Ambassador to the United Nations to . . .

VOICE: What about Israel? *(Silence.)* Why don't you mention Israel, Mr. Secretary of State? He's our prisoner.

(LOCKYER *shades his eyes against the light and peers into the auditorium.)*

LOCKYER: Mr. Simon, is that?

VOICE: Yes.

LOCKYER: Mr. Simon, to date our exchanges with your government on this entire matter have been less than satisfactory. So far as we're aware, and this comprises this morning's cables, your government has taken no official note of Mr. Hitler's apprehension and has made no clarification of its position in respect of a possible trial before a multinational court. In the meantime, this Administration will continue to give the most favorable possible consideration to Israeli concerns.

VOICE: Suppose we get him out on our own?

LOCKYER: That's a hypothetical question, Mr. Simon. It would be irresponsible of me to comment.

VOICE: Gene Jefferson, *Atlanta Constitution.* Mr. Secretary, are Hitler's crimes covered by the statute of limitations?

LOCKYER: The ideal of common law precedents is enshrined in our way of life in these United States and in the policies of this department, and we certainly hold no brief for special retroactive law. However, you will recall that with regard to what have been defined as "crimes against humanity," the statute of limitations has been specifically voided. The current eventuality would appear to emphatically exemplify this category. I should add that we would hope to initiate proper psychiatric checks as soon as possible.

VOICE: Tylden. AP. How do the Russians feel?

LOCKYER: I'd prefer to withhold comment on that, Ed.

VOICE: Mr. Secretary, Anne Carey, *Miami Herald.* Why don't we just send in a helicopter and bring them right out?

LOCKYER: I wish life were that simple, Miss Carey. All the same I want to assure you we're doing everything we can. We're monitoring the situation hourly, and you can be sure my department will keep you informed of any developments of any kind. Thank you. Thank you.

VOICE: Sir, can you give us an assurance due process will be followed? Will the accused be given every legal aid for his defense?

(Blackout.)

SCENE 18

As at the end of scene 16. The murmur of voices gives way to the strident chorus of the jungle. ASHER, *upstage of* HITLER, *takes a step forward and clears his throat uncertainly.*

ASHER: My client would like to . . .

HITLER: Speak.

LIEBER'S VOICE: Mordechai Zathsmar, Leah Burstein, Jakov Kaplan, Rahel Nadelmann, Ruth Levin, Lilian Gourevitch, George Benjamin Dorfmann, Ann Casanova, Samuel Rossbach, Hagadio.

HITLER: First point. *(He raises a hand. The jungle falls silent.)* You must understand that I did not invent. Adolf Hitler dreamed up the master race. He conceived of enslaving inferior peoples. Lies. Lies. It was in the dosshouse I first understood. It was in. God help me. And the lice. Large as a thumb nail. 1910, 1911? What's it matter? It was there I first understood your secret power. *Your* teaching. A chosen people. Chosen by God for His own. The only race on earth chosen, exalted, made singular among Mankind. Grill taught me. You know about Grill? No. You know nothing about me. Jahn Grill. Not that that was his name. Said he was a defrocked priest. For all I know he may have been. That too. But his name was Jacob. Jacob Grill, son of a rabbi, from Poland. Or Galicia. Or. What's it matter? One of yours. We lived close. One sliver of soap between us. It was Grill who showed me the words. The chosen people. God's own and elect among the welter of nations. My promise was only a thousand years. Grill said, to eternity, lo, it is written here. In letters of white fire. The setting apart of the race, like unto no other. Jacob Grill, friend Grill, and Neumann, for whom I painted postcards, they smelt of shit. But they taught me. That a true nation is a mystery, a single body willed by God, by history and the unmingled burning of its blood. You could hear the lice crack between Grill's fingers. God how his breath stank. But he read from the book. Your book. Of which every letter is sacred and every mite of every letter. That's so, isn't it? Read till lights out, and after, sing-song through his nose, because he knew it by heart, from his schooldays. "They utterly destroyed all that was in the city." In Samaria. Because the Samaritans read a different scripture. Because they had built a sanctuary of their own. Of terebinth. Six cubits to the left. They made it seven or five or God knows. Put to the sword. The first time. Every man, woman, child, she-ox, dog. No. No dogs. They are of the unclean things that hop or crawl on the earth, like the Philistine, the unclean of Moab, the lepers of Sidon. To slaughter a city because of an idea, because of a vexation over words. *That* was a high invention, a device to alter the human soul. Your invention. One Israel, one Volk, one leader. Moses, Joshua, the anointed king who has slain his thousands, no his ten thousands, and dances now before the ark. It was in Compiègne, wasn't it? They say I danced. Only a small dance.

The pride of it, the brute cunning. Whatever you are, be it ulcerous as Job, or Neumann scratching his stinking crotch. You should have seen the two of us peddling those postcards. But what does it matter as long as you're one of the chosen people? That's what Grill told me. Jahn Jacob Grillschmuhl Grill or whatever his greasy name was, reeking of piss as he crawled up the stairs. Even he. The apostate. The outcast from Zion. Was still of the chosen. "Listen, Adi, you think you see me as I am, a dosshouse bum. But you're blind. All you goyim are blind. For all you know, Adi, I might be one of the seventy-two chosen, chosen even above the chosen. One of the secret, just ones on whom the earth rests. And listen to me, Adi, here in this barrack, right here, my blind friend, the Messiah may come to me and know me for his own." Then he would roll his eyes and give a little laugh. Which went through me like a knife. But I learnt.

From you. Everything. To set a race apart. To keep it from defilement. To hold before it a promised land. To scour that land of its inhabitants or place them in servitude. Your beliefs.

Your arrogance. In Nuremberg, the searchlights. That clever beaver Speer.[11] Straight into the night. Do you remember? The pillar of fire. That shall lead you to Canaan. And woe unto the Amorites, the Jebusites, the Kenites, the half-men outside God's pact. Rosenberg's[12] Superman. Secondhand stuff. They whispered to me that *he* too. The name. My racism was a parody of yours, a hungry imitation. What is a thousand-year Reich compared to the eternity of Zion? Perhaps I was the false Messiah sent before. Judge me and you must judge yourselves. *Übermenschen.* Chosen ones.

ASHER: What my client means . . .

HITLER: Point Two. There had to be a solution, a *final* solution. For what is the Jew if he is not a long cancer of unrest? I beg your attention, gentlemen, I demand it. Was there ever a crueler invention, a contrivance more calculated to harrow human existence, than that of an omnipotent, all-seeing, yet invisible, impalpable, inconceivable God? Consider the case, gentlemen, consider it closely. The pagan earth was crowded with small deities, malicious or consoling, winged or pot-bellied, in leaf and branch, in rock and river. Giving companionship to man, pinching his bottom or caressing him, but of his measure. Delighting in honey cakes or roast meat. Gods after our own image and necessities. The Jew emptied the world by setting his God apart, immeasurably apart from man's senses. No image. No imagining even. A blank emptier than the desert. Yet with a terrible nearness. Spying on our every misdeed, searching out the heart of our heart for motive. A God of vengeance unto the thirtieth generation—these are the Jews' words, not mine. A god of contracts and petty bargains, of indentures and bribes. "And the Lord gave Job twice as much as he had before." A thousand she-asses where the crazed, boiled old man had only five hundred to start with. Gentlemen, do

11. Albert Speer: Hitler's Minister of Armaments and chief architect; convicted at Nuremberg of war crimes and sentenced to twenty years in Spandau prison.

12. Alfred Rosenberg: Germany's chief antisemitic ideologue and chief exponent of Aryan superiority (the *Übermensch*).

you grasp the sliminess of it, the moral trickery? Why didn't Job spit at that cattle-dealer of a God? Yet the holy of holies was an empty room, a silence in a silence. The Jew mocks those who have pictures of their god. *His* God is purer than any other. And because we are His creatures, we must be better than ourselves, love our neighbor, be continent, give of what we have to the beggar. We must obey every jot of the law. We must bottle up our rages and desires, chastise the flesh and walk bent in the rain. You call me a tyrant, an enslaver. What tyranny and what enslavement have been more oppressive than the sick fantasies of the Jew? You are not Godkillers, but *Godmakers.* And that is infinitely worse. The Jew invented conscience.

But that was only the first piece of blackmail. There was worse to come. The white-faced Nazarene. Gentlemen, I find it difficult to contain myself. But the facts must speak for themselves. What did that epileptic rabbi ask of man? That he renounce the world, that he leave father and mother behind, that he offer the other cheek, that he render good for evil, that he love his neighbor as himself, no, better, for self-love is an evil. Oh, grand castration! Note the cunning of it. Demand of human beings more than they can give, and you will make of them cripples, hypocrites, mendicants for salvation. The Nazarene said his kingdom was not of this world. Honeyed lies. It was here on earth he founded his slave-church. It was men and women he abandoned to the blackmail of hell, of eternal punishment. What were our camps compared to *that?* What could be crueler than the Jew's addiction to the ideal?

First, the invisible but all-seeing, the unattainable but all-demanding God of Sinai. Second, the terrible sweetness of Christ. Had the Jew not done enough to sicken man? No, gentlemen, there is a third act to our story.

"Sacrifice yourself for the good of your fellow man. Relinquish your possessions so that there may be equality for all. Hammer yourself hard as steel. Denounce parent or lover. So that justice may be achieved on earth. So that history be fulfilled and society be purged of all imperfection." Recognize the sermon, gentlemen? The litany of hatred? Rabbi Marx on the day of atonement. Was there ever a greater promise? "Classless society, to each according to his needs, brotherhood for all mankind, the earth made a garden again, a rational Eden." In the name of which tyranny, torture, war, extermination were a necessity, a historical necessity! It's no accident Marx and his minions were Jews—Trotsky, Rosa Luxemburg, Kamenev, the whole murderous pack. Look at them: prophets, martyrs, word-spinners, smashers of images, drunk with the terror of the absolute. It was only a step, gentlemen, a small inevitable step from Sinai to Nazareth, from Nazareth to the covenant of Marxism. The Jew had grown impatient: let the kingdom of justice come here and now, next Monday morning.

Three times the Jew has pressed on us the blackmail of transcendence. Three times he has infected our blood and brains with the bacillus of perfection. Men had grown sick of it, sick to death. When I turned on the Jew, no one came to his rescue. No one. France, England, Russia, even Jew-ridden America did nothing. They were glad the exterminator had come. They didn't say so openly, I grant you that. But secretly they rejoiced. We had to find, to burn out the virus of utopia before the whole of western civilization sickened. To return to man as he is. Selfish, greedy, short-sighted, but marvellously housed in his own stench. The Jew said: "We were chosen to be the conscience of man." And I answered, yes, I, gentlemen, who stand before you: "You are not man's conscience, Jew. You are only his bad conscience. And we shall vomit you so we may live and have peace." A final solution. How could there be any other?

ASHER: The question the defendant is raising . . .

HITLER: Don't interrupt. I won't tolerate interruption. I'm an old man. My voice is tired. I appeal to your sense of justice. Hear me out. *(Silence.)* Third point. You have exaggerated. Grossly. Hysterically. You've made me out some mad devil, the quintessence of evil, hell embodied. When in truth I was only a man of my time.

Average, if you will. Had I been the singular demon of your fantasies, how could millions of ordinary men and women have found in me the mirror, the plain mirror of their appetites? It was, I will allow, an ugly time. But I did not create its ugliness, and I was not the worst. Far from it. How many wretched little men of the forests did your Belgian friends murder outright or leave to starvation and syphilis when they raped the Congo? Some *twenty* million. That picnic was under way when I was newborn. What were Rotterdam or Coventry compared to Dresden and Hiroshima? Did I invent the camps? Ask the Boers. But let's be serious. Who was it that broke the Reich? To whom did you hand over millions, tens of millions of men and women from Prague to the Baltic? Set them like a bowl of milk before an insatiable cat? I was a small man compared to *him.* Yes, Stalin slaughtered *thirty* million. He perfected genocide when I was still a nameless scribbler in Munich. My boys used their fists and whips, I don't deny it. The times stank of hunger and blood. But when a man spat out the truth they'd stop their fun. Stalin's torturers worked for the pleasure of the thing. To make men befoul themselves and obtain confessions which were obscene jokes. It is not I who assert these things: it is your own survivors, your historians. It is the sage of the Gulag archipelago. Ribbentrop told me what contempt he had for us. He found us amateurish, corrupt with mercy. Our camps covered absurd acres; he strung wire and death pits round a continent. Who survived among those who had fought with him, brought him to power, executed his will? Not one. He smashed their bones to the last splinter. When my fall came, my good companions were alive, fat, scuttling for safety or recompense, cavorting towards you with their contritions and their memoirs. How many Jews did Stalin kill? Answer me that. Had he not died when he did, there wouldn't have been one of you left alive between Berlin and Vladivostok. Yet when Stalin died in bed, the world stood hushed before the tiger's rest. Whereas you hunt me down like a rabid dog, drag me through swamps, tie me up at night. Who am a very old man and uncertain of recollection. Small game, gentlemen, hardly worthy of your skills. In a world that tortures prisoners and pours napalm on naked villagers. That continues to do these things quite without my help.

ASHER: I . . . think there is some validity . . .

HITLER: Don't trouble yourself, Herr Advokat. I have only one more point to make. The last. That strange book, *Der Judenstaat.*[13] I read it carefully. A clever book, I agree. Shaping Zionism in the image of the new German nation. But did Herzl create Israel? Or did I? Examine the question fairly. Would Palestine have become Israel, would the Jews have come to that barren patch in the Levant, would the United States *and* the Soviet Union, *Stalin's* Soviet Union have given you recognition and guaranteed your survival, had it not been for the Holocaust? It was the Holocaust that gave you the courage of injustice, that made you drive the Arab out of his home, out of his field, because he was lice-eaten and without resource, because he was in your divinely ordered way. That made you endure knowing that those whom you had driven out were rotting in refugee camps, not ten miles away, buried alive in despair and lunatic dreams of vengeance. Perhaps I *am* the Messiah, the true Messiah, the new Sabbatai,[14] whose infamous deeds were allowed by God in order to bring his people home. "The Holocaust was the necessary mystery before Israel could come into its strength." It wasn't I who said that, but your own visionaries, your unravelers of God's meaning on a Friday night in Jerusalem. Should you not honor me? Who have made you into men of war, who have made of the long, vacuous daydream of Zion a reality? Should you not be a comfort to my old age?

13. Theodor Herzl's 1896 volume, central to Zionism, advocating the founding of a homeland for the Jews.

14. Sabbatai Zevi: the most famous of a number of false messiahs who appeared in the late seventeenth century in eastern Europe.

So, gentlemen of the tribunal:

I took my doctrines from you.

I fought the blackmail of the ideal with which you have hounded mankind.

My crimes were matched and surpassed by those of others.

The Reich begat Israel.

These are my last words.

(Silence. In which HITLER *crosses calmly to the stool and sits. For a moment after that, nobody moves. Then suddenly,* TEKU *crosses swiftly and drops to one knee in front of* HITLER, *who ignores him.* TEKU *hears something and looks up, sharply. A few seconds pass, then, faintly, the sinister thrum of a helicopter. It approaches, the feathery stuttering slowly growing to a deafening roar. There are two of them now. The stage is raked by a fierce wind. Everyone is looking up into the sky, motionless: except* HITLER. *He sits on his throne, unmoved, staring stonily out at us. Cut sound. Blackout.)*

Howard Brenton

H. I. D. (HESS IS DEAD)

As for the present, leaving history aside for the moment, I warn you I shall complain to the management.

—Mikhail Bulgakov, *The Master and Margarita*

Author's Note

H.I.D. (Hess is Dead) was conceived at the Mickery Theatre, Amsterdam, in a series of exploratory and, for me, explosively exciting discussions with the Mickery's Artistic Director, Ritsaert ten Cate, in the autumn of 1987 and the spring of 1988.

The Mickery's Dutch production was performed, under the direction of Lodewijk de Boer, in a translation by de Boer and Anthony Akerman and opened in Amsterdam on 7 December 1989, not in a theatre but in the Waag.

The Waag is an old customs house that once stood at one of the gates of the city. At its center there is a seventeenth-century dissecting room, a place of enlightenment and science. Criminals hanged just outside the gate were rushed, fresh, to the dissecting room, where their humanity was laid bare by the surgeon's knife to medical students and any interested citizens, who paid for admittance. On the domed ceiling the famous doctors, who cut the dead beneath to enlighten the public, had their names and badges of office painted above a lengthy Latin inscription which, more or less, reads, "The lives of the dead examined here were worthless, but in death they aid our understanding of life." The resonances of performing this play, which attempts to dissect the murky entrails of the "truth" of Rudolf Hess's death in Spandau prison using the unscientific precision of drama, in this famous room, are far-reaching. To present such a play there of all places is a typical piece of Mickery cultural mischief-making.

Anyone writing about the death of Hess has to be indebted to *Hess: A Tale of Two Murders* by Hugh Thomas (Hodder & Stoughton), which is not at all the "lunatic fringe" book which the British government wishes it were. I also want to thank Richard Norton-Taylor, who has pursued the story of the "Hess Affair" relentlessly in *The Guardian,* and who very kindly sent me a file of remarkable material. Needless to say, they are not responsible for any of the speculations in the play.

H.I.D. (Hess is Dead) was first staged at the Almeida Theatre, London, by the Royal Shakespeare Company on 29 September 1989.

CHARACTERS

PALMER
CHARITY
NICOLE
OFFICER
RAYMOND
LUBER (*unseen*)

SETTING

A room of tapestries which hang from a great height, but which do not quite reach the ground. The tapestries form a quadrangular room. The tapestries are blue. They have a *trompe l'oeil* effect, describing a room in a late seventeenth century palace. With the movement of performers, members of the audience, or draughts, the tapestries swing. They should be heavy, or if of paper, weighted so that their movement is languid. About the "room" there are gold, upright chairs, for the audience to sit upon and for the performers to use. If because of fire regulations, the audience's chairs have to be bound together, they should be bound in clumps. The audience would then "sit about" the room in irregular groups. Between the chairs are television monitors on trolleys, which the audience can move for their own convenience. A central VCR machine, upon which the performers sometimes play video tapes, is also on a mobile trolley. There should be a sense that the whole space is "bugged," tense with multiple recording devices, audio and visual.

H. I. D. (HESS IS DEAD)

SCENE 1

LARRY PALMER, *sitting upon a chair. He is waiting. By the chair, a large briefcase. Watch and wait. He watches his hands, waiting.*

PALMER: You say
yes, that's
what I
Believe in, that's
my certainty
in the back
Of my head.
No, neck
spine
Lodged between
the shoulder blades
my moral self
What I
believe, a lump
just beneath
The skin. Part
of me, taken
for granted
A bit of bone
a bit of gristle
a vertebra
A sense
of right
and wrong
Part of you

inert, just
lodged there
Year in, year out
not giving
the slightest ache.

(A silence. PALMER *still. Then he straightens his back. Moves a shoulder uncomfortably. He shrugs and slumps, staring down at his shoe. A silence, he is still. Then he leans forward and picks at a piece of dirt, stuck to the shoe top. He stops.)*

Then one day
you are challenged.
It doesn't need
The point of a knife
the muzzle
of a gun
Just a simple
killer
question
A sudden
killer
look
Into your
face—"Right
you bastard
What
do
YOU
Stand for?"
And you are
struck dumb
You panic
your neck
locks solid
You can't
turn
your head
Your spine

is glass, rigid
fragile, it
Could splinter
cripple you
there and then.
"I . . .
believe, I . . ."
but what?

(He pauses. A little laugh to himself, smiling. His smile fades.)

You cannot say
for you have always
at parties
At work
on the phone
assumed that you
Were "in the right"
that of course
you "stood for the good"
But never really
said what
good, what
Right and at the moment
of maximum danger
the knife
Point, the
terrible look
you realize
"I stand
for nothing
at all
I have never had to
in my life
in the West
In the long, long peace
on the long, long march
of democracy

To the McDonald's
hamburger restaurant
chain, I
Need no
belief
at all
I believe
nothing
at all."

(A silence. Then he shrugs.)

Freedom
is
fast food.
That is my position and it suits
me very well, I am a journalist
let others stand, believe and bleed.
For great
causes, I
just want
A
good
story.

(CHARITY LUBER comes on. PALMER stands.)

CHARITY: Mr. Palmer?

(They shake hands.)

PALMER: *Vielen Dank, dass Sie mich empfangen, Frau Luber, ich hoffe es geht Ihnen gut.* [Many thanks for receiving me, Frau Luber, I hope all is well.] *(She waves a hand. A pause. They sit, facing each other, but with an odd distance between them, a little too far from each other for comfort.) Ich bin Ihnen wirklich sehr dankbar fur dieses Interview.* [I'm really very grateful for this interview.]

CHARITY: Please, we'll speak English.

PALMER: A relief, thank you. I am a typical Englishman, locked in my own language. *(He smiles, she does not.)* Frau Luber, I'd like to say . . . how distressed I was to hear of your husband's death. He was the most brilliant man. Please do accept my condolences.

(A silence.)

CHARITY: Did you know Istvan?

PALMER: I did, luckily, interview him once. For the *Atlantic Review.*

CHARITY: Was he rude to you?

PALMER: Not at all.

CHARITY: Then you must have bored him.

PALMER: I was aware of his legendary . . . difficulty? But I found him a delight. He gave me some excellent material.

CHARITY: Oh Istvan always gave excellent material. I was a student of his in Geneva. We married. I was young.

PALMER: Yes. *(A silence.)* Frau Luber, do you want to see the questions I have prepared for this interview, before I ask them?

CHARITY: No, ask what you want. Do you mind if I smoke?

PALMER: . . . Should you?

CHARITY: Zoot. This sanitorium costs a fortune. At these prices the patients can do anything, even die. *(She removes two ashtrays from a handbag. They are small, of clear cut-glass.)* I carry ashtrays, for myself and my guests.

PALMER: How do you know I smoke?

CHARITY: Your teeth are stained.

PALMER: Ah.

(She holds out one of the ashtrays. He stands, leaning forward to take it. She does not release it.)

CHARITY: Do you assume because I'm in this place that I'm sick?

PALMER: I . . .

CHARITY: Sick in my head? "Out of my tree?"

PALMER: I . . . have no idea, Frau Luber.

CHARITY: There is a room here where they hose you down, naked. With high pressure jets.

(PALMER is stuck in his position, the ashtray held between them.)

PALMER: I thought this was the . . . most advanced sanitorium in Europe?

CHARITY: Oh it is. *(She lets go of the ashtray.* PALMER *returns to his seat. He sets the ashtray on the floor beside his foot. He lights a cigarette.* CHARITY *watches him as he exhales and crosses his legs. As if this were a signal, she in turn takes out a cigarette and lights it. Then she continues.)* The most expensive psychotherapy has abandoned psychoanalysis. All that talk? It's out. Now you pay a fortune for a hard cold shower. It doesn't work, of course. But did Freud, Adler, Jung?

PALMER: I . . . *(A shrug at the enormity of the subject.)* . . . have a crude soul, Frau Luber. I have avoided the psychiatrist's couch.

CHARITY: Yes. The crude amongst us always shine with health. *(She watches for the insult's effect. He smiles.)* Please, set up your tape recorder. I assume you have no shorthand?

PALMER: Forgive me, no.

CHARITY: Few journalists under fifty do.

PALMER: Do you object?

CHARITY: Istvan said that the written word tells less lies than the taped.

PALMER: I can send you a full transcript of our conversation, for your comments . . .

CHARITY: No.

*(*PALMER *caught, looking at her.)*

PALMER *(aside):* Playing the Grande Dame.

CHARITY *(aside):* A journalist. Why do Englishmen always seem so . . . damp?

PALMER *(aside):* Tight bum, good tits. German?

CHARITY *(aside):* A wet Englishman, from his ditchwater island.

PALMER *(aside):* Or Swiss? Hard boiled. And young.

CHARITY *(aside):* But I must make him understand, I have no choice.

PALMER *(aside):* The new European woman. Skin cream and enemas, theories of the health of the liver, a skier's calf muscles, all very EEC. Am I intimidated? Yes, I am intimidated.

*(*PALMER *still caught looking at* CHARITY, *who speaks aside.)*

CHARITY: I married
an old
man, with
Profound relief
I left the youthful zoo
of peacock feathers
Motorbikes, hanging about
inadequately hung
young men
(She laughs.)
I
Cut out from
my generation
to go nun-like
To an old
man's bed
an old man's
Dreams, in my arms
and in my dreams
all his ghosts
His dead friends
long gone lovers
clutched to me
With Istvan I made love
to lost hope
lost happiness
The caresses
of the grateful
dead.
(She laughs, throwing her head back.)
Oh the
Desperate
desperate
nights
For the old man

was not defeated
he raged
And a sexist pig
no gratitude
from him
That he'd got his hands
on young flesh, oh no!
No shyness
No shame at the softness
in parts about
his belly
The reversion to babyhood
that old men
endure—
See him play tennis
thwunk! the games—
player, shoulders
Heaved, rounded
in long blue shorts
naked to pot—
Bellied waist
snarling, thwunk!
at the net
An opponent
wrong-footed
smashed. Rage—
In everything
that rage
in love
Rage. Now, I
the widow
carry
The burning
the crucible
of his molten

Fury
condemned
to burn
And talk of a dead husband
to wet young men—
into tape recorders.

PALMER: So I may . . . ?

(She waves her cigarette. He takes out a tape recorder from his briefcase. He stands. He pulls a chair between them, puts the recorder upon it. He returns to his chair. With a remote control he starts the tape. Nothing for a moment. Then the tape is heard. An American woman's voice, rich and calm.)

TAPE: This statement is issued on the 17th of September, 1987 by the four powers, the Union of Soviet Socialist Republics, the United States of America, the United Kingdom, and France. *(*PALMER *stops the tape. He speaks quickly.)*

PALMER: This is the statement put out by the four powers in Berlin after Rudolf Hess's death. This tape was prepared by the Americans for their news agencies. I got this copy off a mate on "Voice of America." It's ace. *(He restarts the tape.)*

TAPE: One. The four powers are now in a position to make a final statement on the death of Rudolf Hess. *(A pause.)*

Two. Investigations have confirmed that on the 17th of August Rudolf Hess hanged himself from a window latch in a small summerhouse in the prison garden, using an electrical extension cord which had for some time been kept in the summerhouse for use in connection with a reading lamp. Attempts were made to revive him, and he was then rushed to the British Medical Hospital where, after further unsuccessful attempts to revive him, he was pronounced dead at 16.10 hours. *(A pause.)*

Three. A note addressed to Hess's family was found in his pocket. This note was written on the reverse side of a letter from his daughter-in-law dated 20th July, 1987. It began with the words: "Please would the Governors send this home. Written a few minutes before my death." The senior document examiner from the laboratory of the British Government Chemist, Mr. P. A. M. Beard, has examined the note and concluded that he can see no reason to doubt that it was written by Rudolf Hess. *(A pause.)*

Four. A full autopsy was performed on Hess's body on the 19th of August in the British Military Hospital by Dr. J. Malcolm Cameron. The autopsy was conducted in the presence of medical representatives of the four powers. The report noted a linear mark on the left side of the neck consistent with a ligature. Dr. Cameron stated that in his opinion death resulted from asphyxia, caused by the compression of the neck due to suspension.

(The tape runs on for a while. A silence. Then PALMER *stops it.)*

PALMER: This is what I reported at the time. The official line.

CHARITY: The official truth.

PALMER: Indeed.

CHARITY: Which you now no longer believe?

(A silence.)

PALMER: May I? The tape . . . *(She waves her hand, looking away.* PALMER *starts the tape.)* Frau Luber, why did your husband predict that Hess would be murdered in Spandau?

CHARITY: Istvan predicted many things. His enemies accused him of being a poet, posing as a critic. As to the reality of what he predicted . . .

(A wave of the cigarette in her hand.)

PALMER: I am aware of the attacks made upon your husband. I have always been suspicious of them, because he was Jewish. *(Nothing from* CHARITY. *Now* PALMER *is careful with his next sentence.)* And he died at the same time as Hess, the very same day as the man whose reality he pursued so relentlessly.

CHARITY: The poetry of coincidence, Mr. Palmer.

PALMER: A difficult concept, Frau Luber.

CHARITY: I'd rather believe in coincidence, rather than in fate, wouldn't you?

PALMER: I don't know. I . . . have a rather prosaic nature.

CHARITY: Yes?

PALMER: It's an English trait.

CHARITY: Nevertheless you've become an obsessive.

PALMER: I'm sorry?

CHARITY: A "Hess freak."

PALMER: Oh I think not.

(She smiles.)

CHARITY: No?

PALMER: I'm just here for a good story, to sell, Frau Luber. I am just a rat-faced journalist, poking my nose into things, into your life, actually, Frau Luber. Twitching my whiskers. *(Still, she smiles. He is unnerved.)* But. But . . . *(*PALMER *sighs. He leans forward, his elbows upon his knees.)* In my trade, facts are all. They are stones. Stones are real. That was said, that was done. But hard facts can, I find, go . . . mushy. The stones turn to marshmallow. The . . . assassination of John Kennedy? Was there a second gunman? The death of Mozart, poisoned by Salieri? The world has seen *Amadeus,* the movie. Actually, Salieri was a good friend to Mozart. Who was not a pauper, but a man with a carriage and servants. Not poisoned, he just caught the flu. But once the world has seen the movie . . . . And the true horror of the Nazi death camps, which cannot be shown on American TV because of the sponsors? Dachau and Sobibor have to be cleaned up for the viewers, and by American TV mini-series, the true horror dies. Hard facts become "beliefs." Puffs of smoke. Phantoms. Stones to burnt marshmallow.

(A silence.)

CHARITY: Istvan said that by 1970 Germany had won the Second World War. *(She eyes him.)* True or false?

PALMER: Frau Luber, your husband was a relentless champion of historical truth.

*(*CHARITY *is exasperated.)*

CHARITY: A champion of . . . Mr. Palmer! *(She regains her temper.)* If you asked most people under thirty, "Who was Rudolf Hess?" how many would say "He was Hitler's deputy"? How many would know that he was the ghost writer for Hitler's *Mein Kampf*? How many would know what *Mein Kampf* was? How many would know that Hess flew a Messerschmidt 110, on a mad solo flight, from Germany to Scotland, on the 10th of May 1941? I'm not talking about students of history, just people, under thirty, around the streets, in London, Paris, Amsterdam, in Berlin. I mean who cares? The death of Rudolf Hess? *(A flick of the hand.)* It was something on TV. Zoot.

PALMER: You care.

CHARITY: I am condemned to. I could . . . Walk out of this place. Get on a motorbike now, with a man my age, go to the south. The mountains of Provence, the Luberon. I could be making love under the stars in the south forty-eight hours from now. *(She stands, suddenly. She approaches the video trolley.)* This is a tape my husband made. *(She laughs.)* Istvan loved fooling about with cameras. He was like you, Mr. Palmer.

PALMER: How do you mean?

CHARITY: "Nosey." A voyeur, a peeping Tom.

PALMER: I didn't . . .

CHARITY: He would even video us making love. But he was always messing up the cameras. Video was just graffiti to him. This tape's typical.

(She touches buttons. The lights change. The monitors fuzz into life.)

SCENE 2

There are three elements in this sequence.

A: A video tape made presumably by ISTVAN LUBER *of* CHARITY *miming Rudolf Hess's physical state and his death. It is in black and white. It has been made in what seems to be a chaotic hotel room, suitcases with their contents pulled out, an unmade bed. The video is shown on the monitors throughout the playing area and the audience.*

B: CHARITY*'s live commentary on the video, and* PALMER*'s reactions to it. She repeats the mimed gestures she makes upon the tape.*

C: A dance which, step by step, in fragments, she builds as she describes HESS *and his death. These dance fragments are very brief and sudden. (The idea of the dance is that from the pitiful, sordid state of* HESS*'s old age that she mimes, she is choreographing something that is unacceptably beautiful—the dance.)*

1. Tape. *(Black and white photographs of Rudolf Hess. A kaleidoscope. Irregular cutting, each held for different lengths of time. ["Graffiti."] His days with Hitler. Uniformed. Then as a pilot. At Nuremberg in the dock, the photograph of Goering laughing at him. The exterior of Spandau. The photograph of Hess dead in the mortuary.)*

2. Live.

CHARITY: The sound's all screwed up. And you'll know these Hess pics.

PALMER: The same old pics. When was this made?

CHARITY: Istvan put it together, now and then.

PALMER: Do you think the pictures of Hitler and Co. will ever wear out?

CHARITY: Istvan was afraid they'd change. Slowly. That even the negatives in the archives would become lies. *(A pause, the montage on the tapes continuing.)* What he was really afraid of was that they would become beautiful.

PALMER: What do you mean? What . . . did Istvan mean?

CHARITY *(casually):* Oh, that the death camps would become art. *(A pause.)* That in the next century there will be advertisements for hamburgers, set in Belsen.

PALMER: No.

CHARITY: No what?

PALMER: Just no. Memory could never decay that much . . .

CHARITY: One of Istvan's themes was that all history decays.

PALMER: But not Belsen.

CHARITY: Why not? Isn't the Emperor Nero just a joke now? Isn't Napoleon used to sell brandy?

(Wait until the image of Hess dead in the mortuary.)

PALMER: Stop.

CHARITY: What?

PALMER: Stop the tape. *(She does so at the image of Hess dead.)* That's Hess in the mortuary. How did Luber get that on to the tape? He died the day Hess died.

CHARITY: I put it there.

(A pause.)

PALMER: Ah.

CHARITY: This montage went on for three cassettes, I cut it down.

PALMER: When? I mean, in here?

CHARITY: Oh yes. There's a full video-editing suite in the sanitorium's basement. My psychiatrists see it as part of my therapy. I paid for it. I am a very rich woman, Mr. Palmer. I inherited everything Istvan had. If I am to go insane, I don't see why I shouldn't do it with state-of-the-art equipment.

PALMER: No. No.

CHARITY: This next sequence is as Istvan left it.

(She runs the tape.)

3. Tape. *(The tape continues. The wrecked bedroom.* CHARITY *stands dead still, seen full-length, a neutral position, arms loose* *at her sides. She is barefoot. She wears a light-colored ballet dancer's leotard.)*

4. Live.

CHARITY: Rudolf Hess in August 1987.
Age, ninety-three.
Imprisoned since 1947.
Much of his physical strength gone. Capable of little effort.
Suffered a minor stroke in the late seventies.
Circulatory problems in the brain.
Both eyes affected, nearly blind in the right.

5. Tape. *(Her hand goes to her left eye. [NB: from here her live commentary follows her twisting distortions on the tape, as detail by detail, her young dancer's body assumes the physical state of the old man. She repeats them live breaking into the dancing steps where indicated.])*

6. Live. *(Following the tape.)*

CHARITY: Left arm.
Elbow bent.
Shoulder frozen.
No grip in the hand, great pain.
Movement restricted.
To the front, arm cannot be raised above the horizontal.
And to the side, no more than forty-five degrees.

7. Dance. *(Suddenly, using the mimed gestures, a dancing movement with her left arm, of a twisted grace.)*

8. Tape. *(She stops the mime and, no sound, she is talking to someone off camera about what to do next. She appears to be angry. She gestures and stamps her foot, turning away from the camera, then back to it.)*

9. Live.

PALMER: Is that Istvan, talking to you?

CHARITY: He should have gone to Hollywood with all the others.

PALMER: Forgive me, but Hollywood this is not.

CHARITY: I meant gone with all the other exiles to America, in 1933.

PALMER: Ah.

(Whatever the discussion on the tape was, it is resolved. CHARITY *continues, following her mime on the tape.)*

CHARITY: Right arm.

Can raise the hand to comb his hair, feebly. Needs a big comb to do so.

His coffee mug.

Since 1979, too heavy to hold by the handle.

Writing.

Cannot with the right hand more than a few minutes.

Cramps, stiffness.

Walking.

Balance bad, affected by arteriosclerosis of the brain stem.

Left knee, gives out.

Cannot walk up stairs without aid.

10. Dance. *(Off balance, the left knee failing, toppling.)*

11. Live.

CHARITY: Spine.

Spinal arthritis.

Now, after the years, he is humpbacked.

Vertebrae at the top of his back, collapsed, the bones impacted, wedge-shaped bodies.

PALMER *(muttering):* So the vicious old bastard was old? What do you want? Pity?

*(*CHARITY *ignores that.)*

CHARITY: Spinal deformity thrusts the head forward.

Limits traverse movement, side to side, no more than a few degrees left, a few degrees right.

Cannot raise his head.
When he tries, he becomes dizzy and can fall.

12. Dance. *(The spine, the fear of falling.)*

13. Live. *(Following the tape.)*
CHARITY: Cannot wash the back of his neck.
Has to shave sitting, with an electric razor.
And so he walks.
Shuffling.
Bent forward at a sharp angle.
Holding the arm of a guard.
To the prison garden.
At half past two in the afternoon of the 17th of August 1987.

14. Tape. *(A montage using and developed from the photograph of Rudolf Hess walking in the garden of Spandau. Black and white charcoal drawings follow the narrative, mixing with and developing from close-ups of* CHARITY *miming the hanging with the length of cord.)*

15. Live. *(*CHARITY *takes a piece of cord, exactly the same as that on the tape, from the video trolley. In her mime she distorts herself into the careful, frail movements of a very old, decrepit body.)*
CHARITY: The garden.
Trees, overgrown.
One prisoner, in the huge building. Year on year.
Guards changed, four nations, each month.
The Soviets in July.
The Americans in August.
In September, the British.
Endless routine.
Old concrete, set.
And in the routine, neglect. In the cracks of the years, little carelessnesses.

The trees in the garden have grown, higher than the watch-towers.
Quarter past three in the afternoon.
The guard in Tower B sees Hess and his duty warder sitting together on a bench.
The duty warder is called back to the main cell block, a telephone call, the subject of the call—never disclosed.
Because of the trees the guard in Tower B cannot see the summerhouse.
The summerhouse, a wooden, rectangular hut, used by the gardener to store his tools.
A beam, six foot from the ground.
A work bench.
A sharpening wheel.
Two pairs of shears.
Rags on the bench.
Old garden chairs.
A garden hose, coiled.
On the floor woodshavings, metal filings.
And two coils of yellow electric cord.
The warder returned.
Hess, crumpled against the garden chairs.
Half-sat, half-lain, bent forward, knees drawn to the chest, round his neck a length of cord, face dark blue.
They came running.
Pulled Hess out of the summerhouse.
Tried to revive. Resuscitation.
Smashed six of his ribs.
Stumbled and shouted.
Routine ended.
(She has followed the mime through to its conclusion, ending as Hess dead.)

16. Tape. *(The tape ends. The screens snow.)*

SCENE 3

CHARITY *stands. Then she dances the steps she has improvised together, ending with a dance presentation of Hess's end. The impossibility of him hanging himself. A death by being strangled from behind. Graceful, beautiful, in silence but for the squeak of her shoes upon the floor. She stops it and is out of breath, collapsed, her head down. She looks up. She shrugs. She takes the cord from her neck and throws it to* PALMER, *who catches it.*

SCENE 4

PALMER, *the length of cord in his hand. He looks at it. A silence.*

CHARITY: The yellow electrical cord. Left by employees of the firm Frohberg Elektrobau. They had been working in Spandau that day. Repairing the four thousand volt wire around the jail's perimeter.

PALMER: But the statement by the four powers said—wait. *(Flicks with his remote control. Rewinds. Plays.)*

TAPE: . . . hanged himself from a window latch in a small summerhouse in the prison garden, using an electrical extension cord which had for some time been kept in the summerhouse for use in connection with a reading lamp. Attempts . . .

(He stops the tape.)

CHARITY: The reading lamp had been removed many years before, when the prisoner's eyes had weakened and he could no longer read.

PALMER: But so trivial a detail.

CHARITY: Yes.

PALMER: Why is it wrong in the official statement?

(A silence.)

CHARITY: The report also did not say that the cord had been wiped with a rag. The rag was soaked in acetone. Acetone is a fat and oil solvent, which gives off a smell of nail polish.

PALMER: Was there mention of acetone being kept in the summerhouse?

CHARITY: No.

PALMER: Acetone. Could its smell, its fumes, knock you out? Like chloroform?

CHARITY: No.

(A silence.)

PALMER: Why was the cord wiped, anyway?

CHARITY: I am sure you know the answer to that. Don't you read detective novels?

(He pauses.)

PALMER: You want me to say the cord was wiped clean by Hess's murderer before strangling him. The murderer would, of course, have worn leather gloves. As all the murderers do.

CHARITY: As all the murderers do. *(She pauses.)* When a man hangs the body's fall drags the knot, up to the highest point of the loop.

PALMER: Ah. *(He pauses.)* Ah.

CHARITY: As the knot pulls away from the back of the neck, it leaves no mark. The marks on the throat will be of equal intensity, all along the throat. But the autopsy on Hess's body showed the mark was not equal on the throat. It was slanting, thickest over the adam's apple, by a twist, by a knot, by a knot twisted, by a hand.

PALMER: A hand in a leather glove.

(He smiles and sighs. Suddenly she snatches the cord from his hand. She whirls away, a fury of movement.)

CHARITY: Old man, hang himself? Tie a cord to a beam, a latch of a window? Tie the cord to his neck?

(She mimes the elderly Hess trying to do so. "He" cannot. He stumbles and falls to the floor, his body stiff, the cord in a shaking hand. Then she relaxes, her body loose.)

PALMER: This material was collected by your husband.

CHARITY: Yes.

PALMER: Your memory is very good.

CHARITY: He was one of them.

PALMER: I'm sorry?

CHARITY: My husband was one of the specialists. *(A pause.)* One of the committee of specialists.

PALMER: There was a committee of which Istvan Luber was a member? A committee to do with the death of Rudolf Hess?

CHARITY: You didn't know? *(PALMER looks down.)* You are making me nervous. Mr. Palmer. You have a reputation of being an investigative journalist, "in the know." A rather fearsome reputation. But you have never heard of the United States and United Kingdom Emergency Coordinating Committee?

PALMER: Forgive me, I feel a fool.

CHARITY: The USUKEMCOC?

PALMER: Specialists? What, to advise . . . ? An ad hoc committee, set up by the British and the Americans?

CHARITY: I did trust you to know. That's why I agreed to see you, only you, and not any of the other freaks . . .

PALMER: I won't disappoint you, Frau Luber. I am a fast learner.

CHARITY: Are you?

(They look at each other. A pause.)

PALMER: Had this committee met before?

CHARITY: Oh yes, at crucial times.

PALMER: Such as? *(*CHARITY *shrugs.)* The Soviets weren't involved?

CHARITY: No, of course not.

PALMER: The French?

CHARITY: There was a French woman there.

PALMER: And the committee's purpose was to . . . what? *(She shakes her head, looking down.* PALMER, *irritated.)* You'll have to tell me more, Frau Luber. I don't want to be rude, but last week I met a man who believes there are two moons circling the earth. What was the brief of this committee?

CHARITY: To tell lies.

PALMER: Disinformation?

CHARITY: Lies.

(She still looks down.)

PALMER: Who were the other members of the committee, beside your husband? *(She stands. She shakes her head.)* I would like to contact them. I need corroboration . . .

CHARITY: They're dead. Like Istvan.

PALMER: I see.

(A silence.)

CHARITY: They went into the walls.

*(*PALMER *takes a deep breath and blows air out. He runs his hand through his hair.)*

PALMER: There is a ship. *The Reefer Rio,* registered in Panama. It is carrying six thousand tons of radioactive beef, from EEC surplus stores. The beef is from Ireland and Denmark; it was contaminated by fallout from the Chernobyl accident. The beef arrived in Venezuela. The authorities refused to let it into the country, because of excessive levels of radioactive cesium. Since then the ship has been sailing around the world for a year, looking for a buyer. It is a good story. I sold it to Reuters. *(*CHARITY *walks away.)*

CHARITY: Where is the ship now?

PALMER: It was last reported to be sailing to Poland. *(*CHARITY *nods, looking down.)* Meanwhile, Rudolf Hess was murdered? As the radioactive meat set out upon its journey around the earth? Is that what you are telling me?

CHARITY: I don't see the connection.

PALMER: There is none. None at all. Except for the insanely paranoid. And the odd poet amongst us.

(She throws the cord on the floor. She turns on him in a fury, fists clenched. A moment, both still, then she turns and goes.)

SCENE 5

PALMER *stands and goes to the video trolley. He leans against it, looking down. Then he realizes it is piled with video tapes, in disorder. He picks up one. It has no markings. He shrugs. He puts it into the player and starts it. The audience see the same tape as he on their machines.*

1. The Tape. *(A palimpsest of old TV shows, old movies, TV advertisements, each very quick. As if it is an old video tape that has been used again and again for recording television programs. Electronic detritus: recorded by an obsessive TV watcher, perhaps a child.)*

2. *(The tape snows, as if going to a different speed of recording.)*

3. *(Then a legend in black and white. The UN sign. Beneath it—UNESCO INTERNATIONAL STANDING COMMITTEE OF CULTURAL COORDINATION [UNISICOC]*
And at the bottom of the screen—
USUK EMCOC/cover 43/sub.P7/4887sectap003)

4. *(In black and white. The room represented by the tapestries. But the room on the video is "real"—solid walls, paneling, a shiny floor. There is a set of grand double doors. In one of the walls, concealed by* trompe l'oeil *decoration, there is a small hidden door, the entrance to secret passages which becomes apparent later. There are three gold chairs in the room. The shots on the video are made by four cameras from ceiling height. They are obviously hidden security cameras. Each can pan in a narrow range. When they do so their movement is even, as if automatic. Each has two sets of focus, a wide shot, a narrow shot. The recording moves from one camera to another, but without the sense of "making a good shot"—as if they are activated by where the voices in the room are coming from. The sound quality is "dry" and loud. The room empty. The cameras rotate their shots evenly.*

The double doors open. NICOLE *and a US Army* OFFICER *come into the room.* NICOLE *is thirty-three. She is dressed in a fine, conservative woman's suit. The* OFFICER*'s uniform is immaculate.* NICOLE, *who is French, speaks English immaculately. She is pedantic. Her voice is deep.)*

OFFICER: This is the facility.

NICOLE: Yes.

(A silence.)

OFFICER: There will be a briefing at 19.00 hours. Thank you, Professor D'Arcy.

(The OFFICER *turns to go.)*

NICOLE: Can I ask . . . *(The* OFFICER *stops.)* Why I am here?

OFFICER: That would be inappropriate at this time. I hope your room is satisfactory?

NICOLE: The room looked excellent. The ceiling a mile high? With cupids and nudes, swimming in the clouds above? But the view through the window, a brick wall?

OFFICER: We had to allocate rooms to members of the committee in a hurry. Perhaps later, we can relocate you.

NICOLE: Can I ask where I am?

OFFICER: This facility is made available courtesy of the Government of the Netherlands.

NICOLE: So I am in Holland.

OFFICER: Ah . . . Forgive me Professor D'Arcy.

NICOLE: Inappropriate? At this time?

OFFICER: The location of this facility is classified.

NICOLE: I did see out of the helicopter? The military helicopter? That whirled me here from Paris? I do have eyes. I saw a lake? A lawn? Stone statues? A palace?

OFFICER: Again, I have to ask you to forgive me, Professor. There is a strictly need-to-know continuity being maintained at this time.

NICOLE: Lieutenant. The meetings of the UNESCO International Standing Committee of Cultural Coordination are not, usually, so . . . glamorous? UNISICOC is one of the most boring organizations I know. One does not usually step out of US Army helicopters into palaces to attend its deliberations.

OFFICER: This is an emergency meeting, Professor.

NICOLE: Can one have a cultural emergency? Has a symphony orchestra machine-gunned an audience?

OFFICER: I have duties to attend to. This facility is being made operational at very short notice. Please forgive any inconvenience. The briefing will be at 19.00 hours.

(Both still. Then the OFFICER *turns and goes, closing the double doors.* NICOLE *alone in the room. Irritable movements. She turns. She looks up at a camera.)*

NICOLE: Hello?

(Her eyes drift from the camera. She has not seen it. But she has sensed the bugging. She goes to the center of the room. Again she turns, then is still. The cameras return to the rhythm of shots they made when the room was empty. The watching LARRY PALMER *shakes his head and leans forward, tired.)*

5. *(The rhythm of the cameras . . . One catches a small door open in the wall, behind* NICOLE*'s back. It closes.* LARRY PALMER *has not seen it.)*

6. *(The rhythm of the cameras . . . Another catches another door, open, out of* NICOLE*'s eyeline. The cameras switch. Again,* LARRY PALMER *has not seen it. He looks at the screen again.)*

7. *(The rhythm of the cameras around* NICOLE*, all four cover the room. There is nothing untoward. Then a camera catches a hidden door open and a figure, just glimpsed, in late seventeenth century costume, a man, falling back into the dark beyond. The door closes. No sound.* LARRY PALMER *starts.)*

LARRY *(under his breath . . .):* What the f . . .

8. *(The double doors open.* RAYMOND TRACE *walks into the room. He is in his mid-forties, casually and rather shambolically dressed.* NICOLE *turns to him. They stare at each other. The cameras change their rhythm, picking up the sound.)*

RAYMOND: Hello Nicole.

(A silence.)

NICOLE: Hello Raymond.

*(*PALMER *stops the video machine. He plays the tape back and forth, searching. He finds the image of the hidden door open. He pauses the machine. The image is blurred and strange, the figure smeared. He rewinds a few frames. He plays it again. This time the figure is even more distinct. It plays on to* RAYMOND*'s entrance.)*

9. *(On the tape—)*

RAYMOND: Hello Nicole.

*(*PALMER *stops the tape. The frame frozen. He scrutinizes the image. He rewinds, stopping every few frames. He reaches the sequence of the hidden door opening. He—and the audience on their monitors—are confronted by the figure. It is, for the third time, different. The resolution is still smeared, but eerily, there are pale streaks of coloring about the clothing. The face is contorted.* PALMER *lights a cigarette. He plays the tape.)*

10. *(. . . The figure falls back into the dark beyond the door. The door closes. The double doors open.* RAYMOND TRACE *enters.* NICOLE *turns to him. They stare at each other. The cameras change their rhythm, picking up the sound.)*

RAYMOND: Hello Nicole.

(A silence.)

NICOLE: Hello Raymond.

(A silence. Then the tape snows, changing speeds. And there is more of the palimpsest of old TV programs and commercials. PALMER *goes to the machine. Fast forwards. The mush of old programs continues. He stops the tape for a few seconds, continues to fast forward. He can find no more of the room. Eventually, the tape snows into an unused section. He turns it off. He sits, smoking.)*

PALMER: Into the walls.

SCENE 6

Live performance. NICOLE *and the* OFFICER *come on.*

OFFICER: This is the facility.
NICOLE: Yes. *(Aside.)* Helicoptered
in, I fell
to dreaming.

OFFICER: There will be a briefing at 19.00 hours. Thank you, Professor D'Arcy.

(The OFFICER *turns to go.)*

NICOLE *(aside):* For fame
is like
love
Fame flatters
fame smiles
fame caresses
And makes your skin
feel just
wonderful.

(To the OFFICER.*)* Can I ask . . .

(The OFFICER *stops.)*

Why I am here?

OFFICER: That would be inappropriate at this time. I hope your room is satisfactory?

NICOLE: The room looked excellent, the ceiling a mile high? With cupids and nudes, swimming in the clouds above? But the view through the window, a brick wall?

OFFICER: We had to allocate rooms to members of the committee in a hurry. Perhaps later, we can relocate you?

NICOLE: Can I ask where I am?

OFFICER: This facility is made available courtesy of the Government of the Netherlands.

NICOLE: So I am in Holland.

OFFICER: Ah . . . Forgive me Professor D'Arcy.

NICOLE: Inappropriate? At this time?

OFFICER: The location of this facility is classified.

NICOLE: I did see out of the helicopter? The military helicopter? That whirled me here from Paris? I do have eyes. I saw a lake? A lawn? Stone statues? A palace?

(Aside.) This is fame's
pornography
the smooth
Secrecy
the call
to the center
Of power
the libertine's
château
The silent pilot
of the roaring
machine
trying not to look
at my legs as I pull
the seat belt tight
I
am
seduced
Aie, aie Nicole
have you come
to this?

OFFICER: Again, I have to ask you to forgive me, Professor. There is a strictly need-to-know continuity being maintained at this time.

NICOLE *(aside)*: All the young dudes
in uniform
he really
Doesn't want to sweat
his collar up, he wants
his collar really clean . . .

(To the OFFICER.*)* Lieutenant. The meetings of the UNESCO International Standing Committee . . .

(Aside.) Blah blah I go
No need to listen
to myself
Always be
difficult on
arrival
At airports
international
hotels
Prickle and
be prickly
let them know
You know
your
worth.

OFFICER: This is an emergency meeting, Professor.

NICOLE: Can one have a cultural emergency? Has a symphony orchestra machine-gunned an audience?

(The OFFICER *"mute," i.e. miming his next line, as* NICOLE *speaks.)*

OFFICER *(mute):* I have duties to attend to. This facility is being made operational at very short notice. Please forgive any inconvenience. The briefing will be at 19.00 hours.

NICOLE *(aside):* Though this
feels
strange
No dust
in the
air. Bugged
Bugged,
I
feel
The air
drawn tight
strained

Silence
　　　　listen-
　　　　　　　　ing, I
Feel
　　　　migraine.
　　　　　　　　I—

(Both still. Then the OFFICER *turns and goes, closing the double doors.* NICOLE *alone in the room. Irritable movements. She turns. She looks up.)*

Hello?

(Nothing.)

SCENE 7

. . . And RAYMOND TRACE *walks into the room. He stops dead still when he sees* NICOLE. *She turns. They look at each other.*

RAYMOND: Hello Nicole.
NICOLE: Hello Raymond.
(A silence.)
RAYMOND: How was Los Angeles? I heard you were in Los Angeles.
NICOLE: In Los Angeles everyone is diseased. Love is coming to a stop.
RAYMOND: So I hear. From promiscuity to celibacy in a generation?
NICOLE: A kind of purity is at work. The sexual plagues will free men and women.
RAYMOND: That pleases you?
NICOLE: It puts me very much at ease.
RAYMOND: Free of love? 'Cos no one will dare to sleep together anymore? If only that were true. *(A pause.* NICOLE *turning from him, in dislike.)* And how are post-semiological synthetics? Have I got that right?
NICOLE: You read my new book?
RAYMOND: Yes your book, great acclaim, great reviews. I must admit I read the reviews, not the work itself.
NICOLE: You are excused. After all we academics only write books to make each other feel bad, don't we?
RAYMOND: Becoming cynical, Nicole? Unlike you.
NICOLE: I . . .
RAYMOND: What?
(A dismissive gesture from NICOLE.*)*
NICOLE: And your work? How is vulgar Marxism?
RAYMOND: In the dog house. *(Aside.)* For I did love her once.
NICOLE *(aside):* Man, man, this man . . . Why do the unhappy have to be so repulsive? *(To* RAYMOND.*)* Why in the dog house?
RAYMOND: Comrade Gorbachev. The new line, glasnost and all that crap. Decades I and a few other comrades, kept the faith with the Soviet Union. Now the Soviets themselves turn round and

tell us that the workers' paradise is a shit heap. All the arguments I spewed out for them, "actually existing socialism" . . . Utterly discredited. The Politburo of the Soviet Union, voting for a free market? Coca-Cola ads on Soviet TV? I feel betrayed.

NICOLE: No more Moscow freebies for you, then?

RAYMOND: I'm still big in Czechoslovakia. *(A pause.)* Well! Surprised to see you at this do.

NICOLE: Really. Why?

RAYMOND: Bit down market for you, I'd have thought.

NICOLE: You know why we're here?

(He stares at her.)

RAYMOND: *In het spoor van Willem en Mary.* [On the trail of William and Mary]. *(She stares at him.) Glorieuze Revolutie.* The Glorious Revolution of 1688. I'm on the International Committee. Organized by the Dutch Ministry of Foreign Affairs in cooperation with the British Council. *In samen werking met de Stichting 1688–1988.* [In cooperation with the 1688–1988 committee.]

NICOLE: Raymond, what are you talking about?

RAYMOND: William of Orange. Rent a King. 1688. They needed a tame academic, to raise the tone, and I am he.

NICOLE: Raymond . . .

RAYMOND: I know, I know. Will'm 'n' Mary, just about the most mind-fuckingly pointless bit of history conceivable, but it pays well. Tricentennial celebrations. International cooperation. It's one big bloody wonderful freebie, actually. They put you up in the American Hotel. They helicopter you to venues like this. When does the meeting start then?

NICOLE: There has been some grotesque administrative error.

RAYMOND: You're not here for the Will'm 'n' Mary committee?

NICOLE: I'm here for UNISICOC.

RAYMOND: UNESCO Cultural Coordination. Bit out of my league, old ducks. Oh to be on a UNESCO committee. That is the flagship of freebies. UNESCO is caviar and champagne, all round the world . . . Well, what's your freebie about?

NICOLE: I was told it was an emergency.

RAYMOND: A cultural emergency? Did an audience machine-gun a symphony orchestra?

NICOLE: Quite. *(A silence.)* The next UNISICOC meeting was going to be on Anti-Heideggerian strategies and feminist linguistics.

RAYMOND: Oh well. We'll do the two together. Heidegger meets William and Mary to discuss feminist linguistics. We are academics, we can bullshit our way out of that. *(Shouting.)* This is fucking typical of the fucking European Economic Community! Utterly fucking meaningless meetings! Everything to do with the European Economic Community is fucking meaningless! I will show you European culture in a mountain of surplus butter!

NICOLE: This room is bugged.

(A silence.)

RAYMOND: How do you know?

NICOLE: Feel it.

(A silence.)

RAYMOND: I see what you mean. *(He turns, calling.)* Hey! Hey! When does the bar open?

(CHARITY comes on. She wears different clothes from before. Now she is in light blue jeans, a pink fluffy sweater and trainer shoes.)

CHARITY: Excuse me, can I ask you whether you smoke? *(NICOLE and RAYMOND look at her.)* If you do, can I ask you not to smoke? *(To RAYMOND.)* Excuse me sir, but I notice you are wearing aftershave.

RAYMOND: Yes I am actually.

CHARITY: May I ask what brand?

RAYMOND: Kouros. You know, the ad on TV, with the racing driver . . .

CHARITY: Is it not Old Spice?

RAYMOND: Bet your sweet life it is not. Look what . . .

CHARITY: Thank you for your help.

(She turns away.)

NICOLE: Oh God. Luber. *(To CHARITY.)* It's Istvan Luber, isn't it?

(To RAYMOND.*)* He is allergic to tobacco smoke and Old Spice aftershave.

RAYMOND: Luber is here?

NICOLE: You are Professor Luber's assistant?

CHARITY *(to* NICOLE*)*: I am his wife. *(To* RAYMOND.*)* My husband has provided historical material for this committee.

RAYMOND: Luber has provided material?

(The OFFICER *enters. He carries folders, a clipboard, and video tapes.)*

OFFICER: Professor D'Arcy, Professor Trace, thank you for your attention and for your presence here, under such pressure of time. *(To* CHARITY.*)* Is Professor Luber . . .

CHARITY: My husband is resting. He suggests the briefing begin. He will join you later.

RAYMOND: Oh will he.

OFFICER: The matter in hand for your consideration is of a highly classified nature. I cannot impress its seriousness upon you too greatly. Professor Trace, you have signed the Official Secrets Act.

(A silence. CHARITY *slips away.)*

RAYMOND: Have I?

OFFICER: For your work on the Home Office Anti-Terrorist Working Party.

RAYMOND: Fuck off soldier . . .

NICOLE: Raymond? You, the left-winger, have . . .

RAYMOND: That was in the early seventies, because of Ireland . . .

OFFICER: I have a photocopy here, of your declaration . . .

NICOLE: The rats of the left, gnaw each other?

(She laughs.)

RAYMOND: Shut up! You don't understand, I knew people.

NICOLE: What people?

RAYMOND: I knew people!

OFFICER *(to* NICOLE*)*: Professor D'Arcy, the French Ministry of the Interior has vouchsafed for you. Your information leading to the arrest of Red Army Faction sympathizers in Lyons, in 1975 . . .

RAYMOND: Ah! Ah! But the lady wrote a famous defense of terrorism in *Libération!*

NICOLE: Cultural terrorism.

RAYMOND: Oh "cultural" terrorism. Pardonnez-moi.

NICOLE: It would seem, Raymond, we have both compromised for our countries: compromised and agonized. It would seem we are about to be asked to do so again.

RAYMOND *(to himself):* The dirt, the dirt, the dirt.

OFFICER *(to* NICOLE*):* The French Ministry of the Interior recommended you, Professor D'Arcy. The French government is as concerned about the incident as are the governments of the USA and of Britain.

RAYMOND: Incident?

OFFICER: The death of Rudolf Hess at 15.30 hours today. *(A silence.)* As expert media consultants and academics, the US and British authorities wish to have your recommendations as quickly as possible. Professor Luber has prepared a briefing tape. Please give your attention to a console.

RAYMOND *(to* NICOLE*):* The death of Rudolf Hess. Tasty.

NICOLE *(to* RAYMOND*):* We are privileged. Perhaps.

OFFICER: This tape has been prepared by Professor Luber. Please attend.

*(*RAYMOND *and* NICOLE *turn to screens. The* OFFICER *puts a tape in the machine—they use the same video trolley as* PALMER *used. The tape is speeding mishmash of Second World War German material. The* OFFICER *walks away from the trolley.)*

SCENE 8

PALMER *goes to the trolley and stops the tape. He pauses.*

PALMER: The big
story
the big
Fish, out on the ocean
a suitcase for a boat
wandering the world
Sails the
investigating
journalist
I
do
think.
(He removes the tape. He scrabbles around amongst others. Some fall to the ground. He picks up one. He puts it on.)

Tape. *(On all the monitors—a palimpsest of TV "channel hopping," in a montage with indistinct, cloudy video of love-making in a bed of many sheets. The man is never seen clearly, there is a glimpse of* CHARITY*'s face. It could be one of the home videos she referred to.* PALMER *watches the screen for a while, then continues to speak.)*
Ernest Hemingway's
"The Old Man
And The Sea"—
(He snorts.)
You lash
the fish
to the boat
And the sharks come
the denials
contradictions

Doubt
hearsay
lies
Gnaw away at the flesh
and when you reach the harbor
what do you have? A
Fishtail
a fishhead
bones. "The
Great story" a wrecked kipper
on your hotel breakfast plate
Ah well, you pay the bill
Your gold card
takes the strain—
the story's dead
But one story
is just like
another
The planet
is crowded
to death
Everywhere
is becoming
like everywhere
Else, the same
beggars
Rangoon to London
The same money
Tokyo
to Delhi
The same TV
Beirut
to Berlin
I travel the world by Holiday Inn
the same room, same cabled porn
Cairo, Manila, Chicago, London

News
is news
is news
Anything
is anything
is anything
And truth?
(He snorts.)
Wearied away
in the weary seas
Of the weary
earth.
(The tape snows.)
Oh come
on, come on.
(He walks away from the video trolley.)

SCENE 9

RAYMOND *goes to the video trolley and switches off the tape. From a projector onto a tapestry looms the photograph of Goering and Hess in the dock at Nuremberg. Goering is laughing at Hess from behind his hand.* NICOLE *has a microphone and is reading from notes, the "recommendations" of the Committee.* RAYMOND *is staring at the photograph as he eats a plateful of food with a fork. They are both exhausted.*

NICOLE: Recommendation three. That the statement by the four powers be short. Five paragraphs, no more.

RAYMOND: The purity of the brief, official statement. *(Musing.)* At Nuremberg, why was Goering always laughing at Hess? *(*NICOLE *looks up.)*

"Old comrades." From the Munich Bierkeller putsch days in Munich. I mean, in the bickering at Hitler's court, Himmler was Hess's enemy, not Goering. Goering let Hess fly his aeroplanes. *(He eats. Mouth full.)* This ris de veau truffé à la crème is excellent. Did they move a cook in for us? *(He stands, holding up his plate. He speaks to the bugging.)* Compliments to the chef.

(He goes to the blown-up photograph.)

NICOLE: Recommendation four. Security after the announcement of the death. Strict control by the military police of all of the prisoner's effects and the prison fabric itself. It is essential that no bricks, window latches, piping, roof slating etcetera etcetera, no artifacts whatsoever from the prison are allowed to leave the site.

RAYMOND *(waving at her, still staring at the photograph):* "Demolition of the myth . . ." Keep that paragraph.

NICOLE *(irritated):* Recommendation five. The site house where the prisoner died and all its contents must be burnt at once. Recommendation six. The demolition of Spandau Prison must begin at once. Military personnel should be used, not private contractors, to guard against any market in souvenirs. It is not a prison that is being demolished, it is a historical, or anti-historical, myth.

RAYMOND: What did Goering mean when he laughed in court at Nuremberg and said to Hess, "Are you going to tell us your big secret now?"

NICOLE: Recommendation six. When the prison has been demolished, it should not be left derelict, or worse still, made into a public park. There must be no shrine. We suggest that the site be sold to a commercial enterprise for immediate development. To demythologize the ground upon which Spandau prison once stood, a supermarket should be built there.

RAYMOND: We didn't discuss that!

NICOLE: Luber sent it down.

RAYMOND: From his sick bed above? *(He waves his fork at the ceiling.)* Nice one Istvan.

NICOLE: Recommendation seven. A strategy against demonstrations at the prison on the announcement of the death. We suggest that, within two hours of the announcement, a small right-wing demonstration be staged at the prison gate by German security forces, posing as Neo-Fascist sympathizers. That television and press be advised of the demonstration in advance. The demonstration to be broken up by uniformed police, without incident. This will one—pre-empt any demonstration by the real right-wing, and two—satisfy the extreme left, that the right has been made to look ridiculous and give the left no reason to demonstrate themselves. There must be neither mourning on the right, nor celebration on the left. Recommendation eight, the Hess family. We suggest that to counter an inflammatory statement by the Hess family the question of the burial be handled in this way. One—an announcement will be made that the body will be buried in the family plot. The world's press is to be encouraged to descend upon the family. The body will be given to the family on the understanding that it will be buried elsewhere, secretly. Cremation would be ideal, but this should not be sought as the Hess family is, nominally, Catholic. A further concession, to

be used in negotiation with the family, can be that the body will be buried in the family plot, in nine months time, but without publicity and at night. I am exhausted.
(She sits down.)

RAYMOND: Are we done?

NICOLE: And I need a bath.

RAYMOND: Why did Hess claim amnesia when he went to England? On his mad flight? This was a powerful political head. But interrogation in England, nothing. All his replies were imprecise. And why . . . in jail, did he refuse to meet his wife? For twenty-eight years in Spandau, he never saw her.

NICOLE: The psychiatric report . . . "An individual of a superior intelligence with schizoid traits . . ." It was a filthy mind. It went to pieces. We have buried the pieces. I am exhausted and I need a long hot bath . . .

RAYMOND: There were six war criminals with him in Spandau at first. The last to be released was Speer. Speer said Hess never reminisced. While the good old boys were going over tales of the good old days with Adolf, Hess always slunk away. Walked in another part of the prison garden. Kept himself apart. *(He goes right up to the photograph, running his hands over it. The tapestry moves.)* We have buried the pieces. I feel kind of dirty, too.

NICOLE: Don't become sentimental. This is cultural warfare. This is against fascism.

RAYMOND: It's gross media manipulation and we know it.

NICOLE: It is . . . an encoding of the truth. No more no less. Our statement is a construct. Like any sentence, or photograph.

RAYMOND: Or the Mona Lisa.

NICOLE: We construct it for the good.

RAYMOND: How Goebbels would have loved modern literary theory. *(He turns and calls out to the bugging.)*
We've done, boys! Come 'n' get it!

SCENE 10

The photograph disappears. Light change. The RAYMOND *and* NICOLE *actors stay where they are, sitting on their chairs.* PALMER *stands. He goes to the video trolley.* CHARITY *comes on. She is dressed as before in the scenes with* PALMER. PALMER *turns to her.*

PALMER: When did your husband die? While the committee was in session?

*(*CHARITY *says nothing. She goes to the video and extracts the tape. She looks at it.)*

CHARITY: You are a spy.

PALMER: Did you smuggle the tapes of the committee out? Copy them illegally?

CHARITY: Everything leaks, somewhere, Mr. Palmer. People leak too. They leave trails in the minds of other people.

(He hesitates.)

PALMER: When you said the members of the committee died . . . *(She stares at him.)* When you said they went into the walls, what did you mean? *(*CHARITY, *upset, fumbles amongst video tapes. She finds the one she is looking for and puts it in the machine. She presses play. On all the monitors, an amateur video of Cologne Cathedral appears. Color, grainy quality. The hand-held camera pans around—the cathedral, towering into a grey sky.)* Cologne Cathedral?

CHARITY: Istvan took this. *(The camera pans away to the shopping area before the cathedral, which is now out of sight.)* Anywhere in Europe, no Mr. Palmer? Any shopping mall. In England, in France. *(He pauses.)* Or where Spandau Prison stood? *(The camera pans to the cathedral again.)* The trouble with Cologne Cathedral is that it's not really there.

PALMER: Another quote from Istvan? *(She stops the tape. She presses a rewind button.)* What happened to your husband and that committee?

(She stops the tape. She presses play. She walks away, ignoring him. PALMER *is left alone staring at the screen. It snows. He wipes his eyes.)*

SCENE 11

The tape plays. PALMER *at the machine, leaning on his knuckles, crumpled before the screen.*

The Tape.

1. *(In black and white a degraded shot of a military jet transport plane with German markings taking off into an overcast sky. It repeats itself, odd cutting.)*

CHARITY *(voice over):* Three hundred years from now history students are shown a tape of a jet taking off. The students are told—this is Hitler, flying to meet Winston Churchill in 1941. But Hitler never met Churchill. And there were no jet planes in the Second World War. But there is the tape, three hundred years old. *(A shot of Hitler from archive footage by a plane's window, looking out.)* There is the plane. Here is Hitler. There is Hitler on the plane.

2. *(A palimpsest of TV gameshows. Then it snows.* PALMER *stops the tape. He fast forwards it. He leans forward, shoulders rounded. He chants, like a child's rhyme.)*

PALMER: See it now, you don't, now you see it, now . . .
(He plays the tape.)

3. *(The room, again recorded by the four cameras.* RAYMOND *is turning to them, calling.)*

RAYMOND: We've done, boys! Come 'n' get it! *(At once the double doors open. The* OFFICER *pushes a trolley into the room. On the trolley there is an immaculate white tablecloth, dishes of food, and two bottles of champagne in ice buckets.)* Hey hey, our masters have opened the bar.
(He lifts a champagne bottle and starts work on the cork.)

OFFICER: We have to thank you for your work here at USUKEMCOC.

RAYMOND: You suck what?

OFFICER: USUK Emergency Command Center, of which your committee is an initiative.

RAYMOND: You heard of this USUK?

NICOLE: Acronyms are the codes of sin. I heard a rumor.

OFFICER: A digest of your report has already been transmitted to Berlin. Your recommendations will form the basis of the Allied position in this matter.

NICOLE: Has . . . this committee been active in the past?

RAYMOND: There will be no answer to that. Will there, soldier? *(Nothing from the* OFFICER.*)* Who will write the history of the rewriters of history? *(He pops the champagne cork.)*

OFFICER: Cars to Schipol Airport are at your disposal. If you wish please continue to use the facility for another twenty-four hours. The kitchen will remain open for another twenty-four hours.

(He turns to go.)

RAYMOND: He abandons us.

OFFICER: You have contributed to the peace, Professor.

RAYMOND: Knocked down Spandau Prison and built a supermarket? Yeah. OK.

(The OFFICER, *irritated for the first time.)*

OFFICER: Peace is a complex status to maintain.

NICOLE: "A complex status."

(The OFFICER *salutes and goes.)*

RAYMOND: Ah well. Back to writing brochures for William 'n' Mary.

(He swigs from the champagne bottle, wipes his mouth on his sleeve. NICOLE *looks directly at camera 1, up in the ceiling's corner.)*

NICOLE: To market history. On the shelves. *(To camera 2.)* To remove impurities. To add artificial sweeteners. *(To camera 3.)* So that tomato soup from the packets may be the color of tomatoes. So that the news of the day may be black and white. *(To camera 4.)* Why was cooking invented? As a measure against the near poison of everything we eat. *(To camera 1.)* So cook the news. Reality is salmonella.

(She looks at cameras 2, 3 and 4 in turn. The tape snows. PALMER *switches the tape off and walks away, as . . .)*

SCENE 12

Live.

RAYMOND: We've done, boys! Come 'n' get it!

(At once the double doors open. The OFFICER *pushes a trolley into the room. On the trolley an immaculate white tablecloth, dishes of food, and two bottles of champagne in ice buckets.)*

OFFICER *(aside):* General Patton
return to earth
zap these schmucks.

RAYMOND: Hey hey, our masters have opened the bar.

OFFICER *(aside):* It's hard
to hear the bugles
forty and more
Years on
Sicily
D Day
The Battle of the Bulge
just sound like old
junk movies on TV.

RAYMOND: You suck what?

OFFICER *(aside):* It's hard to hear the bugles calling
in the traffic on the autobahn
hard in a Hamburg bar.

RAYMOND *(to* NICOLE*):* You heard of this USUK?

NICOLE *(aside):* To market
history
remove
Impurities
add harmless
sweeteners.

OFFICER *(aside):* War graves get forgot
Europe goes to the beach—
soldier boy on guard—
Kids in the sand at the picnic

slop the mayonnaise
on the soldier's boots.

NICOLE *(aside):* Tomato soup
is the color
of tomatoes
The news
is on
the packet.

OFFICER: And peace
is pissed
away.

RAYMOND *(to* NICOLE*):* He means yes.

NICOLE *(aside):* Reality
is sal—
monella.

OFFICER *(aside):* Where is the victory?

(He turns to go.)

RAYMOND: You're abandoning us?

OFFICER *(aside):* Peace is a complex
status to maintain.

RAYMOND: Knocked down Spandau Prison and built a supermarket? Yeah. OK.

NICOLE: "A complex status."

(The OFFICER *salutes and goes.)*

SCENE 13

Live. *(*RAYMOND *sipping champagne.* NICOLE *is making up, with a hand mirror.* RAYMOND *suddenly still.)*

RAYMOND: Hey! The bugging's off.

NICOLE: What?

(A silence.)

RAYMOND: I miss it.

*(*CHARITY *comes on, dressed for the committee, as before. She has a video cassette in her hand. Her hands are dirty. There are smudges of ash on her clothing and her face. They stare at her.)*

NICOLE: What have you done?

CHARITY: Istvan.

RAYMOND: Your hands . . .

CHARITY: Nothing.

NICOLE: What's happened?

*(*CHARITY *refuses to look at her.)*

CHARITY: Istvan . . . has made this tape. He wants you to see it.

RAYMOND: What do you mean he's made a tape, he wants us to see it? Treating us with contempt, sending edicts down through his sidekick. It's bloody outrageous.

NICOLE: Be quiet Raymond. *(To* CHARITY.*)* Has there been an accident? Is your husband alright?

CHARITY: He's sleeping now.

NICOLE: You must tell us . . .

RAYMOND: Yeah, of course. Should we tell the goons here, to get a doctor in?

CHARITY: No. *(A pause.)* When my husband has slept, he will come down to see you. Now, see the tape he has made. Please.

(She holds it out. RAYMOND *and* NICOLE *look at each other again.)*

RAYMOND: If that is what the great man wants.

*(*RAYMOND *takes the tape from* CHARITY. *He puts it into a machine and runs it.* LUBER*'s video is made with a camcorder, hand-held. He has, at times, tried to record himself in a mir-*

ror as he talks, but a camera light shines into the mirror. The screens "white out," colors stream. Sometimes there is a glimpse of the video camera, but never of LUBER*'s face. His breathing is bad. His voice is deep with a faint edge of a German accent.)*

LUBER: My esteemed colleagues, you must forgive me I . . . have wanted to join you, but the vagaries of health, one's tenuous grip on existence. . . . One wakes, one breathes, one has the illusion of safety. . . . One second, one second, forgive me . . . *(Violent coughing, the tape is stopped, then started again, the camera whirling.)*

RAYMOND: Jesus Christ, what's the matter with him?

LUBER: . . . Satisfy your curiosity as to my condition. . . . One pays for a holistic view of life, the holistic assault . . . the absurd project that one lives, that everything will mean everything else, thought, sleep, food, reading, language, love, that all will be imploded into one way of living . . . what you want Raymond, to be the renaissance man, but as your weltanschauung failed, your world view, the Marxist millenium, so has my stomach. . . . It is the oyster in the shell that has done for me . . . where does the drive to human wholeness lead? Like Galileo, to grossness, obscenity, obsession . . .
(A retching fit.)

RAYMOND: What is he gibbering about? *(To* CHARITY.*)* What the hell is wrong with him?

LUBER: I have for some years become inordinately fond of oysters . . . Not for me, the tangerine dreams of alcohol, Raymond, not for me the heady pursuit of power in excellence, Nicole . . . both addictions, corruscating, dissolving all judgment in the end, all self-respect . . . *(Shouts.)* Oh this fucking technology, how can one catch thought . . .

RAYMOND *(to* NICOLE*)*: He's having a go at you, now.

NICOLE *(to* CHARITY*)*: Is this all your husband . . .

CHARITY: Please pay attention.

(The camera steadies. A tray on wheels, stacks of seafood plates piled high with oyster shells, bits of bread, squeezed

pieces of lemon, a table napkin glimpsed, spotted with blood. Then the camera into the mirror.)

LUBER: . . . An intellectual passion to understand the world can, what? Become a desire to eat the world? That is my fate, my dear colleagues, to degenerate to gluttony. With me it is oysters . . . Fragments of shells have perforated my intestine . . . I was always a messy eater, bolted my food, many do who come from where I come from . . . I relish this absurdity, to die . . .

NICOLE: Die?

LUBER: . . . in this way, cut to pieces by a luxury food, the absurdity of someone like me who believes in the unity of mind and body in this predicament . . . *(A violent coughing fit.)* Listen to me! Listen to me! My colleagues of thoughtfulness, my comrade intellectuals, I have information. Look! Look! *(The camera moves along the disordered bed. Documents are spread out. Here and there, an oyster shell.)* I have withheld these documents from you . . . Vanity, vanity, I was going to crack the truth of this hard shell, this pearl in the slime . . .

RAYMOND *(overlapping):* For fucksake, Luber imagery . . .

LUBER: . . . black pearl of disgust, the truth of this vile matter . . . Rudolf Hess, his war record, 1914 to 1918 . . . 8th August, 1917 . . . Severely wounded in the left lung by a rifle bullet . . . The bullet penetrated the chest, right through the chest. Right through the body . . . Hess was in various war hospitals until 10th of December, 1917.

(The camera zig-zags away from the bed.)

RAYMOND: So? The bastard was a war hero.

(The camera is now zooming to the X-ray of a man's chest. The X-ray is pinned up against a photographer's lamp.)

NICOLE: Hess?

CHARITY: Yes.

LUBER: This X-ray was taken in the British Military Hospital in Berlin, September 1973.

RAYMOND: X-Ray. Common image of humanity. Could be you, me, Hitler, Hess, Tutankhamen, Jesus Christ.

NICOLE *(sotto):* No bullet wound.

LUBER: See it, see it, do we see it, history, the trace, the mark left by the truth of a great lie? Look! . . . No sign of damage to the ribs on the left side. No dead tissue track through the lung, which a rifle bullet must leave. *(A silence. On the tape, the X-ray is beginning to smoke with the heat from the light.)* At the X-Ray session, the doctor asked—*"Was ist passiert mit den Kriegsunfallen? Nicht hauttief?"*

NICOLE: "What happened to your war wounds? Not even skin deep?"

(A silence. The X-ray smoking.)

RAYMOND: The X-ray, he's letting it . . .

LUBER: The prisoner replied *"zu spät, zu spät!"*

NICOLE: "Too late, too late."

LUBER: And his bowels opened.

He messed the floor.

They led him away to the bathroom.

At Spandau Prison, on July 7th 1987, there was an emergency . . . The prisoner was raving. He wanted to confess. After all the years, confess what? What?

RAYMOND: The fucking thing is burning!

(And on the tape the camera held anyhow, a hand pulling at the X-ray, now alight . . .)

LUBER: Oh! Oh!

(And the tape cuts to a little later. The X-ray, ruined, a hole melted in its center, lies on the bed, smeared with ash.)

LUBER: Hess not Hess.

The man who died in Spandau was not Hess. *(LUBER now speaking in great pain.)* What is history? The real Hess took off, over the North Sea. To be shot down on Himmler's orders. Raymond, what do you know of the Nazi Party, think! A medieval court. Conspiracy within conspiracy. One of Himmler's agents flew a second plane, out to discredit Hitler. With a message, that Hitler be replaced, along with Churchill.

What is it: This thing, this state of mind . . . History? That we bend, that we distort? From which we want . . . *The truth?*

RAYMOND *(overlapping):* What's the bastard doing? Destroying evidence, wrecking our work, what?

LUBER: Raymond, Nicole, do you understand what we have done? . . . Ours is the new treason of the clerks. . . . We have become specialists, technicians of acceptable truths . . . this is a new age, that only has use for our expertise . . . it has seduced us. . . . We are morticians, we deliver history with an acceptable face . . . acceptable facts, which may or may not be true . . . but they are safe . . . to be taught on the Modern History exam syllabus . . . *(The camera turns to the mirror.)* And it is too late, for us to extricate ourselves, zu spät, zu spät . . . *(The camera turns to the bed,* LUBER*'s hand striking matches, the war records begin to burn. Then as if* LUBER *falls with the camera to the floor. The camera is pointing at the door of the room.* CHARITY *is coming into the room. And, abruptly, the tape stops.)*

RAYMOND: Hess not Hess.

NICOLE: Hess was in prison. He died there. That was what Hess was for. Prisoner number 7. He died in Spandau. It was on the news tonight.

RAYMOND: The news we made, for fucksake!

NICOLE: Yes. *(To* CHARITY.*)* Is . . .

*(*CHARITY *turns away.* RAYMOND *strides to the doors. He cannot open them.)*

RAYMOND: You out there! What has happened to our colleague? You! *(A silence.)* We . . . withdraw our report! Can you hear? You out there!

NICOLE: The report will stand. It's on the news now. And it is inconceivable. The years, years and years, twisted. In twisted loyalty, alone in Spandau. A false Hess? How could he have stood it?

RAYMOND: Maybe he was waiting for orders. *(A silence.)* We must . . .

NICOLE: What? Denounce our own work? What official evidence, what single mark will there be . . . that we ever met? We have been traduced. *(She starts.* CHARITY *moves to a corner.)* The cameras? . . .

*(*CHARITY *puts a finger to her lips.)*

RAYMOND *(low):* Bastards. Bastards. Bastards.

NICOLE: Rudolf Hess killed himself in Spandau Prison on the 17th of August, 1987.

RAYMOND: Yeah. It was on the news, no?

*(*CHARITY *gestures to them.)*

CHARITY: Come, now!

*(*CHARITY *crouches by a wall and pushes open a small concealed door.* NICOLE *and* RAYMOND *approach it carefully.)*

NICOLE: The smell . . . of the air in there.

*(*NICOLE *and* RAYMOND *go through the little door.)*

RAYMOND *(from within):* What's that, hanging there?

*(*CHARITY *closes the door.)*

SCENE 14

PALMER *turns and sees* CHARITY. *He stares at her.*

PALMER: This what they let you do in here? You have the expertise. Didn't you work as a TV producer for RTF?

CHARITY: You have done your research, Mr. Palmer.

PALMER: Oh I do my research. You left French TV, some kind of breakdown even then, wasn't it? You dropped out, became a student in Geneva, shacked up with the great Professor Luber? *(A silence.)* What, the doctors let you fake up tapes? Part of the swish psychotherapy is it, in between sipping the spa waters and being hosed down? To fake up history?

CHARITY: You are cruel.

*(*PALMER *sighs.)*

PALMER: Yeah, sorry about that. *(Putting his tape recorder into his briefcase.)*

CHARITY: Aren't you going to talk to them?

(A silence.)

PALMER: Talk to who?

CHARITY: The walls. *(He stares at her.)* The walls beyond the walls, in the room. That you can get to, through a little door. But you'll get into the paintings, on the walls. Haven't you seen them?

PALMER: I . . .

CHARITY: Huge ugly things, the paint going dark, even the new painting, heavy and thick. The paint . . . hanging there, in folds. We're there, we've been painted in.

PALMER: Look . . .

CHARITY: Istvan. You. Me.

PALMER: What . . . What happened to the other two? Raymond, Nicole? Painted on these walls, you're talking about?

CHARITY: They died, in a plane crash. On an internal flight, Moscow to Riga, in the Soviet Union.

(She huddles against the wall.)

PALMER: Yeah. Those internal flights in the Soviet Union. I sat by a door of some Illyushin crate. Water was pouring in right through the flight. *(A pause.)* So they got together, did they? Across the ideological divide? They seemed to loathe each other. *(Nothing from* CHARITY.*)* If that really was them, eh? On your tape.

(He walks away from her.)

SCENE 15

CHARITY *(aside):* Constanza.

(A pause.)

Constanza
when Mozart died
Held his body in her arms
for four hours
then they had
To drag her screaming
from the bed—
Simone.

(Pause.)

Simone de Beauvoir
when Jean Paul Sartre died
wanted to do the same
A nurse said, "no
don't do that
the gangrene—"

(Pause.)

I made a promise
when you died
to say just once
All the things
you said to me—
in memory
Once to someone
no matter who
a stranger
In the street
to a cold
tape machine
A scribble
on a misted
windowpane
In eternal memory

however fleeting, and when I've done
go south, and be young
Again.
But.

(A pause.)

But
I begin
To forget—
what did you say?
I reinvent—
Constanza
Simone
my love
Rots in my arms
his memory
glues my skin
Constanza
Simone
help me
I am condemned
to the holy fury
of Antigone.

SCENE 16

CHARITY *crouched by the wall.* PALMER, *aside.*

PALMER: I didn't write up the "Was Hess Hess?" story. A mate of mine on *The Guardian* was deep into all that anyway, risking his sanity. *(A pause.)*

So, I just left her there. That was the autumn of '88. The spring of '89, I learnt she'd left that place where I'd interviewed her, the millionaires' funny farm in the Austrian Alps. There was a full color pic of her in *Vogue* magazine. She'd married an American businessman. Big, I read, in the world of transatlantic trusts. *(A pause.)*

In the *Vogue* pic, she looked a million dollars, she was leaning against this guy, the new husband. He had a face like a wall. Deep eyes, of pale aquamarine, going on to blue. A handsome bastard, almost beautiful. And she, ah she . . . was wearing a cream silk trouser suit, NVPL—no visible panty line. I got nowhere near what that woman was about, I thought, nowhere near. I felt . . . abused. And I'd had the nerve to fancy her. *(He shakes his head.)* Ships in the night. *(A pause.)*

And now all this. In the last few weeks, the latest high society New York murder case. That woman, who slammed a hypodermic into her husband's chest while he slept? A massive dose of adrenalin, straight into the heart? That is her.

I've done a piece on it for the *New York Post,* a big break for me. "I met murderess in Nazi loony bin" 'cetera, 'cetera. The thing is though, the second husband, face like a wall, flat like a wall, deep, pale blue eyes, handsome, almost beautiful. He was half the age, but very like Rudolf Hess.

(He leaves.)

SCENE 17

CHARITY, *still crouched, lifts a remote control unit and presses the button.*

Tape. *(On the screens the legend:*
THE WALLS OF SPANDAU SPEAK.
The text is spoken by LUBER'*s voice. The tape shows photographs, some official, some amateur, some black and white, some colored, of the demolition of Spandau Prison.)*

VOICE: The day the Nazi died
his prison walls were just
hard dust
Waiting to be smashed
by demolition balls
swung from cranes to crack
The hardened crust of that dead
history—the walls of Spandau
thought "Why must
They pulverize the memory
of the horror that we held
into thin air? We are free
But the past falls with us—
we are dispelled
the old lies
Are forgotten, we are
condemned, expelled
An unseen cloud
Of molecules blown
over European skies
into the lungs
Of a bureaucrat on the phone
Brussels to Paris, into
the innocent eyes
Of a child in a London park
onto the feet

of irritating flies
Buzzing a Cannes ice cream
onto the dark lips
of a whore in Amsterdam
Into a German's beer—
we are the dirty mark
the rain leaves on a Stockholm
Windowpane. We
do not disappear
we were imprinted
By a monstrous pain
we faced with stone
what you pretend
Was never there
so! Check the food
the water and the air
We are in you
and will rise again
we are cancer, we are there
We will be
revenged
and rise again."

(The screens go dead. In the room, the audience and playing area, a blackout. The tapestries become see-through as lights rise upon wall paintings of the horrors of history, the actors caught, frozen, in the designs.)

SELECTED BIBLIOGRAPHY

CONTRIBUTORS

Selected Bibliography

Friedlander, Saul, ed. *Probing the Limits of Representation.* Cambridge: Harvard University Press, 1992.

Hartman, Geoffrey H. *The Longest Shadow: In the Aftermath of the Holocaust.* Bloomington: Indiana University Press, 1996.

Isser, Edward R. *Stages of Annihilation: Theatrical Representations of the Holocaust.* Madison, N.J.: Fairleigh University Press, 1997.

Lang, Beryl, ed. *Writing and the Holocaust.* New York: Holmes and Meier, 1988.

Langer, Lawrence L. *Holocaust Testimonies: The Ruins of Memory.* New Haven: Yale University Press, 1991.

Langer, Lawrence L. *Admitting the Holocaust: Collected Essays.* New York: Oxford University Press, 1995.

Schumacher, Claude, ed. *Staging the Holocaust: The Shoa in Drama and Performance.* Cambridge: Cambridge University Press, 1998.

Todorov, Tzvetan. *Facing the Extreme: Moral Life in the Concentration Camps.* Tr. Arthur Denner and Abigail Pollak. New York: Metropolitan Books, 1996.

Young, James E. *Writing and Rewriting the Holocaust: Narrative and the Consequences of Interpretation.* Bloomington: Indiana University Press, 1990.

Photograph © Annette Hudeman

ROY KIFT *(Camp Comedy)* studied French and Italian at the University of Wales and trained as an actor at the London Drama Centre. He has been a full-time playwright since 1972 with occasional excursions into directing stage, radio and TV, teaching in drama schools, and lecturing in universities around Europe. He is the winner of many literary prizes and awards including the Thames Television (Stage) Dramatists Award (1974), first prize in the New Plays Competition organized by the German Bundesarbeitsgemeinschaft "Hilfe für Behinderte" for *Stronger than Superman* (1981), the "Förderpreis" of the Würtembergischen Staatstheaters, Stuttgart for the libretto for the chamber opera *Joy* (music: Susanne Erding, 1984) and a Berlin Writer's Award in 1987. Kift is also a translator of stage plays, including works by Molière, Goldoni, Gozzi, Patrick Süskind, Heinar Kipphardt, and Volker Ludwig. He also has contributed to several theatre magazines, such as *DRAMA, Plays and Players, Theatre Quarterly, New Theatre Quarterly,* and *Western European Stages.* He lives currently in Germany.

Photograph © Silvia Jansen

LEENY SACK *(The Survivor and the Translator)* was born in Brooklyn in 1951, a daughter of concentration camp survivors, "and that reality has shadowed and colored my life and my work." Her works include *Our Lady of the Hidden Agenda, Paper Floor, Opening Remarks, Group Show, Watercolor,* and *(Neo-Ventriqual) Thought Clouds.* She has performed and taught extensively in the United States, Europe, and Asia, both as a member of The Performance Group (1974–1978) and as a solo artist. She is a founder and, with her husband, Norman Rosenberg, codirector of Pangea Farm, a center for the study of meditation, psychology, and the arts, where since 1989 she has lived, made new work, and taught practices in breath, sound, kinetic awareness, and performance as an embodiment of insight. Many of her students are from Germany and Austria where she teaches several times each year.

Photograph by Wolfgang Osterheld

BERNARD KOPS *(Dreams of Anne Frank)* is one of England's best known playwrights. He is also an acclaimed poet, novelist, and memoirist. Born in the East End of London of Dutch–Jewish working-class parents, he achieved recognition for his first play *The Hamlet of Stepney Green* (1956). That play was followed by twenty others for the stage, twenty radio plays, eleven novels, and six works of poetry. His Jewish background and the existentialist struggle associated with it play an important part in his dramas, as does the Holocaust. Kops notes that if his father had been able to raise the ten pounds necessary to emigrate back to the Netherlands before the Second World War, he would have perished, along with other members of his family, in the concentration camps. In 1999 four volumes of his collected plays will be published by Oberon Books (England). *Dreams of Anne Frank* won the *Time Out* Award for Best Fringe Play of 1992–1993.

Photograph by Harold Shapiro

DONALD MARGULIES's *(The Model Apartment)* plays have premiered at major theatres around the United States, including the Manhattan Theatre Club, the Actors Theatre of Louisville, South Coast Repertory, and the Jewish Repertory Theatre. The recipient of NEA and Guggenheim Awards, he has twice been a finalist for the Pulitzer Prize. A collection of his work, *Sight Unseen and Other Plays,* has been published by the Theatre Communications Group. Among his better-known and frequently produced plays are *Dinner With Friends, The Loman Family Picnic,* and *What's Wrong With This Picture?* Born in Brooklyn in 1954, Margulies lives in New Haven and teaches playwriting at the Yale School of Drama.

GEORGE STEINER *(The Portage to San Cristobal of A. H.)* was born in 1929 in Paris to a Viennese mother and a Bohemian father. He was educated in the French lyceé, at the University of Chicago, at Harvard, and at Oxford. He has taught at universities in the United States and England and has held chairs of comparative literature at the University of Geneva and at Oxford. He also is a founding fellow of Churchill College, Cambridge. Among his many honors are an O. Henry Short Story award, Fulbright and Guggenheim Fellowships, and the Morton Dauwen Zabel Prize from the American Academy of Arts and Letters. His books, translated into some twelve languages, include *Language and Silence, The Death of Tragedy, In Bluebeard's Castle, After Babel, Real Presences, No Passion Spent, Errata: An Examined Life,* and works of fiction. He lives in Cambridge, England.

Photograph © Jill Furmanovsky

CHRISTOPHER HAMPTON *(The Portage to San Cristobal of A. H.)* was born in the Azores in 1946. He studied French and German at New College, Oxford, and graduated in 1969 with a First Class Honours Degree. He wrote his first play, *When Did You Last See My Mother?*, at the age of eighteen. His work for theatre, television, and cinema includes *The Philanthropist,* his adaptation of *Les Liaisons Dangereuses* by Laclos, translations from Ibsen and Molière, and the screenplays *Dangerous Liaisons, Carrington,* and *The Secret Agent.*

Photograph by Clive Totman

HOWARD BRENTON *[H. I. D. (Hess Is Dead)]* was born in Portsmouth in 1942 and educated at Cambridge University. Brenton has written well over twenty stage plays as well as translations, adaptations, and screenplays. His best-known theatre work includes *Christie in Love, Bloody Poetry, The Churchill Play* (twice revived by the Royal Shakespeare Company), and, for the National Theatre, *Weapons of Happiness, The Romans in Britain, Pravda* (co-written with David Hare), and translations of *The Life of Galileo* and *Danton's Death.* More recently there have been two collaborations with Tariq Ali: *Iranian Nights* at the Royal Court Theatre and *Moscow Gold* for the RSC. *Berlin Bertie* was seen both at the Royal Court and the Deutsches Theater, Berlin, who have commissioned his next piece, *One Once.* He has also written a novel, *Diving for Pearls,* and *Hot Irons,* a volume of essays and diaries.

Photograph © Julia Skloot

ROBERT SKLOOT has been on the Theatre and Drama faculty of the University of Wisconsin–Madison since 1968, teaching courses in theatre literature and serving as a staff director. He has published numerous articles on modern drama and theatre, as well as *The Darkness We Carry: The Drama of the Holocaust* (University of Wisconsin, 1988). He has won several teaching awards and three Fulbright Lectureships to Israel, Austria, and Chile. He holds a joint appointment with the Jewish Studies Program and serves as an associate vice chancellor for academic affairs with a special interest in undergraduate education.

Agai tells "story,"

I write play –

Play produced for radio –

Maria or Laszlo

Miriam writes

not even mine, story of

someone else

I do play as actor –

Maria / Miriam.

voice – performance

my performance based on

Maria / Miriam's performance

of my voice over later

reconstructs in part

of Agai's performance

to wed chars

of her memory,

Agai →

Society [illegible] play. So she may

none like my version [illegible]

by Miriam / Maria's version

[illegible] [illegible] she

[illegible] [illegible] [illegible]

Felt [illegible]